MICAH'S CHALLENGE

MICAH'S CHALLENGE

The Church's Responsibility to the Global Poor

Dr Justin Thacker and
Dr Marijke Hoek (eds.)

Paternoster:
thinking faith

MILTON KEYNES • COLORADO SPRINGS • HYDERABAD

15 14 13 12 11 10 09 8 7 6 5 4 3 2

Reprinted 2009

First published 2008 by Paternoster
Paternoster is an imprint of Authentic Media
9 Holdom Avenue, Bletchley, Milton Keynes, Bucks, MK1 1QR, UK
1820 Jet Stream Drive, Colorado Springs, CO 80921, USA
OM Authentic Media, Medchal Road, Jeedimetla Village, Secunderabad 500 055, A.P., India
www.authenticmedia.co.uk
Authentic Media is a division of IBS-STL U.K., limited by guarantee, with its Registered Office at Kingstown Broadway, Carlisle, Cumbria CA3 0HA. Registered in England and Wales No. 1216232. Registered charity 270162

British Library Cataloguing in Publication Data

A catalogue record for this book is available from the British Library

ISBN 978-1-84227-606-8

Design by James Kessell for Scratch the Sky Ltd (www.scratchthesky.com)
Print Management by Adare
Printed and bound in the UK by J F Print Ltd., Sparkford, Somerset

Contents

Contributors

Dave Andrews and his wife Ange, have lived and worked in intentional communities with marginalized groups of people in Australia, Afghanistan, Pakistan, India and Nepal for more than thirty years. Dave is particularly interested in radical spirituality, incarnational community and the dynamics of personal and social transformation. He is author of many books and articles, including *Christi-Anarchy; Not Religion, But Love; Building A Better World* and *Compassionate Community Work Manual*. Dave, Ange and their friends started Aashiana, Sahara and Sharan – three well-known Christian community organizations working with slum dwellers, sex workers, drug addicts and people with HIV/AIDS in India; and they are currently a part of the Waiters Union, an inner-city Christian community network walking and working alongside Aborigines, refugees and people with disabilities in Australia. Dave is an educator at large for TEAR Australia, a Christian international aid and development agency; a teacher for the Bible College of Queensland, the Brisbane College of Theology; and an elder for Servants to Asia's Urban Poor. www.daveandrews.com.au.

Andrew Bradstock is Co-Director of the Centre for Faith and Society at the von Hügel Institute, St Edmund's College, Cambridge, and Director of the Christian Socialist Movement. From 2000 to 2005 he was Secretary for Church and Society with the United Reformed Church and prior to that lectured in theology at colleges in Southampton and Winchester. Andrew holds degrees in theology, church history and politics from the universities of Bristol and Otago (NZ) and a PhD in political theory from the University of Kent at Canterbury. He has written and edited several books on faith and politics and is co-editor, with Christopher Rowland, of *Radical Christian Writings: A Reader*.

Tony Campolo is Professor Emeritus of Sociology at Eastern University in St Davids, Pennsylvania. He previously served for ten years on the faculty of the University of Pennsylvania. He is a graduate of Eastern College and earned a PhD from Temple University. Founder and President of the Evangelical Association for the Promotion of Education (EAPE), Dr Campolo has worked to create, nurture and support programmes for 'at-risk' children in cities across North America, and has helped establish schools and universities in several developing countries. As well as communicating on religious, social and political matters on television and radio stations across the USA, Canada, UK, Australia and New Zealand, he is the author of 34 books, with the latest releases being *The God of Intimacy and Action*; *Letters to a Young Evangelical*; *Speaking My Mind* and *Everybody Wants to Change the World* (co-authored by G. Aeschliman). An ordained minister, he has served American Baptist churches in New Jersey and Pennsylvania, and is presently recognized as an associate pastor of the Mount Carmel Baptist Church in West Philadelphia.

Tim Chester is part of the Crowded House, a church planting initiative in Sheffield, UK, and co-director of the Porterbrook Network which provides training and consultancy in church planting and missional church. (www.theporterbrooknetwork.org). He was previously Research and Policy Director for Tearfund UK. Dr Chester is the author of a number of books including *The Message of Prayer*; *From Creation to New Creation*; *Good News to the Poor*; *Delighting in the Trinity* and, with Steve Timmis, *Total Church*. He also edited the papers of the first Micah conference, *Justice, Mercy and Humility: Inegral Mission and the Poor*.

Malcolm Duncan lectures, preaches and writes on issues of poverty, community transformation, integral mission and the role of Christians in civil society. He is passionate about emphasizing the importance of holding words, works and wonders in a balanced tension as the church fulfils the Great Commission. His written works include *Building a Better World: Faith at work for change in society* (Continuum, 2006) and *Kingdom Come: The local church as a catalyst for social change* (Lion Hudson, 2007). He is involved in a number of international advocacy campaigns and he leads a local church on the Berkshire/Hampshire border.

Joel Edwards is the General Director of the Evangelical Alliance, UK, and is a passionate advocate of both diversity and unity within the church, but unity with a purpose; to see real change for real lives and real communities. Joel also serves on a number of faith, government and public agency advisory groups and is a regular broadcaster for UK and international media. He is committed to seeing long-term change for the world's poor and chairs the Micah Challenge International Board and Council, and is a Micah Challenge UK Board member. He is an honorary canon of St Paul's Cathedral and has an honorary doctorate from the University of St Andrews.

Marijke Hoek is coordinator of Forum for Change, facilitated by the Evangelical Alliance, which aims to bring together prayer, strategic thinking and action in media, education, arts, politics and business. She is part of Network (Local Evangelical Fellowship), which represents the Alliance in Greater Manchester. Her Masters degree in applied theology and PhD from Regents Theological College, Nantwich, concerned the topic of suffering and weakness. She is part of the Micah Challenge UK media team.

Jon Kuhrt works for Shaftesbury as Director of Community Mission. Shaftesbury has been active in urban mission for over 160 years and the role of the community mission team is to challenge and equip the church in social action and community development, working in particular with churches in urban areas to help them impact their communities. In conjunction with Tearfund, the team has developed *'Just People? The Micah Course'*. Previously, Jon worked with homeless people and managed hostels for rough sleepers in Soho, London. He is passionate about how the Christian faith connects to social activism and politics.

Melba Padilla Maggay is President and Chief Executive Officer of the Institute for Studies in Asian Church and Culture (ISACC), a conscientizing voice in politics and in church-and-culture issues. She had been cited for her outstanding leadership in organizing the evangelical Protestant presence at the EDSA barricades during the February People Power Uprising in 1986. She holds a doctorate in Philippine studies, a Masters in English literature and a first degree in mass communication. A writer, social anthropologist and specialist in intercultural communication, she was Research Fellow on the subject at the University of Cambridge under the auspices of Tyndale House, applying it to the question of culture and theology. She has lectured on this and other cross-cultural issues worldwide. Her many writings include, *Transforming Society*; *A Clash of Cultures, Intercultural Communication Problems in the Interface Between American Protestantism and Filipino Religious Consciousness*; *Culture and Economic Empowerment*, a study of grassroots communities struggling to rise from poverty, and 'Culture, Globalization and Development', a paper for the Micah Network Consultation on Globalization. She currently sits on the governing boards of a number of NGOs and serves as part of the International Board of Reference of the Micah Network.

Njongonkulu Ndungane was Archbishop of Cape Town from 1996 to the end of 2007. He decided to enter the church while serving a three-year sentence on Robben Island as a political prisoner following his involvement in the anti-Pass Law Demonstrations in 1960, which resulted in his eventual arrest under apartheid law. Njongonkulu was ordained as a priest of the Anglican Church in July 1974 in the Diocese of Cape Town. He received a Bachelor of Divinity and Master of Theology degree in Christian ethics at King's College, London, and became an associate of the college. His book *A World With A Human Face: A Voice From Africa* was published in 2003. He is currently President of 'African Monitor', a pan-African not-for-profit body harnessing the voice of the continent's civil society in monitoring and promoting the effective implementation of promises made by the international community, and Africa's own governments, for the continent's development. He has been awarded several honorary degrees including Doctor of Divinity from Rhodes University, Grahamstown, from the Protestant Episcopal Seminary, Virginia, and from Episcopal Divinity School, and Doctor of Humane Letters from Worcester State College, Massachusetts, and is international Patron of Micah Challenge.

C. René Padilla was born in Quito, Ecuador, and reared in Bogotá, Colombia, and has lived with his family in Buenos Aires, Argentina, since 1967. He obtained his BA in philosophy from Wheaton College, Illinois, USA, his MA in theology from the Wheaton College Graduate School, and his PhD in biblical exegesis and criticism from the University of Manchester, UK. For 22 years he was on the staff of the International Fellowship of Evangelical Students (IFES), first as travelling secretary, then as the Associate General Secretary for Latin America, and finally as Director of Certeza, the IFES publishing house. He was one of the founders of the Latin American Theological Fellowship in 1970, and of the Kairos Community in 1976, which in 1989 was organized as the Kairos Foundation. He is at present the Director of Kairos Books and Secretary of Publications of the Latin American Theological Fellowship. He has lectured in colleges, universities and theological institutions around the world and has written or edited several books and many articles. He is President of the Micah Network.

Ronald J. Sider (PhD, Yale) is Professor of Theology, Holistic Ministry and Public Policy and Director of the Sider Center on Ministry and Public Policy at Palmer (formerly Eastern Baptist) Theological Seminary and President of Evangelicals for Social Action. A widely known evangelical speaker and writer, he has spoken on 6 continents, published 31 books and scores of articles. His *Rich Christians in an Age of Hunger* was recognized by *Christianity Today* as one of the one hundred most influential religious books of the twentieth century. His most recent books are *The Scandal of the Evangelical Conscience: Why Are Christians Living Just Like the Rest of the World; Just Generosity: A New Vision for*

Overcoming Poverty in America and *Churches That Make a Difference: Reaching Your Community with Good News and Good Works* (with P. Olson and H. Unruh). He is the publisher of PRISM magazine and a contributing editor of Christianity Today and Sojourners. He has lectured at many colleges and universities around the world, including Yale, Harvard, Princeton and Oxford. Dr Sider is international Patron of Micah Challenge.

Justin Thacker is the Head of Theology at the Evangelical Alliance UK, and an associate research fellow at the London School of Theology. His first book *Postmodernism and the Ethics of Theological Knowledge* was published in 2007 and he co-edited *The Atonement Debate*. Justin's first career was as a medical doctor, specializing in paediatrics. He worked as a doctor in the UK for five years and for one year in Kenya before training in theology at the London School of Theology, and King's College London. Justin is an elder of the United Reformed Church, has an active preaching ministry, is on the council of Scripture Union and has led a Scripture Union holiday for children with special needs for the last nine years.

Jim Wallis is a bestselling author, public theologian, preacher, speaker, activist and international commentator on ethics and public life. His latest book, *God's Politics: Why the Right Gets It Wrong and the Left Doesn't Get It*, was on *The New York Times* bestseller list for four months. He is President and Executive Director of Sojourners/Call to Renewal, where he is Editor-in-Chief of *Sojourners* magazine and also convenes a national network of churches, faith-based organizations and individuals working to overcome poverty in America. Jim Wallis has appeared in major newspapers such *The New York Times, The Washington Post, The Los Angeles Times* and *The Boston Globe,* among others, and appears regularly on radio and television programmes. He teaches a course at Harvard University on 'Faith, Politics, and Society', and is the author of eight books, including *Faith Works; The Soul of Politics: A Practical and Prophetic Vision for Change; Who Speaks for God? A New Politics of Compassion, Community, and Civility* and *Call to Conversion.* Jim is on the Council of Reference for Micah Challenge UK.

Preface

In the summer of 2007, when this book was compiled, the UK Prime Minister Gordon Brown delivered a significant address at the UN in which he acknowledged the lack of progress that had been made in delivering the Millennium Development Goals at this crucial halfway stage (31 July 2007). While the establishment of those goals had been a historic moment, Brown reflected that 'seven years on it is already clear that our pace is too slow, our direction too uncertain and our vision at risk'.

Micah Challenge represents one way in which the international Christian community has responded to this challenge by campaigning for the delivery of the Millennium Development Goals. It concerns the church's responsibility to the global poor and aims to deepen the commitment of the Christian community and strengthen its advocacy in relation to injustice and poverty. It unites Christians from both hemispheres, urging our respective governments to grasp this historic opportunity to deliver on the promises they have made.

In 2006, the Board of Directors of Micah Challenge UK rightly assessed the need for 'underpinning thinking' for the movement, and this book is the result. It aims to reflect biblically and theologically on our responsibility to the global poor in order to generate a greater motivation and sense of direction. It would also further develop a conviction and a confidence that the gospel is a significant force for change: social, political and personal. At the same time, though, this book is not just a call to transform our thinking, but also our lives.

Hence, this book adopts a wide-ranging approach in its efforts to outline the parameters of our global responsibility.

Following an introductory chapter, which sets out the history and vision of Micah Challenge, the chapters move progressively from biblical and theological reflections on issues of poverty, through more practical explorations of social ethics, to a corporate and personal call, which asks the question, 'What are we doing about all this?' The overall vision is determined by the gospel of God's Son who shapes the identity and character of his community and furnishes the church with a perspective that determines its mission, lifestyle, advocacy and dedication to a politics of compassion, mercy, humility and justice.

We considered that a book consisting of contributions by theologians and practitioners from various continents would be of interest to all. As such, you will find within this book a range of styles (from more academic approaches to more popular), a range of content (from theological reflection to community action), a range of voices (from the global South to the economically rich West), and even a range of views, or at least emphases.

Many thanks are due to the authors, whose variety of background, style and experience have formed this colourful array of thoughtfully crafted essays. It is furthermore a privilege that the Prime Minister of the UK, Gordon Brown, has written a foreword to this book. More than many, he has demonstrated a genuine concern for issues of global poverty, and we are grateful to him. We also thank Andrew Tanswell, former coordinator of Micah Challenge UK, for his enthusiasm and support of the book in its initial stage and Andy Clasper, Executive Director Micah Challenge UK, for his subsequent involvement.

We hope that this book will spark further critical dialogue and passionate action, and contribute to the creation of what Gordon Brown calls, 'the greatest coalition of conscience in pursuit of the greatest of causes', so that the Christian community will play its part in inspiring the worldwide transformation that is needed.

Justin Thacker and Marijke Hoek
November 2007

10 DOWNING STREET
LONDON SW1A 2AA

THE PRIME MINISTER

In 2000, the Millennium Development Goals focused the world's attention on ending the scandal of poverty. These eight commitments have united governments, civil society and faith communities from around the globe in an unprecedented bid to improve the lives of those who are all too easily forgotten, silenced and marginalised.

Christianity and other world faiths have a vital part to play in reaching out to help the poor and marginalised – and reminding those of us in government of our special responsibilities to men, women and children affected by poverty. The values of Christian belief emphasise compassion, generosity and social responsibility. These values strike a chord with our desire to see a world that is just and fair, and free from poverty. For many people faith is an important part of their lives, guiding the everyday actions of millions and shaping the fabric of communities. Micah Challenge is harnessing that faith to unite Christians globally from across church denominations to deepen that commitment to people living in poverty through prayer, service and advocacy. You are already making a huge difference.

I warmly welcome this book and your wider campaign. As we pass the mid-point to achieving the Millennium Development Goals, we are off track. I believe we face a development emergency. In the coming year we must redouble our efforts to build a global coalition of faith, NGOs, private sector and government to galvanise the action needed. I know your efforts will be an inspiration to Christians and church communities around the world who tirelessly seek an end to poverty.

Gordon Brown

November 2007

1

Micah Challenge: The Story So Far

Joel Edwards

When we stepped into the vestibule of the United Nations building, it was like walking into a dream. Earlier, a small group of us had imagined a Christian movement that mobilized people around the Millennium Development Goals: eight promises to reduce poverty, which the United Nations initiated at the dawn of the Third Millennium. These eight promises to the poor came about when 191 nations committed themselves to half absolute poverty by 2015.

We were there because we believed that something was happening in global evangelicalism which increasingly embraced God's heart for the poor as an integral part of the gospel agenda. From the very outset, the campaign was regarded as an effective vehicle harmonizing growing evangelical concern for the poor with its biblical witness to the world. Micah Challenge was to be more than a programme: it was to become a global evangelical response to the poor. We were without excuse, for evangelicals committed to the authority of Scripture already had a biblical mandate to respond to the poor. In this mission to the poor we hoped that Micah's prophetic impulse allowed no escape clause on such a historic response from our world governments.

Micah Challenge was therefore, primarily a response to God but it was also a response to our governments. If world leaders were prepared to commit to these measurable promises to the poor it seemed inconceivable that the Christian church should not hold them responsible in the spirit of transparency that they themselves had offered in the MDGs. If the government of Nigeria or Brazil committed themselves to fight corruption, reduce infant mortality and work for greater gender equality, for example, how could the church in these countries – with their moral mandate – fail to hold them accountable? And if governments in Switzerland, Britain and Canada had promised to tackle issues of aid and debt then Christians in these nations already had a basis for dialogue on behalf of the world's poor. The pincer movement of North and South responses harmonizing local churches and Christian NGOs provided an effective platform for action. And this action would not be an overnight wonder. This campaign was never envisaged as a short-term sprint but rather as a long-haul marathon towards and even beyond 2015.

But this was also to be a redemptive movement. Micah never envisaged itself as a hostile anti-government protest. Instead it would stand as critical partners with government, critiquing, highlighting injustices and condemning where necessary but always as partners committed to fulfilling the promises made and bringing the wealth of our constituency in order to accomplish this.

None of us were naïve: this unusual project would have to be sustained through a great deal of faith and tenacity, marrying short-term gains with long-term vision. As we met we were fuelled by the thought of a world in which these promises were kept. But we were also haunted by the image of a world in which this covenant was abandoned.

So, as we entered the UN building on Friday 15 October 2004 to launch Micah Challenge we walked with determination. We were being hosted by the United Nations Millennium Campaign, and the 4 p.m. event, which took place in the Dag Hammarskjöld Auditorium, featured a line up of key spokespersons from the two founding bodies, Micah Network and the World Evangelical Alliance, along with representatives from Africa, Latin America, directors of the Millennium Campaign and a Manhattan gospel choir.

The Right Revd Njongonkulu Ndungane, Archbishop of Cape Town, who presented the main address, reminded all of us that 'The Millennium Development Goals are the most comprehensive and ambitious commitment that the world has ever made to combating the evils of poverty.' In his view, 'The Micah Challenge presents a significant new movement in global civil society to address the evils of poverty. It is God's challenge to us to be his agents of hope in this hurting world.'[1]

But this promising launch was no more than the start of a long journey that had begun some three years earlier.

2000–2002

Towards the closing decade of the twentieth century something of a social and political revolution took place. The enormous groundswell of public protest against global poverty championed by superstars and celebrities such as Bob Geldof and Bono made poverty an inescapable political issue. Live Aid in the 1980s, followed by Jubilee 2000, then the 'Drop the Debt' campaign generated a tidal wave of public opinion that could not be ignored. But these campaigns did something else: they recognized that the Christian church, as a founding contributor, belonged at their heart. Christian organizations such as CAFOD, Christian Aid and Tearfund played a central role in mobilizing people to attend G8 meetings in Birmingham, Cologne and London. As Isobel Carter described it, Jubilee 2000 was 'a huge and challenging vision to change the world'.[2] When the final curtain fell on the Jubilee 2000 campaign, Gordon Brown, the then Chancellor of Exchequer, publicly recognized the role of the Christian church.[3]

The status of Christian churches as serious partners was well established by our presence at the quarterly breakfasts, which were jointly hosted by Gordon Brown and Clare Short – then International Development Secretary – at No. 11 Downing Street. But, as we approached the culmination of Jubilee 2000, everyone knew that in spite of the unprecedented levels of public interest, poor countries would not have their unpayable debts cancelled by December 2000.

In the autumn of 2000, a modest but ambitious conversation began between me and Stephen Rand, campaigns and prayer coordinator for Tearfund UK. Given that heads of state had only recently launched the Millennium Development Goals, evangelical Christians globally had an excellent and unprecedented opportunity to act as critical partners with governments, encouraging them to keep their promise to the poor. A brief paper recommending some basic ideas to mobilize evangelicals became the initial discussion point. Many evangelicals were increasingly becoming involved in poverty eradication but this development, which appeared to be a *kairos* moment, opened up the way for the global evangelical family to commit itself to the poor more deeply. In the earliest conversations, there was a feeling that a global evangelical movement of this nature would have authenticity because evangelicals were already present in every nation involved, and an additional incentive was that we could prod American evangelicals to become more committed to the poor!

Such a movement would not be exclusively evangelical, and neither would it be a tool of the United Nations. Instead, it would seek to be prophetic and professional, by mobilizing Christians who could draw from the expertise of Christian NGOs.

This embryonic dream was intimated in a letter to the Chancellor of the Exchequer in 2001.[4] During the sasme period, Andy Atkins, Advocacy Director for Tearfund UK and involved in the J2000 campaign, furthered the thinking of ways in which the MDGs could become a focal point for Tearfund's advocacy, and influenced much of the strategic thinking behind the scenes. As a result of the dialogue between Evangelical Alliance UK and Tearfund UK, Stephen Rand crafted a historic resolution, which was adopted by the Assembly of the World Evangelical Fellowship in Kuala Lumpur on 10 May 2001. As a global movement with 120 national alliances and some 104 organizations in its global membership, the WEF was an ideal vehicle to carry what many of us believed to be the 'mood' of the Holy Spirit in our world.

> As a global Christian community seeking to live in obedience to Scripture, we recognise the challenge of poverty across God's world. We welcome the international initiative to half world

> poverty by 2015, and pledge ourselves to do all we can, through our organisations and churches, to back this with prayerful, practical action in our nations and communities. . . . In this Jubilee year of the World Evangelical Fellowship, we urge governments and financial institutions of both North and South to act decisively, transparently and with integrity to combat corruption. . . . Taking the necessary steps to break the chains of debt and give new start to the world's poorest nations.[5]

This was an unprecedented resolution in the history of the World Evangelical Fellowship, later to become the World Evangelical Alliance.

In the same year, evangelical relief and development stepped into a new era with the birth of the Micah Network. In September 2001, the 'coalition of evangelical churches and agencies' represented by 140 leaders of Christian organizations from 50 countries met in Oxford, UK, for its first international conference 'to listen to God and each other for mutual learning, encouragement and strengthening as we serve the cause of the Kingdom of God among the poor.'[6]

At that conference, the Micah Network ratified its Declaration on integral mission:

> Integral mission or holistic transformation is the proclamation and demonstration of the gospel. It is not simply that evangelism and social involvement are to be done alongside each other. Rather, in integral mission our proclamation has social consequences as we call people to love and repentance in all areas of life. . . . If we ignore the word of God we have nothing to bring to the world. Justice and justification by faith, worship and political action, the spiritual and material, personal change and structural change belong together. As in the life of Jesus, being, doing and saying are at the heart of our integral task.[7]

Without any deliberate orchestration, both organizations were experiencing a spiritual and missional metamorphosis. In both cases they were prepared to restate their commitment to an integral approach to mission from an evangelical perspective. Given the historic relationships and the global nature of both these bodies, it soon became evident that a partnership around the aspirations of the MDGs was a serious possibility. The steps towards 2015 soon began in earnest.

Throughout 2002 conversations around the idea of a global Christian movement addressing the MDGs accelerated, and the World Evangelical Fellowship, which was morphing into the World Evangelical Alliance, pursued a deeper conversation with Micah Network.[8] The first comprehensive discussion paper emerged,[9] and in May 2002, at a special meeting of WEA general secretaries, Doug Balfour, director of Tearfund UK, introduced the emerging vision.[10] In the ferment of a new global evangelical identity and the appointment of a new international secretary,[11] the idea was warmly endorsed. Even before anyone had settled on an official name for this new idea, the vision was sufficiently compelling to instigate an invitation for Micah Network partners to get involved.[12] And in December that year, the first attempt to outline a potential structure of such a global movement was submitted to the fledgling steering group.[13]

2003

This turned out to be a year of significant steps. It was effectively the pivotal point at which the ideas of a global movement took practical shape. A great deal of momentum was provided by a small secretariat with Michael Smitherham's appointment as international coordinator and a small office housed by Tearfund UK. A significant amount of support came from Tear Australia and the expertise of the Micah Network community.

But among the many significant steps taken in this period two events were seminal in shaping the future: the Seattle Council in February and the September meeting in Mexico.

Seattle 24/25 February

From the outset it was clear that no one wanted to be part of a movement that did no more than mimic a political agenda. While the MDGs were an important launch pad, they were, 'no more than a starting point'.[14] There was a recognition that issues of trade and justice were not fully covered in the MDGs. The soul of the campaign, it was agreed, was to, 'capture God's heartbeat for the poor' and campaign for the fulfilment of the MDGs in order to, 'promote awareness and provoke the church in terms of the secular response to the issues of poverty'.[15] The MDGs remained central to the campaign not because they were comprehensive weapons in the war against poverty but because there was 'symmetry with the campaign goals and the message from the church . . .'[16] In any event the group concluded that the campaign should continue for at least five years beyond 2015.

In Seattle, Doug Balfour's *Shalom 20–15* proposals provided the discussion point for the infrastructure of the campaign. The shape of its council, its basic governance, budget, formal launch and a road map towards 2015 were all under discussion. The first Steering Group of the new 'Joint WEA/Micah Council' was identified with joint chairs from both parenting groups.[17] From the very outset, the group was deeply committed to supporting national campaigns in the South and tried to ensure that voices from the South were present as decision-makers. Of the nine Steering Group members, four were from the global South.

However, something important happened in Seattle: the campaign was given a name and two primary objectives. Here is how the first record described them:

- To provide the global evangelical community with a means of influencing national and international policies affecting key areas (also described as getting policy makers to do it). Key measure is therefore policy change.
- To significantly increase the involvement/action of evangelicals in favour of the poor (also described as doing it ourselves). Key measure is the register of participants.[18]

In addition, 'Micah Challenge' became the official name of the campaign.[19] Clearly, this title was derived from the already existing Micah Network and the positive ownership that the Micah Network had demonstrated towards the campaign. The fact that Micah Challenge also adopted Micah 6:8 as its biblical motif was a direct influence of the Micah Network, which had incorporated this text in 2001.[20]

When we left Seattle, a lot had changed. For the first time evangelical churches and agencies had collaborated in a global initiative to mobilize Christians and register their prophetic contribution to the global struggle against poverty. An idea was becoming a campaign.

Mexico 27/28 September

When we gathered in the old town of Queretaro, Mexico, for the second Micah Challenge council meeting, we did so in the aftermath of a global summit on climate change and poverty and immediately after a Micah Network gathering. A lot of preparatory work had already taken place, including the development of a National Campaigns Resource, which enabled national campaigns – particularly in the South – to get off the ground. In August, the secretariat published a 'Core Elements Discussion Document' that clarified the two objectives, developed the idea of a Micah Call and launched the campaign's logo. The logo was in effect a merger of Amos's passage of rivers of righteousness[21] with Micah's ideas of mercy, justice and humility.[22]

The Call was recognized as one of the central tools providing a global identity across the national campaigns. The idea was that the Call be targeted 'at a broad and inclusive audience; inspiring; clear, compelling and comprehensive, to include something of the MDGs' content.'[23] The Council's aim was to gather 25 million signatures and in excess of a million local churches.[24]

During the course of the meeting, two draft Micah Calls appeared for discussion:

> We commit ourselves, as followers of Jesus, to work together for the holistic transformation of our communities, 'to act justly, to love mercy and to walk humbly with our God.' (Micah 6:8)
>
> We call on the international and national decision-makers of both rich and poor nations to fulfil their public promise to achieve the Millennium Development Goals and so halve absolute global poverty by 2015.

We call on Christians everywhere to be agents of hope for and with the poor, and to hold their national leaders accountable in securing a more just and merciful world.

Micah Chullenge Council
28th September 2003

This is a unique moment in history when the stated intentions of world leaders echo something of the mind of the prophets and the teachings of Jesus on behalf of the world's poor.

Compelled by the Scriptures we commit ourselves, as followers of Jesus to work together for the transformation of our communities, to pursue justice, be passionate about mercy and to walk humbly with God.

We affirm world leaders in their promise to halve world poverty by 2015. We call on the international and national decision-makers of both rich and poor nations to act effectively on their commitment to achieve the Millennium Development Goals.

For our part we will do all in our power to deepen our Christian commitment to building hope, reducing poverty and keeping our leaders accountable for their role in securing a just and equitable world.

Micah Challenge Council
28th September 2003[25]

These early drafts, which were tested in the cross-cultural dialogue at the Council, went through further interrogation and nuancing from a range of theologians and Christian leaders across the world. Vinoth Ramachandra, the Sri Lankan theologian, provided some final drafting comments.[26]

The 2003 leg of the journey not only laid down some of the critical steps in its governance, structure and purpose, but also in terms of the vision, identity and character of the campaign. With the publication of a National Campaigns Resource Pack there was a sense that the campaign – now anticipating its official launch – was underway.

2004–2007

The years since 2003 have been a combination of anticipation and global developments for Micah Challenge. For one thing, it became increasingly clear that a global campaign needed a stronger infrastructure to survive the demands placed upon it. Consequently, the council meeting that took place immediately following the launch was particularly traumatic. It was not just a matter of getting structures sorted out; it was also the challenge of balancing representation between the global North and South, of sharing the responsibilities between the Micah Network and WEA – the two parent bodies – and ensuring that above everything else, priority was given to developing national campaigns on the ground.[27] But so much is also due to the contribution of the staff team, Michael Smitheram, Regine Nagel and Jill Howard, and key members of the Council such as Steve Bradbury (Tear Oz), Alfonso Wieland (Paz y Esperanza, Peru) and Paul Mususu (Evangelical Fellowship of Zambia), whose contributions helped Micah Challenge's glocal profile.

In the same period before the launch, national campaigns had emerged in a number of countries such as Canada, Australia, Switzerland, Netherlands, Sierra Leone, Ghana and Kenya. In May 2004, a small delegation from Micah Challenge UK went to visit the newly appointed International Development Secretary, Hilary Benn.[28]

In addition there was a real concern to ensure that a viable American model was up and running. As everyone knew, America's response to the MDGs and the critical issues of trade and debt would always be influential in the fight against global poverty. Consequently, American evangelicalism would have a key role to play. Few people thought this would be a viable proposition. But those of us who attended the lunch meeting to explore this possibility a few hours before the official launch sensed that something tangible was emerging on US soil.

Inevitably, Micah has had to adapt to the presence of other significant campaigns and events. Make Poverty History was prominent in the UK, and to some extent legitimately siphoned energy away from Micah. In the United States, the One

Campaign committed to bringing poverty alleviation to the US government and public. With significant backing from Gates, Google and Bono, it will increasingly become an important factor in the development of Micah Challenge USA and elsewhere in the world.

Council meetings in 2005 and 2006 struggled to match the expanding vision to limited resources. Despite the generosity of its principal members in the Micah Network[29] and contributions from the national campaigns,[30] Micah Challenge International struggled financially. A further practical challenge was the decision to operate the secretariat from two locations: Canberra and London.

From 2004 the campaign began to look ahead to 2007 – the halfway point for the fulfilment of the MDGs. It was largely from the global South that the idea of a 'Blow the Whistle' campaign emerged as a way to mark this transition point.

Now present in 34 countries, Micah Challenge has a potent vision and a positive future. Those of us who have been close to the centre of things are aware that it still has a long way to go in coming into its own. Micah Challenge is not a self-contained movement but has come to define itself as, 'a part of a global movement campaigning for the fulfilment of the Millennium Development Goals'.[31] And it is equally aware that such a movement can never be an exclusively evangelical club. In the battle to eradicate poverty, Micah Challenge presents itself not as an evangelical mission to the world but rather as an evangelical contribution to God's mission in the world. And in doing so it contributes to the wider ecumenical struggle against poverty. If Micah Challenge remains true to itself it will retain its evangelical heart. If it is to remain true to its task, it will also refuse to limit itself to evangelicals, drawing instead from the wider Christian family and civic society.

The campaign's two goals continue to drive the strategies and programmes: to deepen our commitment to the poor and to advocate for and with the poor against injustice and poverty.

In seeking to fulfil its role as an effective advocate with the poor, Micah Challenge is already an integral member of Global Call to Action Against Poverty (GCAP). It is also highly respected by the United Nations Millennium Campaign. In a recent meeting with the UN, discussions took place which would strengthen the relationship between Micah Challenge Sunday[32] and the Guinness Record 'Stand Up' against poverty Day. In the USA, the National Association of Evangelicals and Micah Challenge US hosted an October 2007 meeting of some 30 international church leaders. The meeting was sponsored by the UN development office in the USA with the UN secretary general as the guest of honour.

In a recent conversation with the assistant director of the UN Development Programme for Africa, Micah Challenge received a striking endorsement. 'If I could get the churches in Africa to adopt Micah Challenge,' she said, 'it would reduce my work by 50 per cent!'[33] In the events that accompanied Micah Sunday 2006, it was clear that in countries such as Australia, Malawi and Zambia governments were responding to these campaigns.

But Micah Challenge has never been *primarily* concerned with political advocacy. Its principal concern is to deepen Christian commitment to the poor. From the outset, the campaign has been convinced that the church's credibility in this long-term campaign depended on its own willingness to live in accordance with God's heart for the poor. In seeking to deepen our commitment, Micah Challenge is passionate about pushing Christians beyond passive giving to lifestyles that more accurately reflect the biblical appeal to 'pour out your soul to the poor.'[34] This accounts for the steady and continued emphasis on prayer, which rests at the heart of the campaign. Micah Sunday is, in fact, a commitment to root the campaign in the local church with an appeal to the wider society.

But the campaign has also drawn together Christian NGOs and churches from a range of traditions. Indeed, it has also sparked real partnerships between churches in Africa and the USA in order to model what it means to deepen our commitment to the poor.

The value of this campaign as a long-term response to measurable targets is that it presents Christian witness as a prophetic voice in critical partnership with governments who have, perhaps unwittingly, expressed the heart of the Scriptures in terms of God's commitment to the poor.

2

Loving Mercy: Restoring Personhood, Restoring Society

Archbishop Njongonkulu Ndungane

It was my singular honour and privilege in October 2004 to be invited to be the founding Patron of Micah Challenge, and to address the launch held in New York. I spoke then of how when Jesus began his public ministry, he read from the scroll of the prophet Isaiah, almost as a way of setting out the 'manifesto' for the course he intended to pursue, 'The Spirit of the Lord is upon me, because he has anointed me to bring good news to the poor . . .' (Lk. 4:18)

It is as if the opening shot of the gospel (a word which itself means 'good news') is indeed 'Good news for the poor, for the afflicted, for the oppressed . . . and the favour of the Lord.'

One aspect of God's favour is his loving kindness towards us, the loving kindness of Micah 6:8, which he expects us also to show to others. As I said in New York, 'to love loyalty, kindness, mercy, loving kindness' means 'to recognize in every human being the spark of the image of God, and grant them the same dignity, the same respect, the same opportunities that we enjoy, in this life as well as in the life to come.'

This is something we are called upon to do for individuals, and for communities: to restore personhood and restore society where both have been denied the dignity, respect and opportunities that are God's gift to his children. So let us consider further what this 'loving mercy' is all about.

'*Hesed*' is one of the great words of the Old Testament. It has no exact English equivalent. Generally it is translated as loyalty, faithfulness and goodness. Whenever the Bible speaks of the 'steadfast love' of the Lord, it is *hesed* we are talking about. And therefore, in the words taken up by Micah Challenge, when our Lord requires us to 'do justice, to love kindness and to walk humbly with our God,' it is *hesed* to which we are called, alongside justice and humility.

Within Scripture, the word *hesed* occurs on almost 250 occasions (and just over half of these are in the Psalms). While three-quarters of all the citations speak of *hesed* as a quality of God and of his dealings with his people, a full quarter refer to the relationships there are, or ought to be, between human beings.

The call from the prophet Micah is that we should emulate God, showing to others the same kindness and mercy that he shows to us. Of course, to Christians this should come as no surprise. To be Jesus' disciple means not only to study his teachings, but to learn to follow his lifestyle. He is the One who told his followers to 'love one another as I have loved you.' When it comes to showing *hesed* to others, we can be entirely sure this is one answer to the question of 'what would Jesus do?'

One important aspect of *hesed* is that it cannot exist in a vacuum. An isolated individual cannot be a person of *hesed*, there needs to be someone else to whom *hesed* is shown. God extends his loving kindness and mercy to us. For us to be kind and merciful means that there must be others to whom we show it.

According to biblical scholars, those who have the upper hand in a relationship are those who are expected to show *hesed*: the rich to the poor, the strong to the weak, the powerful to the insignificant, the influential to the marginalized and the insider to the outsider. What is particularly interesting is the extent to which this obligation exists where people already have some prior connectedness. *Hesed* is an intrinsic responsibility that comes with the relationship of mutual belonging, for example, as a result of the covenant God makes with his people, or through being fellow members of the people of God.

Hesed is part of the daily oiling of the wheels of relationship and community that maintains the bonds of unity.

It is not surprising therefore that we find the call to *hesed* in the words of the prophet Micah, with his condemnation of the way the leaders of 'Jacob and the house of Israel' exploit the people (see Mic. 3). Morally obliged to safeguard those in their care, they instead exploit them.

I wonder if this is ringing bells for you, as you consider the world today! No wonder this powerful verse symbolizes Christian commitment to strive for global economic justice through the Millennium Development Goals, and has provided the rallying call, and even the title of, Micah Challenge.

There is another aspect of *hesed* we should note. Many of us for years have sung the chorus, 'The steadfast love of the Lord never ceases, his mercies never come to an end; they are new every morning (new every morning), great is your faithfulness.' These words come from the Book of Lamentations (Lam. 3:22,23). In the midst of Jeremiah's lengthy laments over the fate of Jerusalem, he can say 'but this I call to mind, and therefore I have hope . . .'

What moves Jeremiah to have hope is that the *hesed* of God is not found in one-off gestures here and there; it is an attitude characterizing and encompassing all his dealings with his people. It is steadfast, unchangeable, unceasing, persisting through thick and thin with unending faithfulness.

This should encourage us as we are halfway through the timescale of the Millennium Development Goals. We are in this for the long haul, through thick and thin. We know that the progress with many of the goals has been more than disappointing. But, moved by God's loving kindness and mercy to us, we are not going to give up in our efforts to ensure our governments and international institutions fulfil the promises that they have made. Drawing strength from God's faithfulness to us, we will be faithful to others also. We know he has given us this responsibility.

Perhaps you know the rabbinical saying that If the Lord does not come himself, he will certainly send.

There is a story about a man trapped on the roof of his house as the floods are rising. First the fire brigade come by with a long ladder, giving him the chance to cross to higher ground. 'No, no' he answers, 'I am waiting here in faithful prayer, for the Lord will save me.' A little later, the floods are still rising, and a man passes in a rowing boat and offers to take him to dry land, but he gives the same answer. The waters keep rising, and a helicopter comes and hovers overhead, and one of the crew is winched down to pull him to safety. But his answer is the same as he sits tight on his roof. Finally, the floods carry him away and he is drowned. He dies and goes to heaven, and meets the Lord. 'Lord!' he cries in indignation, 'there I was on the roof of my house, praying faithfully to you to save me, and you did not answer my prayer!' 'What do you mean, I didn't answer your prayer? I sent the fire brigade, the navy and the air force!'

Of course, the joke is about a man who has too narrow a view of faith and of the way God works in this world. But we should also draw the lesson that sometimes we are the ones whom the Lord is sending to answer the prayers of others. Almost everyone who reads this book will be among the world's prosperous. All of us who enjoy such advantages must therefore recognize that we have a God-given obligation towards everyone else within our human family who is not so privileged, an obligation that includes exercising *hesed*.

The God who shows us loving kindness and mercy is of course far superior to us. Yet, it is important to recognize that he does not show us *hesed* in order to lord it over us, Lord though he truly is. He shows us *hesed* in order to bind us to him in love. *Hesed* is far more practical than merely an attitude of generous magnanimity. Often it is linked to the tangible protection that God offers, a refuge to his people in times of trouble, or to the provision of food in times of need. In Joshua 2:12, the prostitute Rahab is able to speak of the *hesed* she has shown in hiding the Hebrew spies who have come to Jericho, and then asks that they in turn, when the city is captured, should show *hesed* to her and her family. Thus there can be a dynamic reciprocity between human beings who share *hesed* with changing circumstances. *Hesed* draws both parties closer, strengthening their relationship so that it is ever more characterized by Christlike living with one another. Family members, for example, are expected to show *hesed* to one another, demonstrating the aspect of mutual loyalty that *hesed* also carries.

Therefore for us to show *hesed* to others is to declare our commitment to them in love, and our loyalty, even respect, for them. *Hesed* honours the other person, underlining the fact that we consider ourselves bound in relationship to them. In development terms, we can see this as reflecting the need to consider ourselves partners with, rather than benefactors towards, the developing world

Partnership is a vital aspect of the Millennium Development Goals. It is only when those on the ground participate fully in the process of developing the policies and programmes designed to help them that we are likely to make lasting progress.

Within Africa, civil society is now becoming a far more active partner in this pursuit of prosperity for all. You will not be surprised to hear that it is the churches, in partnership with other faith communities, who are taking a lead. There are three particular ways in which we are helping to make a difference.

The first is through our activities within local communities. We often have networks where governments do not reach. In many African countries, faith groups provide an average of 40 per cent of all health care. Our potential role as partners in development has only recently been recognized; but I am delighted to say that this recognition is now bearing much fruit, as we increasingly become partners in projects with donors and NGOs who previously wanted to work only on a secular basis.

Second, the real test of the Millennium Development Goals is whether they make a tangible and sustainable difference to the lives of the very poorest. Faith communities, to which these people belong, are often best placed to give accurate feedback on what is actually being achieved. We must make the voice of the poorest heard in the corridors of power; they must know the power of *hesed* exercised on their behalf, so that they may experience its inclusive embrace.

The third area where faith communities within the developing world can use their networks is to help our civil society bring a coordinated and focused grass-roots perspective to the development debate, both in holding our own governments to account, and in calling on donors to meet their commitments swiftly, efficiently and effectively. In this way, we can be an effective and complementary counterpart to the voice of civil society, through organizations like Micah Challenge, in the global North.

'African Monitor' is an initiative I launched last year, which is aimed precisely at these last two aspects. Please pray for us as we develop our capacity to fulfil this important role. We are not explicitly a Christian body as we embrace all of our continent's people, but God's love and God's *hesed* are at the heart of what we are working to achieve.

Acting together, Christians can play a vital role in helping global partners meet their commitments. When we work with one another, united across nationalities and races, across rich and poor, across men, women and children, we have an enormously powerful and influential voice. We must speak up loud and clear.

There is no doubt that the world can afford to do all that is necessary to meet the Millennium Development Goals. But there is a large question mark against whether or not we have the willpower. Governments and business can say the words, but they need all the encouragement, all the pressure, that we can give, to deliver the goods. They need to hear that their citizens truly want them to take the hard steps that are required, so we may live in a world where there is some for all, not all for just some; in a world where loving kindness and mercy are valued above naked profit at the expense of the poor and weak.

'Love one another as I have loved you' said Jesus, and one aspect of the love of God which we have come to know is the *hesed* of his steadfast, loving, mercy and kindness. It comes from his unfailing committing of himself in covenant to his people, committing himself to our flourishing, to our enjoyment of abundant life. He calls on us to recognize the global interconnectedness of the whole human family, bound together as his children, and to live out a similar long-term commitment to the well-being of every human individual, and every society with whom we share this planet.

Therefore, as Paul writes to the Thessalonians, let us 'never tire of doing what is right' (2 Thess. 3:13).

3

Walk Humbly with Your God

Tim Chester

He has told you, O man, what is good;
and what does the Lord require of you
but to do justice, and to love kindness,
and to walk humbly with your God? (Mic. 6:8)

It is easy to see what justice and kindness have to do with a concern for the poor. It is easy to see why they might have caused this verse to have been chosen to give a name and identity to the Micah Network. But what about humility? Have we moved into different territory, another area of Christian discipleship unrelated to social justice? Does humility simply describe the manner in which we go about development and advocacy? Or is humility more integral to Christian social involvement?

Back in the sixth century, Gregory the Great said, 'belief in inequality arises from the spring of pride'.[1] In other words, people accommodate inequality by reasoning that their wealth and privileges arise from some kind of superiority, whether skills, experience, entrepreneurial drive or national character. According to research by George Barna in the United States, the most widely known Bible verse is: 'God helps those who help themselves.'[2] The tragic irony, of course, is that this is not from the Bible at all; it comes from the Greek storyteller Aesop, entering the consciousness of modern Western culture through the 1736 edition of Benjamin Franklin's *Poor Richard's*

Almanack. Instead, the Bible says God helps those who humble themselves (Jas. 4:6,10).

Consider the effect on a culture of the proclamation that God helps those who help themselves. Such a culture will see prosperity as a reward for self-attainment. 'Wealth is my achievement,' people will suppose, 'I deserve it and it entails no moral responsibility toward those who do not deserve it. The poor must be at fault in some way, receiving a just outcome for their fecklessness which I have escaped as a result of my virtue.' We can begin to see how Gregory's assertion might play out in practice: 'Belief in inequality arises from the spring of pride.'

The point is not that the poor are never responsible for their poverty. It seems to be a commonplace in development circles that the poor must be exonerated if we are to promote social involvement. The culpability of the powerful is highlighted to the virtual exclusion of personal responsibility and local corruption. But we must not romanticize the poor. At times, the poor do make bad decisions, pursue idolatrous desires and live in slavery to sin.

No, the point is that the blessings enjoyed by the prosperous are a generous gift from God. Paul's 'evangelistic pitch' in Lystra was to invite his hearers to acknowledge the God who 'did good by giving you rains from heaven and fruitful seasons, satisfying your hearts with food and gladness.' (Acts 14:17) Our upbringing, education and intelligence should not make us feel superior; they should make us feel thankful. They are gifts from God. They should make us grateful. And never far behind true gratitude are her sister virtues: generosity and humility.

The humility of Jesus

'What do you want me to do for you?' It was a strange question for Jesus to ask the blind man who had called out to him for mercy. Surely it was obvious. 'Rabbi, let me recover my sight' (Mk. 10:51). The blind man wants to see. But Jesus' words echo his response to another recent delegation.

> And James and John, the sons of Zebedee, came up to him and said to him, 'Teacher, we want you to do for us whatever we ask of you.' And he said to them, 'What do you want me to do for you?' And they said to him, 'Grant us to sit, one at your right hand and one at your left, in your glory.' (Mk. 10:35–37)

The word-for-word repetition of Jesus' question to both the blind man and the brothers Zebedee highlights the links between the two events. James and John are blind. They do not see the true nature of Jesus' kingship and kingdom. They want the positions of highest honour and the top jobs in the coming kingdom. But, says Jesus, 'You do not know what you are asking. Are you able to drink the cup that I drink, or to be baptized with the baptism with which I am baptized?' (Mk. 10:38) The route to the throne is via the cross. When the blind man receives his sight he follows Jesus 'on the way' and in Mark 8 – 10 the way is the way to the cross. Those who truly see, see that following Jesus means following the way of the cross. They see the true nature of honour, authority and greatness in the kingdom of God. Sandwiched between these two stories Jesus says to the twelve:

> You know that those who are considered rulers of the Gentiles lord it over them, and their great ones exercise authority over them. But it shall not be so among you. But whoever would be great among you must be your servant, and whoever would be first among you must be slave of all. For even the Son of Man came not to be served but to serve, and to give his life as a ransom for many. (Mk. 10:42–45)

'Clothe yourselves, all of you, with humility toward one another,' says Peter, 'for "God opposes the proud but gives grace to the humble."' (1 Pet. 5:5) It may well be that Peter had in mind the example of Jesus on the night before he died. John 13 describes how Jesus 'got up from the meal, took off his outer clothing, and wrapped a towel round his waist' (v. 4). He clothed himself with the apron of humility. And then 'he poured water into a basin and began to wash his disciples' feet' (v. 5). What makes this all the more remarkable are the three things that John highlights Jesus knew as he performed this act of humble service; things that utterly undermine our excuses for not serving others:

- Jesus knew his time had come (v. 1). If anyone could have said he was too busy, it was Jesus.
- Jesus knew he had all authority (v. 3). If anyone could have said he was too important, it was Jesus.
- Jesus knew Judas would betray him (v. 11). If anyone could have said he was too often let down, it was Jesus.

When he had washed their feet, put on his outer garments and resumed his place, Jesus himself comments by saying:

> Do you understand what I have done to you? You call me Teacher and Lord, and you are right, for so I am. If I then, your Lord and Teacher, have washed your feet, you also ought to wash one another's feet. For I have given you an example, that you also should do just as I have done to you. Truly, truly, I say to you, a servant is not greater than his master, nor is a messenger greater than the one who sent him. If you know these things, blessed are you if you do them. (Jn. 13:12–17)

While we vie for positions of honour, Jesus was wearing an apron. While we pursue power and cling to authority, Jesus was among us as one who serves. While we compete for publicity or esteem, Jesus was at our feet.

But the example of Jesus is not enough. On its own, it leaves us with an unattainable model. Worse, it can be a self-defeating model. In *The Screwtape Letters*, C. S. Lewis creates a fictional correspondence between two demons outlining the strategies to be employed to harm Christians.

> Your patient has become humble; have you drawn his attention to the fact? All virtues are less formidable to us once the man is aware that he has them, but this is especially true of humility. Catch him at the moment when he is really poor in spirit and smuggle into his mind the gratifying reflection, 'By jove! I'm being humble,' and almost immediately pride – pride at his

> own humility – will appear. If he awakes to the danger and tries to smother this new form of pride, make him proud of his attempt – and so on, through as many stages as you please. But don't try this too long, for fear you awake his sense of humour and proportion, in which case he will merely laugh at you and go to bed.[3]

Humility cannot be *achieved!* Lewis goes on to define humility as self-forgetfulness. When you meet a humble person you do not leave them thinking, 'What a humble person.' You leave thinking, 'That person was really interested in me.' Humility is not falsely thinking our abilities are less valuable than they really are: 'clever men trying to believe they are fools.' 'The great thing,' advises the demon Screwtape with his inverted logic, 'is to make him value an opinion for some quality other than truth, thus introducing an element of dishonesty and make-believe . . . Since what they are trying to believe may, in some cases, be manifest nonsense, they cannot succeed in believing it and we have the chance of keeping their minds endlessly revolving on themselves in an effort to achieve the impossible.'[4] Humility is self-forgetfulness and so it will never be attained through continual self-monitoring. But if humility is self-forgetfulness, how are we to remember to forget ourselves?

The great English Puritan John Owen may help us. He said, 'There are two things that are suited to humble the souls of men and they are first, a due consideration of God and then of themselves – of God in his greatness, glory, holiness, power, majesty, and authority; of ourselves, in our mean, abject, and sinful condition.'[5] We look at ourselves through the prism of God's glory, seeing ourselves as small creatures of a vast God and unworthy servants of a great King. We look at ourselves through the prism of Christ's cross, seeing ourselves as sinners saved by grace pointing other sinners to the fountain of grace.

The glory of God

The call to walk humbly before God is addressed in Micah 6 to 'you, O man': 'He has told you, O man, what is good . . . to walk humbly with your God?' (v. 8) It is an expression that emphasizes our creatureliness. It is the word *ADAM* from which the first man takes his name. We are transported back to Eden and our fashioning by God from 'the dust from the ground' (Gen. 2:7). We are put in our place. '*Man* is frequently used in the OT as a contrast to divine power and glory, stressing what is creaturely in the human constitution. Here it is intended to remind the people of their subordination to God and to cut them down to size after their presumptuous retort.'[6]

Humility begins with a vision of God and his glory. We remember our place in the universe. We were made for God's glory. He, and not me, is the Almighty, the Holy One, the Creator, robed in splendour. He, and not me, is central and sovereign. God's aseity, immutability, eternity and omnipresence humble us. They are his incommunicable attributes for we cannot share them, not even in part. Matthew Henry said, 'The greatest and best man in the world must say, By the grace of God *I am what I am*; but God says absolutely – and it is more than any creature, man or angel, can say – *I am that I am*.'[7] The Puritan, Thomas Watson, says, 'When we have done anything praiseworthy, we must hide ourselves under the veil of humility, and transfer the glory of all we have done to God.'[8]

The earth is part of our solar system. But our sun is only one star among 100,000,000,000 that make up our galaxy, the Milky Way. The Milky Way is so vast that light travelling at 186,000 miles a second takes 100,000 years to pass from one end to the other. And yet the Milky Way itself is only one galaxy among at least 100,000,000 others. Isaiah tells us that God marked off the heavens with the breadth of his hand (Isa. 40:12). It is a spatial metaphor for a God who exists outside of space, but it gives us a sense of 'the scale of God': the whole universe fits in his hand. Hold your hand up: the universe is that big to God. If we ever think we are important or necessary or great, then we have been afflicted with a massive and preposterous loss of perspective.

God is not only glorious, but his glory is our chief end. Pride is not just a sin, but part of the very definition of sin. Pride puts us in the place of God. We turn from our chief end of glorying God and make our chief end glorifying ourselves.

C. J. Mahaney speaks of 'cosmic plagiarism'.[9] To pursue honour, praise or pre-eminence is a sinful pursuit that seeks to rob God of his glory. We reveal that we value the praise of ourselves above the praise of God. We reveal that we value approval from people above approval from God.

This is why humility is a paradigm of repentance. To humble ourselves before God is to repent of our god-complex. This is why to walk humbly before our God is what God requires. This is 'what is good'. We turn from our desire to be God and submit to the sovereign rule of God.

> *For thus says the One who is high and lifted up,*
> *who inhabits eternity, whose name is Holy:*
> *'I dwell in the high and holy place,*
> *and also with him who is of a contrite and lowly spirit,*
> *to revive the spirit of the lowly,*
> *and to revive the heart of the contrite.'* (Isa. 57:15)

Where does 'the One who is high and lifted up' dwell? Perhaps he dwells with the powerful? Perhaps he lives with the great ones of this world? No, his ways are utterly unlike our own. The One who is high and who dwells in a high place lives with him who is of a lowly spirit. The One whose name is Holy and who dwells in a holy place lives with those who are contrite.

In Isaiah 66:1 the LORD proclaims his glory, 'Heaven is my throne, and the earth is my footstool.' He does not depend on humanity in any way, '"What is the house that you would build for me, and what is the place of my rest? All these things my hand has made, and so all these things came to be," declares the Lord.' (vv. 1–2) 'But,' he continues, 'this is the one to whom I will look: he who is humble and contrite in spirit and trembles at my word' (v. 2).

The statement in Hosea 12:6 that parallels Micah 6:8 says: 'So you, by the help of your God, return, hold fast to love and justice, and wait continually for your God.' What God requires of us is to return or repent and that means humbling ourselves before God and continually trusting in (or waiting on) him. It is the same as the call for faith and repentance with which Jesus begins his ministry: 'The time is fulfilled, and the kingdom of God is at hand; repent and believe in the gospel.' (Mk. 1:14–15)

The cross of Jesus

The life of Jesus provides a wonderful model of humility to follow. But if we want to be humble people we must move from looking at the life of Jesus to look at the cross of Jesus. His life shows us humility; his cross humbles us. It is at the cross that we see ourselves as we really are. Here are two quotes from the two 'greats' (in the spirit of Mk. 10:43) of twentieth-century British evangelicalism, Martyn Lloyd-Jones and John Stott:

> There is only one thing I know of that crushes me to the ground and humiliates me to the dust, and that is to look at the Son of God, and especially contemplate the cross . . . Nothing else can do it. When I see that I am a sinner . . . that nothing but the Son of God on the cross can save me, I'm humbled to the dust . . . Nothing but the cross can give us this spirit of humility.[10]

> The cross tells us some very unpalatable truths about ourselves, namely that we are sinners under the righteous curse of God's law and we cannot save ourselves. Christ bore our sin and curse precisely because we could gain release from them in no other way. If we could have been forgiven by our good works, by being circumcised and keeping the law, we may be quite sure that there would have been no cross. Cf. Galatians 2:21. Every time we look at the cross Christ seems to be saying to us, 'I am here because of you. It is your sin I am bearing, your curse I am suffering, your death I am dying.' Nothing in history or in the universe cuts us down to size like the cross. All of us have inflated views of ourselves, especially in self-righteousness, until we have visited a place called Calvary. It is there, at the foot of the cross, that we shrink to our true size.[11]

On the cross we see our sin and we are cut down to size. And on the cross we see God's grace. Micah 6:8 calls on us 'to walk humbly with your God'. 'Your God' here is one half of the covenant formulation, 'You shall be my people and I shall be your God.' The other half comes a few verses earlier in verse 3: 'O my people, what have I done to you? How have I wearied you? Answer me!' The people have nothing to say in response and so God answers his own question: 'For I brought you up from the land of Egypt and redeemed you from the house of slavery, and I sent before you Moses, Aaron, and Miriam,' (v. 4). God is being ironic: what God did for his people that was so wearying was graciously to redeem them! The wording is taken from the introduction to the Decalogue, 'I am the Lord your God, who brought you out of the land of Egypt, out of the house of slavery,' (Ex. 20:2). The people find God's law wearying, but they have forgotten that it was set in the context of redemption and grace. The 'kindness' or 'mercy' that we are to love is *hesed* – covenant love, faithful love, loving-kindness. It is not first and foremost our love, but God's covenant faithfulness to his people. It is the love for his people to which God binds himself in covenant promises. It is God's gracious loving kindness to us that creates both the foundation and pattern for our loving kindness to others.

Micah writes to a culture obsessed by money. 'What is good' is measured by the people in monetary terms much as it is in our day. Verses 6–7 apply the same values to our relationship with God.

With what shall I come before the Lord,
and bow myself before God on high?
Shall I come before him with burnt offerings,
with calves a year old?
Will the Lord be pleased with thousands of rams,
with ten thousands of rivers of oil?
Shall I give my firstborn for my transgression,
the fruit of my body for the sin of my soul? (Mic. 6:6–7)

The result is a dreadful parody of the true meaning of sacrifice and atonement. That which was a pointer to God's grace and his promise of atonement becomes a deal struck between equals. Sacrifice becomes a means by which we buy off God. A relationship with God is given a price, 'a thousand rams'. And if that will not do then add a few noughts, 'ten thousands of rivers of oil'. But God cannot be bought and sold.

If verses 6–7 are a parody of sacrifice, the cross is the reality. The Levitical system of sacrifice was never a means for buying off God. It was, as the writer of Hebrews explains (Heb. 9:1 – 10:20), a pointer to the sacrifice for sin that God himself would provide just as he had promised to Abraham (Gen. 22:14). 'Shall I give my firstborn for my transgression, the fruit of my body for the sin of my soul?' asks Micah 6:7. The answer is that we do not need to give our firstborn because God himself gives his firstborn. It is an allusion not only to Abraham and Isaac, but also to the Passover. A firstborn lamb was sacrificed as a substitute in the place of 'my firstborn'. Now God has given his first and only Son (Rom. 8:32) as a substitute Passover Lamb to redeem us from the penalty and power of our sin. On the cross I see the depth of the 'sin of my soul'. Only the blood of God's firstborn, the most precious thing in the entire universe, could pay the price of my redemption. 'You were ransomed from the futile ways inherited from your forefathers, not with perishable things such as silver or gold, but with the precious blood of Christ, like that of a lamb without blemish or spot.' (1 Pet. 1:18–19) Walking humbly in the light of the cross means an inevitable and resolute rejection of all self-confidence and all self-righteousness.

Micah 6:8 calls on us to *walk* humbly with our God. It may be that Paul had Micah's statement in mind in Ephesians where he repeatedly describes the Christian life as walking with God. Ephesians 2:1–2 says 'you were dead in the transgressions and sin in which you once *walked*'. And the section ends in verse 10 with 'we are his workmanship created in Christ for good works, which God prepared beforehand, that we should *walk* in them.' We move from walking in sin to walking in good works. The 'meat' in this sandwich is the wonderful grace of God, raising us with Christ and seating us in heavenly realms. We move from death to life, slavery to freedom, wrath to grace. And this transformation is not in any way the result of our work so there is no room for boasting. Instead it stands as an eternal testimony to God's glorious grace (1:6,12,14; 2:7). 'Walking' becomes a key theme in the latter half of the epistle: We are to take care how we walk, walking in a manner worthy of our calling, not walking as the Gentiles do, but instead walking in the light and walking in love (4:1,17; 5:2,8,15). But this is all built on the foundation of grace laid in chapter 2.

The secret of humility is never to stray far from the cross. It should often be in our thoughts, often on our lips, often in our songs, determining our actions, shaping our attitudes, captivating our affections. This is why the remembrance of the Lord's death in communion is so integral to Christian discipleship.

The cross subverts all human notions of glory. The message that we proclaim – the message of Christ crucified – is folly and weakness in the sight of the world. 'We preach Christ crucified, a stumbling block to Jews and folly to Gentiles, but to those who are called, both Jews and Greeks, the proclamation of Christ crucified is Christ the power of God and the wisdom of God. For the foolishness of God is wiser than men, and the weakness of God is stronger than men.' (1 Cor. 1:23–25) And with this foolish, weak message of the cross goes a foolish, weak community of the cross.

> But God chose what is foolish in the world to shame the wise; God chose what is weak in the world to shame the strong; God chose what is low and despised in the world, even things that are not, to bring to nothing things that are, so that no human being might boast in the presence of God. (vv. 27–29)

The cross leaves no scope for human boasting. Instead our one boast is in Christ Jesus, 'our wisdom and our righteousness and sanctification and redemption.' So, 'Let the one who boasts, boast in the Lord' (vv. 30–31). We need to ditch our worldly notions of success. We need to ditch our modernistic preoccupation with numbers and size. We need to turn our notions of success upside down so that we align them with God's kingdom perspective (Mk. 4:26–32).

And we are not finished yet. With the message of the cross and the community of the cross goes a ministry shaped by the cross:

> And I, when I came to you, brothers, did not come proclaiming to you the testimony of God with lofty speech or wisdom. For I decided to know nothing among you except Jesus Christ and him crucified. And I was with you in weakness and in fear and much trembling, and my speech and my message were not in plausible words of wisdom, but in demonstration of the Spirit and of power, that your faith might not rest in the wisdom of men but in the power of God. (1 Cor. 2:1–5)

Our *modus operandi* is not eloquence or wisdom, but weakness and fear. 'We have this treasure in jars of clay, to show that the surpassing power belongs to God and not to us' (2 Cor. 4:7).

It is tempting for us to think that what we need most is political influence, media profile, national campaigns or mega-churches. But Jesus says the kingdom of God has been given to his 'little flock' (Lk. 12:32). Martin Luther distinguished between a theology of glory and a theology of the cross. The theology of glory seeks the revelation of God in the power and glory of his actions. The theology of the cross sees the ultimate revelation of God in the cross. By faith we see in the cross power in weakness, wisdom in folly and glory in shame. We need to develop a corresponding understanding of the *church of the cross*[12] of which the phrase 'Christ's little flock' is an image. The problem is that 'power made perfect in weakness' (2 Cor. 12:9) is so counter-intuitive and counter-cultural that we do not believe it. We believe that God will use the powerful and important and impressive. But he does not. We need the radical change of perspective that the cross brings.

A community of the broken

Humility has everything to do with the poor. In Luke 14 Jesus observes guests vying for positions of honour at the table: the antithesis of humility. He calls on his hearers to take a low position so that the host may promote them to a position of higher honour. It is not advice on social etiquette; it is an eschatological warning. Jesus' conclusion is: 'For everyone who exalts himself will be humbled, and he who humbles himself will be exalted' (Lk. 11:14). One of the recurring themes of Luke's Gospel is that a day of eschatological reversal is coming (see, for example, Lk. 1:51–53; 6:20–26; 13:30). God will include the marginalized and Gentiles who have faith in his Son, and exclude (judge) the self-important, self-serving and self-sufficient, exemplified in the religious elite of Israel. The first shall be last and the last shall be first. The certainty of this assertion is found in the ministry of Jesus (Lk. 1:4). Repeatedly in Luke's Gospel, Jesus welcomes and eats with sinners, thereby declaring and embodying the riches of God's grace, while at the same time confronting the self-confident and self-righteous.

In Luke 14 Jesus goes on to tell the parable of a great banquet. The master of the banquet sends out invitations, but people make excuses. So he sends his servants to 'bring in the poor and crippled and blind and lame,' (v. 21). God graciously invites the broken people to his messianic banquet. But this story follows an exchange in which Jesus says, 'When you give a dinner or a banquet, do not invite your friends or your brothers or your relatives or rich neighbours, lest they also invite you in return and you be repaid. But when you give a feast, invite the poor, the crippled, the lame, the blind,' (vv. 12–13). It is the same four categories that are invited to God's banquet. We are to reflect God's grace to us in the way we treat the marginalized. We are not to prioritize our rich neighbours. Our focus is to be on the poor and needy. Indeed part of our evangelism to the rich is our evangelism to the needy. We subvert their preoccupation with power and success as they see us loving the unlovely. We expose their self-righteousness and selfishness as they see us eating with outcasts. They begin to see Jesus living through us.[13]

There is a considerable debate about whether the proclamation by Jesus of good news to the poor (Lk. 4:18–19; 7:22) and his pronouncements of blessing to the poor (Mt. 5:3; Lk. 6:20) refer to the economically poor or the spiritually humble. I will not rehearse the arguments again. But my experience of thinking through these issues in the context of church planting among the urban poor in the United Kingdom makes me wonder whether the debate represents a false polarization. There are economically poor people and economically rich people, but the truth is we are all broken people. Sin ravages everyone's life. The impact of that sin varies, but we are all broken. And, paraphrasing the first Matthean beatitude, blessed are the broken people for the kingdom of God belongs to them. I count it a great privilege to be a broken person serving broken people for this is where God's blessing is found.

The real divide that the first beatitude opens up is not between the economically poor and the spiritually humble. It is between Christian communities that hide their brokenness and Christian communities that are open about their brokenness. The former value respectability and order, maintaining this through a culture of pretending in which 'mess' is hidden or ignored. Communities of broken people in contrast are comfortable with 'mess' and messy people do not feel exceptional or uncomfortable. Problems are out in the open where they can be addressed. Above all, such communities are communities of grace. Every person lives as a sinner who has received divine grace and relates to others on this basis. Grace treats sin neither as something that is unimportant, nor as something that must remain hidden. These are the communities that Jesus came to establish.

The beatitudes of Matthew 5 are not statements of piety or advice for happy living. They are declarations of liberation. Matthew's many quotations from, and allusions to, the Old Testament in chapters 1 – 4 present Jesus as the one who will bring the exile to an end and effect the promised new exodus. He is the one who will liberate God's people from slavery to sin and its effects – personal, social and economic. The community of Jesus will be restored to life under the reign of God (v. 3). They will receive the comfort promised to the exiles in Isaiah 40:1–3 (v. 4). The promise to the meek or humble in verse 5 is a reference to Psalm 37:11, which promises that 'the meek will inherit the land'. In the context of exile, it is the promise of return to the land, except that Jesus now has the whole earth in view. To hunger for justice is to seek God's liberating intervention and to be satisfied is to enjoy the land of milk and honey again. 'Sons of God' is what Israel was called when Moses demanded that Pharaoh set them free (Ex. 4:22–23). The 'sons of God' are the liberated ones. Jesus is declaring liberation to the broken, the mournful, the meek.

The fullness of this liberation is eschatological, but it is already anticipated in Jesus' new jubilee community. Jesus follows the beatitudes in Matthew by saying: 'You are the salt of the earth, but if salt has lost its taste, how shall its saltiness be restored? It is no longer good for anything except to be thrown out and trampled under people's feet' (Mt. 5:13). Salt in the Old Testament was a sign of covenant faithfulness (Ex. 30:35; Num. 18:19; Lev. 2:13; 2 Chr. 13:5). But the community of Israel has not been faithful to the covenant. Being thrown out and trampled under foot is the language of exile and conquest. Israel was exiled, but now God is creating a new people through Jesus. So Jesus calls his disciples to be God's covenant community, warning them not to be unfaithful as Israel was. He continues, 'You are the light of the world. A city set on a hill cannot be hidden. Nor do people light a lamp and put it under a basket, but on a stand, and it gives light to all in the house. In the same way, let your light shine before others, so that they may see your good works and give glory to your Father who is in heaven' (Mt. 5:14–16). Again this is the language of Israel's calling to be a light to the Gentiles reapplied to the nascent Christian community. The Christian community is to be God's light in the world, demonstrating that it is good to live under God's rule. The liberated community is to be a liberating community – a community of the broken for the broken.[14]

The community of the broken will be a community that welcomes the poor and marginalized. The recognition of our brokenness is crucial for this. Those who see themselves as superior will either dismiss the poor as undeserving or patronize the poor as objects of charity. The discipline of community development has taught us the importance of participation, developing Participatory Reflection and Action (PRA) or Participatory Learning and Action (PLA) as a collection of methodologies to facilitate this. But when development professionals talk about participation they mean in effect participation in projects. The church can and should go a step further. As a woman in my church put it to me, 'I know people do a lot to help me. But what I want is for someone to be my friend.' People do not want to be projects. The poor need a welcome to replace their marginalization; they need inclusion to replace their exclusion; they need a place where they matter to replace their powerlessness. They need Christian community. The Christian community is more than a community in which the rich help the poor. It is a community in which broken people saved by grace struggle together to demonstrate to a lost world the liberating reality of Christ's loving rule. The proud have no place in this community for they do not recognize themselves as broken people. 'Humble yourselves before the Lord and he will exalt you' (Jas. 4:1).

4

New Heavens and New Earth

Justin Thacker

In a book that primarily addresses issues of global poverty, some might think it odd to include a chapter on heaven. After all, the traditional challenge to Christians is that because life after death is all that matters to us, we neglect the real issues of this life. Of course, as with many of the arguments against Christianity, this one has little empirical evidence to support it. In response to Christ's command, the Christian community has been at the forefront of a whole series of campaigns that seek to change this world for the better, Micah Challenge being the most recent. The purpose of this chapter then, is to explore why that might be the case. In a faith that considers this world as passing and the one to come as eternal, why is it that by word and deed we seek to transform that which will not last? We can attempt an answer to this question by examining in the first place the nature of the life to come.

New heavens and new earth

Among contemporary theologians, there is significant agreement that the nature of our eternal hope is not some disembodied, ethereal existence in which we float around as souls; rather the hope to which we are called is an embodied existence in a new or renewed earth.

So, Professor Edward Donnelly writes,

> Perhaps the great obstacle to a true appreciation of heaven is our inability to imagine our bodies there. Though we believe in the resurrection of the body, 'heaven' still brings to mind a realm which is immaterial, not physical in any real sense . . . Yet the Bible tells us that heaven is the ideal environment for them. At Christ's second coming this earth, which God created for our habitation and his glory, will be restored and renewed . . . heaven and earth will come together in a wonderful unity.[1]

This hope of an embodied existence in a new earth has not always been the case though. John Colwell has noted that a description of the afterlife in terms of 'the immortality of the soul', rather than the 'resurrection of the body' has frequently been the more popular motif across the ages. However, he describes this as a departure from the early apostolic hope and goes on to refer to the 'widespread repudiation of this development, particularly among scholars of the New Testament'[2] in the last hundred years or so. Our hope of paradise, then, is a renewed earth with a new body. Yet, the question remains what further can be said regarding its nature – what will it be like beyond this mere affirmation?

Revelation 21:1–4 is probably where we should begin to look in answer to this question.

> Then I saw a new heaven and a new earth, for the first heaven and the first earth had passed away, and there was no longer any sea. I saw the Holy City, the new Jerusalem, coming down out of heaven from God, prepared as a bride beautifully dressed for her husband. And I heard a loud voice from the throne saying, 'Now the dwelling of God is with men, and he will live with them. They will be his people, and God himself will be with them and be their God. He will wipe every tear from their eyes. There will be no more death or mourning or crying or pain, for the old order of things has passed away.' He who was seated on the throne said, 'I am making everything new!'

Here we have the clearest affirmation of what most of us look forward to in the new heavens and new earth: 'There will be no more death or mourning or crying or pain, for the old order of things has passed away.' It is this absence of physical suffering that becomes, for many of us, the defining feature of heaven. Whatever else heaven is, heaven is a place where pain no longer exists. It is perhaps for this reason that, far too often, heaven is pictured in a disembodied fashion. If, in this life, it is our bodies that experience pain and if, in the life to come, the characteristic feature is the absence of pain, then it is a short step to imagine a disembodied life in the hereafter. For whatever else a disembodied life is, it must be a pain-free life.

Interestingly, one can raise the hypothesis that one of the reasons that we have rediscovered in the last hundred years the notion of an embodied paradise is the reality that our lives – at least in the West – are to a large extent free from physical suffering and pain. We certainly do not experience, either first- or second-hand, the physical torment that would have been commonplace in earlier centuries. It may be the case, then, that we are more ready to accept an embodied eternity, because such embodiment does not fill us with the dread of physical pain that would have affected the ancients – or our contemporary brothers and sisters in the global South.

Yet, having said all that, perhaps we could have avoided at least some of these theological wanderings if we had paid closer attention to the biblical texts themselves in their description of the paradise to come. For I would suggest that the primary idea in the biblical descriptions of the life to come is not the *absence* of pain and suffering, but rather the *presence* of God. And importantly, a re-evaluation of heaven in terms of God's presence, rather than pain's absence, leads us to some significant conclusions regarding our present existence and mandate.

In the seminal passage from Revelation quoted earlier, our eyes rapidly skate over the first few verses until we get to those that address our real concern: pain. However, it is in those first few verses that the framework for the life to come is laid out.

> Then I saw a new heaven and a new earth, for the first heaven and the first earth had passed away, and there was no longer any sea. I saw the Holy City, the new Jerusalem, coming down

> out of heaven from God, prepared as a bride beautifully dressed for her husband. And I heard a loud voice from the throne saying, 'Now the dwelling of God is with men, and he will live with them. They will be his people, and God himself will be with them and be their God. He will wipe every tear from their eyes.'

There are three essential points in this passage, some of which we too frequently ignore in our consideration of heaven. Firstly, something *new* is taking place here. We are told three times of that which is *new*: heaven, earth and Jerusalem. And, in case we did not get it, the point is hammered home by indicating that the old has gone; it has 'passed away'. Indeed, based on this language some have suggested that what takes place at the eschaton, the end of times, is a complete destruction of the cosmos followed by an entirely new act of creation. Whether this is correct, or whether a renewal of the existing creation is the correct interpretation, we cannot know. The important point, though, is that something distinctively different is occurring: things will not be the same.

Secondly – and perhaps most surprising – the direction of movement in relation to the new heavens and new earth is not of us leaving this physical world, ascending through the clouds, and then joining God in some spiritual (as in non-material) realm. Rather, the trajectory that occurs is that heaven comes down and joins earth. The direction of travel is *downwards* not *upwards*.[3] 'I saw the Holy City, the new Jerusalem, *coming down out of heaven from God*, prepared as a bride beautifully dressed for her husband,' (my emphasis). The same point is made in Revelation 3:12, which describes the new Jerusalem as, 'coming down out of heaven from my God' (see also Rev. 21:10). We must not overstate the significance of this trajectory, but the relevant point is that paradise is paradise not because we leave this earth, but because heaven joins us here.

That leads us to the third and most important motif in this passage: the presence of God. 'Now the dwelling of God is with men, and he will live with them. They will be his people, and God himself will be with them and be their God. He will wipe every tear from their eyes.' This idea of God being or living with his people is one that runs throughout the whole of the Scriptures, both Old and New Testaments (Ex. 29:45; Lev. 26:11–12; Ezek. 37:27; Zech. 2:10,11; Jn. 1:14; 2 Cor. 6:16). It is the concept of God's *shekinah*, the *presence* of God. For the Jews, this was exemplified by God's presence in the temple in Jerusalem, which is why the author of Revelation, in describing the eternal presence of God with us, puts it in terms of, 'The new Jerusalem, coming down out of heaven from God'. The author is not really trying to persuade us that an actual city, complete with utilities, will descend from the clouds, but rather is speaking metaphorically of God's *presence*, his *shekinah* joining us on earth. The point, though, of these biblical descriptions of God's active presence is not just geographical, but sociological or relational. Their emphasis is that we truly become the people of God, not when God is absent, but rather when God is present – in close proximity. 'I will live with them and walk among them, and I will be their God, and they will be my people' (2 Cor. 6:16).

Of course, this is borne out by what happened in the Garden of Eden, and by the presence of Christ with us. In Genesis, we have this picture of the Lord God 'walking in the garden in the cool of the day', and yet, due to their sin, the first man and woman are hiding. Although God is there, it is his *presence* that their sin cannot bear. And so, the result of the Fall is banishment from the *presence* of God. In other words, at the point at which humanity lost its perfect relationship with God and the created order, that loss is expressed in terms of a separation from the *presence* of God. The corollary of this is the fact that when the Saviour that restores that relationship is described, he is named in terms of God's active presence with us. 'The virgin will be with child and will give birth to a son, and they will call him Immanuel, which means, 'God with us.' (Mt. 1:23; cf. Isa. 7:14). The sense we are getting, then, is that the people of God are truly the people of God when God is with them. Moreover, it is by means of his presence that the blessings associated with being the people of God are realized (Jer. 32:38–41).

This is especially evident when we consider an evocative phrase from the passage in Revelation above: 'He will wipe every tear from their eyes.' Here we see that the *presence* of God is not merely spatial proximity, but also the presence of intimacy. In being near, God demonstrates his concern. Moreover, it forms the bridge to our usual conception of heaven in terms of the absence of pain. The point that seems to be made is that the reason that there is no more pain or suffering or death or mourning is not because, in the abstract, these things have been removed, but rather because God's *presence* banishes them, or prevents them from being realized. When God is absent, then fear, pain and suffering may flourish. But where God is present, these things simply cannot be. So, for instance, the struggles for Adam and Eve began not when they were still in the garden, but when they left. And in Revelation 7:16–17, where another description is given of the suffering-free paradise that awaits, it is clear that the absence of such suffering is entirely down to the *presence* of God. 'Never again will they hunger; never again will they thirst. The sun will not beat upon them, nor any scorching heat. *For the Lamb at the centre of the throne will be their shepherd; he will lead them to springs of living water*. And God will wipe away every tear from their eyes.' (My emphasis; see also Rev. 21:22,23; 22:1–5.) We have here a wonderful description of the paradise that awaits, but the author is clear that what makes our experience so different in this setting is not so much that hunger or thirst have been banished as such, but rather that the Christ will be with us to lead us – direct us – to that which meets our needs.

Hence, what makes heaven heaven is not so much the absence of pain and suffering – however welcome that may be – but rather the unhindered presence of God.[4] As I will go on to show, this has profound consequences for our responsibilities in the here and now, but we will approach those responsibilities by first exploring the difference that the *presence* of Jesus made to those in first-century Palestine.

Jesus and the kingdom

One of the toughest challenges to those of us who would support the notion of an interventionist God is simply this: if God can heal the blind man, why not cure all blindness? If God can cure the lame, then why not cure all paralysis? If God has the power to intervene for some, then why does he not intervene for all? It was on precisely this question that Alister McGrath, Professor of Historical Theology at Oxford University, and one of the most gifted British apologists, came unstuck – albeit temporarily – in a recent debate with Richard Dawkins.[5] It certainly is a difficult question.

However, the beginnings of a response to this challenge are evident as we examine Jesus' own declarations in relation to the kingdom of God.

> [Jesus] went to Nazareth, where he had been brought up, and on the Sabbath day he went into the synagogue, as was his custom. And he stood up to read. The scroll of the prophet Isaiah was handed to him. Unrolling it, he found the place where it is written: 'The Spirit of the Lord is on me, because he has anointed me to preach good news to the poor. He has sent me to proclaim freedom for the prisoners and recovery of sight for the blind, to release the oppressed, to proclaim the year of the Lord's favour.' Then he rolled up the scroll, gave it back to the attendant and sat down. The eyes of everyone in the synagogue were fastened on him, and he began by saying to them, 'Today this scripture is fulfilled in your hearing.' (Lk. 4:16–21)

All commentators on the life of Jesus acknowledge that this is a pivotal passage in understanding the nature of his ministry and identity. In the midst of the synagogue, Jesus draws attention to a passage in Isaiah – a passage that for hundreds of years had been understood as declaring the kingdom of God – heaven on earth if you will, and Jesus says: 'This scripture is fulfilled in your hearing.' We must not lose sight of the sheer audacity evident here.

Jesus was not just saying that the kingdom was coming – many had said that; he was not just outlining the nature of the kingdom – the passage itself did that; rather he was declaring that now, in his person, by means of his presence – this kingdom would be realized. As N. T. Wright puts it, 'The Kingdom of God, he said, is at hand. In other words, God was now unveiling his age-old plan, bringing his sovereignty to bear on Israel and the world as he had always intended, bringing justice and mercy to Israel and the world. And he was doing so, apparently, through Jesus.'[6] Or, as Steve Chalke and Alan Mann summarized it, 'The Kingdom, the in-breaking *shalom* of God, is available now to everyone *through me*.'[7] This is huge.

The point of note is the personal manner in which Jesus draws this conclusion. 'The Spirit of the Lord is on *me*, because he has anointed *me* to preach good news to the poor. He has sent *me* to proclaim freedom for the prisoners and recovery of sight for the blind, to release the oppressed, to proclaim the year of the Lord's favour.' Jesus was not just saying, God's Spirit is now here for everyone, so that we all preach the good news, proclaim freedom, cure blindness and so on. No, this was a personal declaration. Even in Isaiah, from where the quotation is taken, the messianic subject does not merely announce the good news, but also brings it about. And consider Jesus' dramatic declaration on finishing his reading: 'Today this scripture is fulfilled in *your* hearing.' Once again, it is not: 'Today this scripture is fulfilled', but rather it is fulfilled in '*your* hearing', in the presence of those who were there – and this is so, because Jesus was there, personally present.

What should we conclude from this? That God's in-breaking kingdom is present and available in the person of, and by means of, the actions and teaching of his anointed servant, Jesus Christ. In the same way that the absence of suffering that characterizes the new heaven and new earth is made possible by the *presence* of God, so the *shalom* of God that characterizes the kingdom is made possible by the presence and actions of Jesus Christ. In neither case is the absence of pain, or peace that is promised, available in general, or in the abstract. Rather, they are possible because Jesus makes it so.

A similar conclusion can be drawn from Jesus' use of parables. N. T. Wright has drawn attention to the fact that in the parable of the sower, Jesus is not so much making a general point regarding the propensity or otherwise of people to respond to God's message. Rather, his emphasis is 'what God was doing in Jesus' own ministry'. Similarly, in the parable of the prodigal son, it is not, once again, a universal principle regarding the love of God. 'The parable was not a general illustration of the timeless truth of God's forgiveness for the sinner . . . It was a sharp-edged, context-specific message about what was happening in Jesus' ministry. More specifically, it was about what was happening through Jesus' welcome of outcasts, his eating with sinners.'[8]

The kingdom, then, does not come in the abstract. It comes in and through the person and work of Jesus Christ. Even when the disciples heal and forgive, it is not because they have some general ability to do so, rather it is because Jesus has specifically given them the authority to go and continue his kingdom work. It is for precisely this reason that we have Jesus' otherwise remarkable statement at the time the Seventy-Two were sent out. 'He who listens to you listens to me; he who rejects you rejects me; but he who rejects me rejects him who sent me.' (Lk. 10:16) The point Jesus is making is that any ability the Seventy-Two have to enact the kingdom is only realized because Jesus is there in power. Moreover, any ability Jesus has is only because God is at work in him. The kingdom never comes in the abstract, but only by means of God's active presence, whether in his Son or Spirit, or in us as we allow the Son and Spirit to work through us.

The answer, then, to the question of why God healed the blind man, but not blindness is simply this. God does heal blindness, and lameness and so on, but only where he is fully present. It is his unhindered presence that brings *shalom*, not the casting of some universal magic spell. In the age to come, his *shekinah* – his full and unveiled presence – will be operative everywhere (consider Rev. 22:5), and hence there will be no more suffering or pain. However, in this age, in the time before he comes again, his presence is experienced in veiled form. In the first place, this was true of his Son, who though fully God, had his glory hidden as he lived among us.[9] Such a veiled presence meant that shards of light could and did break through to bring healing, forgiveness and restoration – but this was not the unhindered presence that we will all experience in the age to come, when we will see him 'face to face'. In the second place, though, that task of bringing God's presence to the world – and so the all-encompassing *shalom* of God – is now ours. Our job is to continue in the glorious building project that God in Christ has begun.

Heaven on earth

> Consequently, you are no longer foreigners and aliens, but fellow citizens with God's people and members of God's household, built on the foundation of the apostles and prophets, with Christ Jesus himself as the chief cornerstone. In him the whole building is joined together and rises to become a holy temple in the Lord. And in him you too are being built together to become a dwelling in which God lives by his Spirit. (Eph. 2:19–22)

> What Jesus was to Israel, the Church must now be for the world. Everything we discover about what Jesus did and said within the Judaism of his day must be thought through in terms of what it would look like for the Church to do and be this for the world. If we are to shape our world, and perhaps even to implement the redemption of our world, this is how it is to be done.[10]

In John 20:21, when he has risen from the dead, Jesus says this to the disciples: 'As the Father has sent me, I am sending you'. The phrase has occurred before in John 17:18, and in both places the Greek uses a tense that refers to an ongoing state of being resulting from some past action. The sense, then, is not that at some point in the past, Christ was sent and now it is our turn, but rather that Christ is in an ongoing state of *having been sent*. The significance of this is that it indicates the way in which what we are doing is merely the continuation of what Christ was doing. In fact, it is not so much that we do it for God, or on behalf of God, but rather that God continues his work through us as we are united to Christ, and empowered by his Spirit. And what is that task? To be the presence of God in the world and so bring his *shalom* to bear. The importance here is that both these aspects go together: being the presence of God and bringing his *shalom* to bear.

One of my favourite preachers[11] has a stock phrase regarding our mission in this world: 'It's not rocket science, it's just this: love God, and love others'. I think he is right. And yet it is remarkable how the history of Christianity, perhaps evangelicalism in particular, has managed to divorce these two commands. The reason they are integrally related[12] is because of what we have been saying that the absence of suffering is only possible because of the presence of God. Given that it is only by God's presence that peace and justice can reign on earth, then to try and love God without loving your neighbour is either to worship a different god, a false idol, or to ask God to be a different kind of God – but the only God the Bible knows is one whose concern is to bring *shalom* to the whole world. Similarly, to say that you will love your neighbour while ignoring God is to believe that a reign of righteousness is possible in the absence of God. Yet, as I have shown, the biblical witness is that righteousness is only possible, not in the abstract, but by means of God's presence. Hence, to divorce these commands, or even to seek to follow one but not the other is just impossible. Now, of course, the challenge to this is to ask whether atheists or those of other faiths can do good works. My answer is of course they can. In Romans 1:14ff, Paul makes it clear that the Gentiles of his day do good works by means of the conscience that God has given them, 'the requirements of the law are written on their hearts.' This is not then, a debate about whether Christians or atheists do more good, but it is to say that wherever justice and mercy are evident, it is because God's righteousness is operative in that place – whether acknowledged or not.

In conclusion, then, I have suggested that the new heavens and new earth, the kingdom of God on earth, will be characterized by the absence of suffering primarily because its defining feature is the presence of God. I have, therefore, indicated that our task in this life, before that kingdom is fully realized, is to continue the work that Jesus inaugurated by being God's presence and bringing his reign of *shalom* to the world. In this sense then, there is a direct continuity between what we do now, and our experience in the age to come. To put it bluntly, our eternal life starts now – the moment we get on with it!

This is further highlighted by Revelation 22, where there is a curious phrase that occurs in the middle of the wonderful vision of heaven that is outlined. After talking of the river of life, the throne of God and the Lamb, the glorious fruit that is there, we find this: 'But the throne of God and of the Lamb will be in it, and his servants will serve him' (Rev 22:3). It echoes a similar verse in Revelation 7:15, but what is their point? Well, it is possible to interpret them both in terms of the elders and angels singing and praising God as the relevant Greek verb, *latreuo*, can be translated worship as well as service. However, there are good reasons for thinking that the latter idea is the predominant one. In the Septuagint, the Greek translation of the Old Testament, *latreuo* is primarily used for the whole of the people's service towards God, everything they do in their lives for him.[13] In this sense, then, the continuity between our present existence and the one to come is that in both we seek to offer our full response to the God who brings us peace.

However, is it not also possible to see in this passage in Revelation 22:3 echoes of another vision in which the Lamb is on his throne, with all his angels in attendance, and the nations before him?: Matthew 25: 31–46. On that occasion, reference is also made to those who served the king, 'For I was hungry and you gave me food, I was thirsty and you gave me something to drink, I was a stranger and you welcomed me, I was naked and you gave me clothing, I was sick and you took care of me, I was in prison and you visited me' (Mt. 25:35,36).[14] And if we recall the point that the king makes on that occasion that, 'just as you did it to one of the least of these who are members of my family, you did it to me,' then the theological point to be made here is that our practical service of the poor now, and our ongoing service and worship of God in the age to come are both from the same stable: a heart responding fully to God.

Given this, the challenge before us is that we join with the angels in heaven and participate in heavenly worship not so much by singing songs, but by feeding the hungry and poor, speaking out on their behalf, challenging injustice and critically monitoring our lifestyle. In a strange paradox, then, heaven on earth is experienced most where we least expect it: among those in need, for is that not where we would find Jesus?

5

Divine Power in Human Weakness

Marijke Hoek

Although the world is full of suffering, it is also full of the overcoming of it. (Helen Keller, 1880–1968)

In his letter to the Romans, Paul addresses a small Christian community in the heart of the most powerful empire. His agenda in writing has universal dimensions. It is about God's restoration plan, starting with Christ who is the beginning of the new creation and continuing with his people in whom his image is being formed. Uniquely, he refers to a groaning and enslaved creation and aligns this suffering world and its expectation with the presence and destiny of the Christian community.

> The creation waits in eager expectation for the sons of God to be revealed. For the creation was subjected to frustration . . . in hope that the creation itself will be liberated from its bondage to decay and brought into the glorious freedom of the children of God. We know that the whole creation has been groaning as in the pains of childbirth right up to the present time. (Rom. 8:19–22)

While 'slavery' is a powerful image for suffering, oppression and captivity, and 'groaning' reflects the world's pain, 'labour' implies the promise of new birth. Here, Paul sets creation's groaning in the context of great potential: release from its bondage and participation in the glorious freedom of God's people. In turn, the believers are also hopeful. God's children, adopted and led by the Spirit, are heirs of a new world and marked by their hope for the fulfilment of a new reign. At the same time, however, they are also aware of their weakness (8:26). This probably concerns their numerical, economic and sociopolitical weakness. It certainly refers to their limitations in knowing what to pray for as well as their vulnerability in a harsh context. While Paul acknowledges this weakness, his theological perspective is, however, focused on the assurance and demonstration of God's power. Hence, the church's weakness is placed in God's sphere of reign rather than that of any other power.

The strengthening of God's people takes place in their vocation to reflect his image into the world. In Romans 1:21–23, Paul describes how mankind denied the image in which it was created. His reflection on our place in creation, knowledge of God and loss of that knowledge calls Genesis 2 – 3 to mind, a passage which connects mankind's 'image' and stewardship of creation in a way that promotes life. In Romans 8, Paul reflects that, while the world has suffered dysfunction since the Fall, it hopes to share in the restoration. He does not speak of a 'new earth' or 'new creation' but more reservedly in terms of creation's hope to participate in the glorious freedom of God's children. The new creation has, after all, begun in God's people who are a herald to his liberation, who recognize the potential and have both the faith and the moral imagination to seek the birth of something new.

In view of the cosmic scope of this redemption plan and the promise of inheriting with Christ, we may expect Paul to expand on a glorious church; however, he refers instead to its weakness. Earlier, he mentions 'weakness' in the context of God's plan for the world, noting that, while Abraham acknowledged the reality of the human situation, he did not weaken but was strengthened in his faith concerning the fulfilment of God's promise (4:19–21). When Paul revisits 'weakness' in 8:26, it is again in the context of the full scope of salvation history, the destiny of the world. Thus, he places the church on a dramatic worldwide stage in which 'our weakness' also concerns the immense challenge we face in our vocation as God's people in responding to the groaning in his world.[1]

Although weakness may characterize the Christian community, Paul is aware of the Spirit's role in enabling them to recognize that hope is their true context of living, due to the power of the Spirit. While the believers' vocations emerge in the midst of an array of opposing power dynamics, and Roman power would have significantly affected the church, these heirs with Christ are part of his overcoming reign. Thus, the community's weakness is placed next to the Spirit's powerful help, forming a distinct theological motif: our human weakness is the showcase of God's power.[2]

Paul's choice of verb with reference to the Spirit's help contains the idea of coming alongside and sharing burdens with the believers, even implying an element of empathy with them. In their weakness, the empowerment and companionship of the Spirit would not merely form Christ's image within them but also build a public witness to God's reign and destiny. N. T. Wright challenges that the sociopolitical implications of Paul's letters need to be studied in more detail,[3] especially when read against the background of the Caesar cult. When reading Paul's texts against the background of a powerful empire, it appears that the activity of the Spirit applies not only to religious, but also to social and political aspects of life. While the worship of the emperor and Rome was the fastest growing religion at the time and the imperial cult constructed a definition of the world, Paul's gospel and his redefinition of concepts such as 'weakness' and 'victory' construct a challenging Christian worldview based upon the foundation of the cross. His understanding of the role of the Spirit is crucial in reshaping this worldview in which he calls attention to our responsibility to exercise a Christlike authority that brings a travailing creation within the domain of Christ's reign.

This image of a groaning creation is of significant interest when we consider the challenge we face in our time. The world is groaning under the yoke of poverty and injustice. Significant parts of the human community are in pain while nature itself suffers damage. In our commitment to Micah Challenge, Paul's view of destiny will undoubtedly motivate and sustain us in our work, advocacy, prayer, endurance, hope *and* in our weakness.

A world full of power dynamics

To understand the nature of 'weakness', it is important to appreciate the harsh conditions of first-century life on the one hand, and the imperial construct in which religion and politics formed a web of power on the other. At the time, the followers of Christ were a small and powerless minority in society, whereas Rome was the seat of prestige and the centre of power. Caesar claimed to be 'son of god', his ascension was portrayed as 'good news' (the same word as used for 'gospel') and he was regarded as 'lord of the world' whose powerful rule had brought justice and peace. Paul wrote Romans at a time when the imperial agenda ascribed a cosmic status to its rulers and the emperor was portrayed as the reconciler and ruler of the world who offered a new beginning. While the imperial cult constructed the reality of the empire, Paul's gospel constructs the new reality of Christ's reign whose death and resurrection initiated a new era. His thesis in Romans 1:16–17, which introduces the gospel and lordship of Christ, inevitably poses a challenge to the claims and reign of Rome.[4]

In this imperial context, 'sonship' is a significant theme. The Roman dynasty portrayed the heir as 'the second hope of great Rome'. So, when, in the early first century, the two adopted heirs died, the continuity of the imperial reign was threatened. However, the subsequent adoption of Tiberius filled the city with joy since it realized the hope of the empire's perpetual security and reign.[5] In Romans 8, Paul presents a similar matrix of ideas as found in the imperial context: adoption–sons–heirs–hope. He communicates the reality of salvation in a term that is borrowed from Graeco-Roman law and custom. Not only would he have been indebted to the prominent practice of adoption, but also in the context of the empire, his 'Spirit of adoption' phrase has clear political connotations. Indeed, the expansion of God's family and co-heirdom with Christ are topics that resonate with the claims of the eternal reign of the imperial family secured through adoption.

The Spirit of adoption is creating a new community, a new social and ethical order in the existing structures of society. While citizenship defined the ethics and allegiance for Roman citizens who were part of the most powerful empire in the world, defining the believers as 'sons of God' (8:14) emphasizes the major reorientation Paul envisaged (12:1ff). Roles in life are assigned by God and exercised by faith (12:3–8), thus putting all former social distinctions assigned in society in the shadow of the Christian vocation.[6] This view would have reshaped the believers' self-understanding, as the community would have experienced corporate weakness that was of a numerical, sociopolitical, judicial and economic nature. Poverty and food shortages were significant economic aspects of first-century life. Considering that the church included labourers, slaves and recent immigrants, some would have had citizenship, while others would have encountered the discrimination experienced by non-citizens, which characterized the Roman judicial system.[7] Yet, despite their experience of powerlessness and hardship, believers are encouraged to remember their status as 'sons of God' and 'heirs with Christ'. Paul is thus calling into being an entire new identity, a new morality and structure of society. He is also calling into being a strong confidence in the transforming power of the gospel.

The key question in the letter is how God's justice will be realized in a world that is dominated by evil powers.[8] In Romans 8:32–35, Paul identifies the human power dynamics that pervade society and oppose the believers, referring not only to hardships such as 'famine', but also to things done by 'someone' ('who'). Moreover, in 8:38f, he lists a variety of opposing cosmic forces. However, in the face of much that is 'against us', God is 'for us'. So, how will his justice be realized? Paul presents Jesus as the embodiment of a new humanity whose sovereignty is qualified in terms of obedience within the limitations of human existence and weakness.[9] His emphasis on the *abundance* of Christ's reign of grace (5:20) would have evoked associations with the 'Augustan age of grace'.[10] While many people believed the emperors were divine, Paul presents Christ as the social and cosmic healer. A first-century listener may have assumed Paul's text on the lordship of Christ in Romans 14:9 to be a comparison and contrast with the emperor.[11]

In a world in which Caesar's reign is secured through terror and in which he is portrayed as the 'unconquered hero', Paul's claim of Christ's ultimate sovereignty and the description of his followers as 'more than overcomers' testify to his lordship and superior reign (8:34–37). While the cross shows Jesus' incarnational weakness, it simultaneously redefines power. Hence, weakness does not equate to powerlessness but rather it forms *the* occasion for God's power to overcome. Christ's sovereignty marks the church out as being different; it has a different ruler and a different way of overcoming. The victory 'through him who loved us' celebrates his lordship, love and faithfulness. This victory lies first of all in the fact that we are inseparable from God's love in Christ. Secondly, 'overcoming' concerns our exercise of the right rule, our stewardship and the restoration of glory lost at the Fall (8:29–39). Living according to the Spirit (8:2ff) thus generates a community that experiences the reality of divine power at work in weakness. In Christ's followers, a restoration movement has begun and, through us, he will work to reclaim a groaning world.

A world full of suffering

Paul is concerned with the rebellion of the creature against the Creator and the world groaning under such corruption. The Fall not only directly affected creation, it also affected humanity's stewardship that was intended for its development (1:21–25). While this world is finely tuned for life,[12] mankind threw the whole creation off balance. Ever since the Fall, a cosmic drama has been unfolding in the form of floods, droughts, earthquakes, hurricanes, famines and the like, vividly described by the prophets.[13] In the context of such desolation, the term 'groaning' appears. Job, for example, links the groaning of the land, its barrenness and human suffering to injustice:

> If my land cries out [lit. 'groans'] against me and all its furrows are wet with tears.
> If I have devoured its yield without payment or broken the spirit of its tenants,
> Then let briers come up instead of wheat and weeds instead of barley. (31:38–40)

The relation between the desolation of creation and the disobedience of Israel is widespread in Jewish thinking. Philo, a Jewish author in the first century, reflects on the relation between selfish humanity with its irrational pleasure, desire of glory, power, riches, injustice and crop failure.[14] Included in the groaning of creation are the provoked disasters, political oppression and tragedies of injustice.[15] Thus we see that the transgressions of God's people, the social balance and the ecological concerns are interwoven.[16] When stewardship is corrupted, everything falls with it.

Paul places the groaning of creation and the church in a deeply relational context; it is not only God's creation that groans, but also his people (8:23). The term is in fact regularly found in Jewish texts when the righteous cry to God in their oppression.[17] Such groans move God to action: 'Because of the oppression of the weak and the groaning of the needy, I will arise'.[18] The redemption from slavery that followed is a foundational experience through which the biblical writers interpret divine power. In the Exodus, the community experiences deliverance in which the tide of groaning and powerlessness is turned. Welker describes the effect of the Spirit concerning a people who experience the restoration of an internal order, a new sense of community and capacity for action. The descent of God's Spirit results in the joining together of people who find themselves in distress, and thus, he argues, 'a process of emergence sets in . . . that constitutes a new beginning, new relations, a new reality'.[19]

Besides suffering endured due to their Christian vocation, the believers suffer with the rest of creation in the groaning of this age, such as war, famine, oppression, terror, illness, natural catastrophes, and anguish. Believers are not exempt from the world's pain; rather, they stand in this world and take part in its groaning. Moreover, they ache over the world's aching. In Jewish texts, the groans of God's people also concern their grief over a suffering world. Job sighs: 'Have I not wept for those in trouble? Has not my soul grieved for the poor?' (30:25) The followers of Christ agonize when they see injustice, starvation, indignity, slavery, illness, tears and death. These mourners of the world, writes Wolterstorff, are aching visionaries who have a glimpse of God's new day. They weep over humanity's weeping in this light. They will be comforted (Mt. 5:4).[20] Such weeping invites God's kingdom to come.[21]

The Spirit further heightens the believers' sympathy for the world's wounds, for the new covenant was understood to bring a renewal of the heart that implied a new sensitivity to the various interdependent relationships.[22] No longer having a heart of stone, the Spirit makes us sensitive again to a right relationship with God's world and draws us into its groaning. Having received the first fruit, having glimpsed perfection, the imperfect begins to hurt because in the context of such hope, the present pain, bondage, decay, suffering, poverty, barrenness and brokenness ache even more.[23] Creation's transformation is part of his redemption plan or rather, integrally linked to the redemption of humanity, which reflects a typical eschatological Jewish hope.[24] Adoption effects new agents of freedom, a new community and relationships that carry the potential of redemption for the world.[25] Not only does the church live under the rule and reign of God, our vocation to reign in life (5:17) concerns the responsibility to make the nature and reign of Christ present in the world. While our transformation is an ongoing, Spirit-empowered process of embodying God's word (12:1f), Paul is not just concerned with the new humanity but with God's entire world. Since we belong to Christ, we live as witnesses to the standard of his faithfulness (8:9,14ff). Such lifestyle coheres with the theological vision emerging from Paul's letter, described by Byrne, '. . . the vision of a God who in the person of the Son faithfully engages in a costly and vulnerable intervention into the world in order, through the gift of the Spirit, to roll back human selfishness and empower human beings to live faithfully in and for the world.'[26]

A world full of overcoming

Although the Fall interrupted God's purpose, his intent is continued in Christ, who is first in the line of the authentic restored humanity. 'God knew what he was doing from the very beginning. He decided from the outset to shape the lives of those who love him along the same lines as the life of his Son' (Rom. 8:29, The Message). Characterizing Jesus as, 'the firstborn among many brothers' is part of Paul's prominent 'family' language. In the social structures of the time, siblings constituted the longest lasting relationship, fulfilling a crucial function in the family, including upholding the honour of the father's house. This 'sibling' metaphor is central in Paul's ecclesiology and, thus, has consequences for the community's ethics and lifestyle.[27] The siblings are being conformed into Christ's image. Paul, however, describes little about Jesus' life and instead focuses time and again on the cross. Consequently, 'what the Son is like' needs to be derived from the way Paul characterizes his death; his love, obedience, self-giving and suffering (5:18f; 8:3,32). Being shaped along these lines sets high demands for the call upon his disciples. Hence authentic life, or reclaimed life, is to become like Jesus, an ever-closer conformity to the one who is, after all, the express image of God. So, how do we mirror him? In our quest for justice, in our identification with, and concern for, the vulnerable and poor, in our self-giving, weakness, humility and in our love.

And we also mirror him in the radical righteousness and costly servanthood defined by him. As he stayed faithful, so too will the cross give sense to our weakness. Consequently, the way we exercise dominion bears the characteristics of the way Christ exercised his.[28] While the 'more than conquerors' motif is popular in the Western church, the idea seems disconnected from the prominent dynamics of the cross, from the pathos, groan and lament,[29] which may explain its often-hollow ring. Paul's view of overcoming is, however, anchored in weakness, in the midst of life's laments. In the toughness of the Christian cause, the church bears testimony to God's power and love and brings his reign into the world. To overcome is to remain faithful to him. N. T. Wright states, 'The call of the gospel is for the church to *implement* the victory of God in the world *through suffering love*'.[30] This is the community that creation is waiting for (8:19).

While Paul's thought on 'image' is clearly influenced by the Jewish tradition, the imperial background also forms part of his context. The bestowing of the image of a lord or ruler was a typical sign in political life of extending his power and conserving his property. A first-century Roman citizen would have been surrounded by images in public spaces and temples that celebrated the cosmic reign of Roman rule. And so Paul's audience would probably have heard imperial political overtones in the term 'image'. Subversively, Paul claims that in the midst of a powerful empire, an image is being formed in this Christian minority that accords with the likeness, the reign of Christ. This image, then, is both a reflection of, and a signpost to, the new order.

Thus, in a first-century society dominated by power and against the background of the empire, Paul redefines concepts of 'weakness', 'power', 'conquering' and 'reign'. The cross fundamentally re-evaluates the seat, definition and exercise of divine power. The Spirit empowers believers for sacrificial living, a reigning dynamic by which they are transformed into the image of their Lord in the midst of their weakness. The willingness to sacrificial living is itself a participation in the character of God's victory.[31]

While the church may consider itself the weaker party in a worldwide arena with its powerful dynamics, the promise of God's empowering in weakness stands. The Christian faith stimulates a commitment to the politics of justice. In recent history, Christians have led the US civil rights movement, campaigned against communism, apartheid, forms of slavery and called for the cancellation of international debt. Such commitment to a greater liberty and compassion is transforming the world and shows that a movement of people who face up to injustice and pay the price can bring about a seismic shift in their time, affecting moral, social, historical, economic, spiritual and legal dynamics in society while also testifying to the capacity to overcome. Blessed are those with an aching hunger for justice, for they will be filled (Mt. 5:6).

Divine help in the church's weakness

To walk according to the Spirit contains a sociopolitical dimension of discipleship. While this involves costly sacrifice, the Spirit's help in our apparent human weakness is generous and multifaceted:

The Spirit helps in our ignorance

Paul's reference to 'not knowing' in 8:26 echoes a core theme that Isaiah refers to, namely the road Israel will take. This road is a central theme in Isaiah 40:1 – 42:13, forming the immediate background for the second part:

> For a long time I have kept silent; I have been quiet, and held myself back:
>
> But now, like a woman in childbirth, I cry out, I gasp and pant; . . .
>
> I will lead the blind *by ways they do not know; along unfamiliar paths* I will guide them
>
> I will turn the darkness into light before them, and make the rough places smooth. These are things I will do: I will not forsake them. (Isa. 42:14–16, italics added)

Here, Isaiah speaks about travail in the experience of God, which precedes the birth of a new order and the display of his strength. The road Israel walks in this new exodus is a road he will walk with them (40:3,10), guiding and accompanying them on these unfamiliar paths. Paul's reflection 'we do not know what we ought to pray for' concerns an aspect of our weakness: we are limited in knowledge. The reference to the Spirit's help in accordance with God's purpose in 8:26–28, reminds us of Israel's experience. Leaving familiar roads and venturing into unconventional ways, we are assured of divine help in view of divine purpose. This awareness of weakness creates a people who strongly rely on him. In our not-knowing, the Spirit sustains, guides and is our advocate.

The Spirit provides advocacy

While we hope for what is not yet seen, we are assured of an advocate who prays in accordance with God's will with groans (8:26–28). Here, Paul communicates the invaluable truth that in a challenging cosmic arena, the Spirit helps in our human weakness: when it is beyond us to know what to pray; when experiencing hardship, when faced with, and partaking in, the cosmic groaning with its tragedies; in the awareness of creation's expectation; while having a hope, yet aching for the fullness of the promise, the Spirit intercedes for us in accordance with God's will, finely tuned towards his purposes. Thus, 'weakness' is not merely a reflection of being human, but it is taken up in God's purpose and transformed by his power.

The knowledge that the Spirit of God intercedes would undoubtedly have given the early church confidence in the realization of God's reign in the midst of its weakness. In first-century civic life and its judicial bias towards those of superior social status, people of lower status sought the help of an influential patron who could speak in court on their behalf. Paul's choice of legal language in 8:16 and 26 ('testifies', 'intercedes') portrays that the church has its own unique advocacy as part of the reign under which it functions. Though socially, numerically and politically weak and experiencing hardship, the church is part of a kingdom where ultimate power is defined and located. God's community is not dependent on the Roman system of patronage or on the gods of the imperial cult. Whereas *Spes* served as a protectress over affairs for citizens and the imperial family,[32] Paul skilfully paints the picture of the Spirit witnessing and interceding in the affairs of God's family.

In fact, compared to any other advocate, this divine advocacy is of a superior quality. This idea of the Spirit's advocacy is unknown in Jewish or New Testament writings. Not only does Paul introduce here a new idea but he also constructs a unique verb in which the '*hyper*'-prefix reflects the idea of 'super-intercessions'. This prefix marks the language of excess in the imperial claims and propaganda, typifying a range of virtues that reinforce the emperor's superiority: the greatness of Caesar's mind, good will and superior courage.[33] The cumulative effect of Paul's reference to Christ's intercession portrays that we are part of a domain in which we can rely on powerful advocacy amidst power dynamics and structures (8:32–39). Moreover, in 8:37, he uses this '*hyper*'-prefix again to typify the community as 'more than overcomers'. Probably, he is thus engaging with the imperial claim that portrays Caesar as the 'unconquered hero'. Thus, Paul formulates his view in language that places our weakness in the domain of Christ's ultimate sovereignty. Pinnock poignantly writes, 'A mission whose goal is transformation of the world is stupendous. A powerless church can hardly consider it. It presupposes the anointing and empowerment of Spirit . . .'[34]

As such, the 'advocacy' and 'overcoming' ideas contribute to the subverting of the imperial conception of 'power'. The verb's present tense in the Greek text indicates that the victory achieved through Christ is already visible. Belonging to him, we are called to demonstrate the characteristics of Christ in our daily act of worship (12:2). Daily expressions of mercy and justice such as providing a home for the refugee or buying fair trade products express the nature of his kingdom. Christ's reign thus invades the world, not hindered by the church's weakness but rather displayed in it.

The Spirit guarantees and strengthens hope

People who in their weakness call upon their Lord, not only look to him but also adopt his viewpoint for they look through a lens of hope. Romans 8:20–25 is permeated with the theme of hope: it is woven into creation, marks our salvation and faith, is deposited and guaranteed by the Spirit, and directs our future expectation. The texts on hope are, however, sandwiched between the 'suffering' and 'weakness' themes (8:17f,26). While this demonstrates the hard reality in which life is played out, it also indicates that hope is a structural element of life. Paul reflected earlier how central the Spirit is to hope: 'And hope does not disappoint us, because God has poured out his love into our hearts by the Holy Spirit . . .' (5:5).

You can hear the echo of Joel 2:28: God promised to pour out his Spirit, causing his people to dream dreams and have visions. Imagine justice flowing like a river, righteousness like a never-failing stream. Imagine, once again, elderly men and women sitting in the streets, with cane in hand, overlooking playing children (Amos 5:24; Zech. 8:4). Imagine orphans being placed in a family, receiving education and fulfilling their potential. Imagine medical help being available to all. Imagine people being set free from forms of bond-slavery and able to steer their destiny. Imagine food, clothes, shelter and water for all. Imagine restoring broken dwellings. Imagine just that.

Hope for the transformation of creation, the manifestation of God's children and the restoration of the glory as we share with Christ sounds like the new social order in the prophetic writings.[35] This hope for God's reign increasingly to break into our life and affect a groaning creation is a power that will sustain and motivate us, creating a resilient, imaginative and trusting people. Thus, as we take part in the ongoing creation of the world, this hope equates a 'staying-power'.[36] Throughout history, God's people have stood out from the crowd because they have had hope based on his promise of transformation, deliverance and redemption.[37] The idea of 'waiting with endurance' describes the circumstance of this hope (8:25f). In those who hope for what is not yet, there is then an active enduring, a passionate waiting, while anticipating the new creation and walking in the way of love.

The shape of God's redemption plan has always been cruciform. His faithfulness to the world requires that those who belong to Christ embody faithfulness at great cost. Hope not only concerns future ultimate redemption, it also concerns the present work of healing and liberation, often most powerfully displayed in weakness and suffering. Hope is medication for your child, clean water, a home, seed funding for a business. The community of faith consists of those who spend themselves on behalf of the poor, live with the needy, ache about injustice, who refuse to believe that extreme poverty is part of the world's DNA. Such defiant faith, empowered advocacy and enduring compassion herald a new order in the presence of powerful empires. Blessed are the merciful (Mt. 5:7). Nothing is more powerful than the way of the cross. Love overcomes.

A time full of potential

Paul sets the community's transformation and its vocation in a time frame. He appeals to them to understand the time (Rom.13:11–13). By choosing '*kairos*', he emphasizes the sense of opportunity: the day that is breaking forth sheds its light upon the character of the present. Thus, life is placed in the context of the new creation or, as Hays writes, the texts are read 'through the lens of new creation'.[38] Paul even chooses *kairos* in 8:18 in reference to the present suffering, since it not only constitutes an opportunity for divine help but also for revealing the characteristics of the Christlike life, reflecting a measure of his glory, character and reign in the world.

The challenge is to understand the time. When Martin Luther King, Jr led the civil rights movement in the USA, Gandhi led a peoples' movement in Asia, liberation theology flourished in Latin America, while in Africa many nations gained independence. King ascribed this human rights revolution to the *Zeitgeist*, a time when time itself is ready for change. He warned against 'the myth of time', as if there is something in the flow of time that would correct all wrongs: 'Social progress never rolls in on wheels of inevitability. It comes through the tireless effort and the persistent work of dedicated individuals.'[39] In a time when a cosmic groan went through the continents, a contraction that laboured towards the birth of a new order, King and others arose.

When Gordon Brown was the UK Chancellor of the Exchequer, he acknowledged that we are in a unique point in history in which it is economically possible to deal with extreme poverty. He also discerned the lack of moral resolve in political quarters, suggesting that therein lies the challenge to the church. Micah Challenge recognizes the significant opportunity in our time as well as the need to rise to the challenge in a radical faith-filled engagement to act justly, love mercy and walk humbly with our God. *Kairos*: it is a promising word for a promising time, and a poignant word for a demanding time.

Conclusion

Romans is rightly viewed as 'the charter of the counter-empire.'[40] Although society may ascribe a marginal position to the church and 'Rome' may be the centre of power, Paul places the Christian community in a central, authoritative role and recaptures its imagination. He paints a picture of the grandeur of God's plan, the costs connected to its realization and the provision of a relational framework. Our human weakness, socio-economic and political powerlessness form the setting for the Spirit's advocacy. Paul is not merely concerned with the Spirit's role in salvation, prayer, ethics and resurrection, but with the experience of the Spirit who provides help in the outworking of God's will and infuses us with hope to be a transforming power. The church already testifies to the overcoming power of divine love in its own groaning, weakness and partly fulfilled hopes. Though creation's complete liberation from bondage and the 'new earth' are future expectations, which, as known from biblical texts, will be a divine accomplishment, our conformity to Christ's image has profound implications for life. Hence, belonging to his family places a responsibility upon us to display a measure of godly dominion that affects this groaning creation.

Three groans; one redemptive plan. In the chronological timeline, each generation needs to understand the opportune time. Paul's faith is not negated by the church's weakness but, rather, weakness is the occasion for divine enabling in view of our destiny. Our partaking in Christ's suffering love effects sympathy with, and responsibility towards, the world's groans and generates sacrificial living. Paul's image of a suffering world looking in expectation to the people of God is a strong incentive to work in anticipation of the new creation, to reflect signposts that point to this eventual future. In our time, we can commend Micah Challenge to the wider world, appealing to its conscience, inspiring its response and providing the dynamics for worldwide transformation. While change has to be worked out through policies that contribute towards eliminating poverty and developing a greater level of justice, and while we should hold governments to account on delivering the Millennium Development Goals, we can only be good stewards of this vision if we are willing to pay the cost and take up our cross ourselves.

6

The Kingdom of God and the Mission of the Church

C. René Padilla

The kingdom of God provides the basis for the church and its mission. It is an eschatological reality that marks the starting point as well as the goal of the church, 'the community of the King'[1] that lives between the times of Christ – between the incarnation and the second coming.

The expression *kingdom of God* (or its equivalent *kingdom of heaven* in the Gospel of Matthew) occurs more than one hundred times in the gospels, quite often in the records of Jesus' teaching. Since its meaning can only be understood against the background of the Old Testament, in the first section of this chapter we shall examine the Old Testament basis for the Jewish messianic hope, while in the second section we shall explore the meaning of the expression in the gospels. On that basis, in the third section we will draw a few conclusions regarding the importance of the kingdom of God for our understanding of the mission of the church.

The messianic hope; in the Old Testament

Scholars have generally agreed that God's promise given to David through the prophet Nathan in 2 Samuel 7:12–16 lies at the basis of the Jewish messianic hope. According to Kaiser this promise 'is matched in importance and prestige only by the promise made to Abraham in Genesis 12 and later to all Israel and Judah in Jeremiah's new covenant (Jer 31:31–34).'[2] According to Sicre, without this text 'it is impossible to understand many of the prophetic affirmations.'[3] Through Nathan's oracle, God tells David:

> When your days are over and you rest with your fathers, I will raise up your offspring to succeed you, who will come from your own body, and I will establish his kingdom. He is the one who will build a house for my Name, and I will establish the throne of his kingdom forever. I will be his father, and he will be my son. When he does wrong, I will punish him with the rod of men, with floggings inflicted by men. But my love will never be taken away from him, as I took it away from Saul, whom I removed from before you. Your house and your kingdom will endure forever before me; your throne will be established forever.

The following comments are here appropriate. First, the promise assumes that God's governance of Israel will not be *directly* exercised by God, but will be mediated through a king who will succeed David. In other words, theocracy as synthesized in the affirmation that 'Yahweh is king' is no longer to be regarded as incompatible with monarchy. This position stands in sharp contrast with the view expressed in 1 Samuel 8:7, according to which, when the elders of Israel requested the appointment of a king to lead Israel, 'Such as all the other nations have,' Samuel was told, 'It is not you they have rejected, but they have rejected me as their king' (cf. Judges 8:22–23).

Second, the promise ties God's blessing to the house of David unconditionally and on a permanent basis. This is a covenant relationship with David and his offspring: it transcends the monarchy as an institution and is liturgically celebrated in Psalm 89:20–37:

> I have found David my servant; with my sacred oil I have anointed him.
>
> My hand will sustain him; surely my arm will strengthen him.

No enemy will subject him to tribute; no wicked man will oppress him.

I will crush his foes before him and strike down his adversaries.

My faithful love will be with him, and through my name his horn will be exalted.

I will set his hand over the sea, his right hand over the rivers.

He will call out to me, 'You are my Father, my God, the Rock, my Saviour.'

I will also appoint him my firstborn, the most exalted of the kings of the earth.

I will maintain my love to him forever, and my covenant with him will never fail.

I will establish his line forever, his throne as long as the heavens endure.

If his sons forsake my law and do not follow my statutes,

if they violate my decrees and fail to keep my commandments,

I will punish their sin with the rod, their iniquity with flogging,

but will not take my love from him, nor will I ever betray my faithfulness.

I will not violate my covenant or alter what my lips have uttered.

Once for all, I have sworn by my holiness – and I will not lie to David –

that his line will continue forever and his throne endure before me like the sun;

it will be established forever like the moon, the faithful witness in the sky.

Third, the promise is related to an earthly political kingdom established by God, with a king – a 'messiah' – from the Davidic dynasty who will enjoy God's special favour. The Norwegian author Sigmund Mowinckel[4] claims that 'The word "Messiah" is not found in the Old Testament as a title or as a name applied to an eschatological king, but occurs for the first time in the literature of late Judaism and then as an abbreviation of the more complete expression, "Anointed of Yaweh".'[5]

The fact remains, however, that the promise does refer to a *future* king. Accordingly, late Judaism interpreted the promise in eschatological terms and this interpretation is basic to the understanding of Jesus' proclamation of the good news of the kingdom of God.

Many Old Testament passages make a close connection between the monarchy as a historical reality and the development of the messianic hope in the people of Israel. Space does not allow a detailed discussion of the topic within the confines of this chapter. A good illustration of this connection, however, is provided by the prophet Jeremiah, who lived in one of the best epochs of Judah's history, under the reign of Josiah (640–609 BC), but also suffered under the reign of evil kings, including Jehoahaz (609), Jehoiakim (609–598), Jehoiachin (598–597) and Zedekiah (597–586), who was taken with bronze shackles to Babylon, where he died.

It is not difficult to imagine the feelings of utter desolation and despondency that took possession of Israel as a result of the fall of Jerusalem and the exile that followed. Had God forgotten them? The prophetic answer to that question may have simply been expressed in words that common people believed: that the humiliating defeat was the outcome of the separation that the monarchy had made between governance and justice. The link between injustice and exile – the 'scattering' of the sheep – is made explicit in Jeremiah 23:1–2:

> 'Woe to the shepherds who are destroying and scattering the sheep of my pasture!' declares the LORD. Therefore this is what the LORD, the God of Israel, says to the shepherds who tend my people: 'Because you have scattered my flock and driven them away and have not bestowed care on them, I will bestow punishment on you for the evil you have done,' declares the Lord.

Quite clearly, the assumption is made that power, whether political or economic or military, is not given to the kings for their own benefit but for the service of justice. The duty of the shepherds is to 'bestow care' on the sheep. In like manner, the duty of the kings is to enable each person, family, clan or tribe to get the right portion of power and goods. When they fail to fulfil this duty, both the rulers and the people suffer the consequences.

In order to illustrate the great difference between a king that uses public power for his own benefit and a king who regards himself as a mediator of Yahweh's justice, Jeremiah appeals to the radical contrast between Jehoiakim and his father Josiah. Jehoiakim's self-serving use of power is made evident by his large and luxurious palace built by unrighteousness and injustice, by workers whom he has openly exploited (22:13–14). The portrayal of this evil king can hardly be more demolishing: 'Your eyes and your heart are set only on dishonest gain, on shedding innocent blood and on oppression and extortion' (v. 17). Josiah, on the other hand, is described as a king that, 'Did what was right and just . . . defended the cause of the poor and needy, and so all went well' (vv. 15–16a), and his practice of justice is equated to knowing God, 'Is this not what it means to know me? declares the LORD' (v. 16b). In the same tenor, 2 Kings 22:2 states that Josiah, 'Did what was right of the Lord, and walked in all the ways of his father David; he did not turn aside to the right or to the left.' He thus becomes a model king who by practising justice mediates the knowledge of God as a God of justice in Israel.

The same eloquence used to describe Jehoiakim's moral bankruptcy is also used by the prophet to portray God's judgement on the evildoer, 'Therefore this is what the LORD says about Jehoiakim son of Josiah king of Judah: "They will not mourn for him: Alas, my brother! Alas, my sister! They will not mourn for him: Alas, my master! Alas, his splendour! He will have the burial of a donkey – dragged away and thrown outside the gates of Jerusalem"' (vv. 18–19). To stress the finality of God's judgement, Jeremiah adds, 'O land, land, land, hear the word of the Lord! This is what the Lord says: "Record this man as if childless, a man who will not prosper is his lifetime, for none of his offspring will prosper, none will sit on the throne of David or rule any more in Judah"' (vv. 29–30).

Time after time, however, the prophetic word of judgement comes together with God's promise of restoration, often expressed in terms that point to the Davidic covenant. Such is the case in Jeremiah 23, where the announcement of punishment on the kings for the evil they have done is followed by a word of hope:

> The days are coming, declares the Lord, when I will raise up to David a righteous Branch, a King who will reign wisely and do what is just and right in the land. In his days Judah will be saved and Israel will live in safety. This is the name by which he will be called: The LORD of Righteousness [Justice]. (vv. 5–6)

In contrast with the kings who caused the ruin of Israel by their failure to do justice, David's descendant will be characterized by justice. The same prediction is ratified in 33:15–16. The messianic hope is the hope focused on the coming of a king who will fully qualify as a faithful mediator of God's justice: a king who will use his power to insure that all the members of society, including the economically poor or socially marginalized, will be fully taken into account. As Brueggemann has put it, 'Out of the concrete political practice arose an expectation of the coming messiah: a historical agent to be anointed, commissioned, and empowered out of David's house to do the Davidic thing in time to come, to establish Yahweh's justice and righteousness in the earth.'[6]

A number of Old Testament passages reflect that hope. Space does not allow a more detailed discussion of this topic, but the three following examples taken from Isaiah are worth mentioning:

- Isaiah 9:2–7, which predicts the coming of a king about whom it is said that, 'Of the increase of his government and peace there will be no end. He will reign on David's throne and over his kingdom, establishing and upholding it with justice and righteousness from that time on and for ever' (v. 7).
- Isaiah 11:1–9, which announces the coming of a Spirit-filled ruler who 'with righteousness . . . will judge the needy, with justice . . . will give decisions for the poor of the earth' (v. 4). Under his government paradise will be restored and even superseded, 'for the earth will be full of the knowledge of the Lord as the waters cover the sea' (v. 9).
- Isaiah 16:4b–5, which foresees an era when oppression will be over and, 'In love a throne will be established; in faithfulness a man will sit on it – one from the house of David –

one who in judging seeks justice and speeds the cause of righteousness' (v. 5).

Similar messianic expectations are attached to the suffering Servant of the Lord in the Isaianic Canticles, as is seen in the two following passages:

- Isaiah 42:1–4, which foretells the coming of the Servant of the Lord who, 'will bring justice to the nations' and 'will not falter or be discouraged till he establishes justice on earth. In his law the islands will put their hope' (vv. 1, 4).
- Isaiah 61:1–3, which views the Servant of the Lord as anointed by the Spirit 'to preach good news to the poor . . . to bind the broken-hearted, to proclaim freedom for the captives and release from darkness for the prisoners, to proclaim the year of the Lord's favour, and the day of vengeance of our God, to comfort all who mourn . . .'

Aside from the Davidic king and the Servant of the Lord, a proper understanding of the messianic expectations that, rooted in the Old Testament, were current at the time of Jesus requires us to take into account the figure of, 'One like a son of man, coming with the clouds of heaven,' of whom it is said in Daniel 7:14: 'He was given authority, glory and sovereign power; all the peoples, nations and men of every language worshipped him. His dominion is an everlasting dominion that will not pass away, and his kingdom is one that will never be destroyed.' This vision of the 'Son of Man' played an important role in apocalyptic literature, especially in the so-called Similitudes of Enoch (first century BC) and in II (or IV) Ezra (first century AD), both of which provide evidence that in apocalyptic circles this Danielic figure was identified with the Messiah through whom God was to establish his kingdom of justice and peace.

Jesus, Messiah and Lord

Quite early in the history of the church Jesus' death was given a theological interpretation. The Apostle Paul makes that clear when he writes: 'For what I received I passed on to you as of first importance, that Christ died for our sins according to the Scriptures' (1 Cor. 15:3). We must not assume, however, that this theological understanding of Jesus' death is unrelated to Jesus' public career.

The historical evidence provided by the gospels leaves no doubt regarding the political dimension of his crucifixion. He was not crucified because of promoting a new religion. He was crucified because he proclaimed that the kingdom of God was coming and many people, especially in Galilee, were responding positively to the enactment of his message in his person and action. As a result, a growing movement was taking shape around him and the leaders of Israel felt that their position in relation to the Roman Empire was under threat. According to John 11:45–53, after Jesus raised Lazarus from the dead,

> Many of the Jews who had come to visit Mary, and had seen what Jesus did, put their faith in him. But some of them went to the Pharisees and told them what Jesus had done. Then the chief priests and the Pharisees called a meeting of the Sanhedrin. 'What are we accomplishing?' they asked. 'Here is this man performing many miraculous signs. If we let him go on like this, everyone will believe in him, and then the Romans will come and take away both our place and our nation.' . . . So from that day on they plotted to take his life.

At the centre of the plot was the accusation that Jesus was a political subversive, opposing payment of taxes to Caesar and claiming to be a king (Lk. 23:2). To this messianic charge point both the title on the cross – 'Jesus of Nazareth, the King of the Jews' in Aramaic, Latin and Greek (Jn. 19:19) – and the mocking of Jesus by the Roman soldiers, who put on him a purple robe and a crown of thorns and pretended to pay homage to him as, 'King of the Jews' (Mk. 15:16–20).

The plot of the Jewish authorities aimed at having Jesus condemned to death by the Romans as a messianic claimant who was subverting Caesar's good order. The subversion that Jesus came to embody and to initiate, however, was not what the Romans and the Jews (including Jesus' own disciples under the influence of common Jewish messianic expectations) could be led to imagine. To be sure, right from the beginning of his ministry Jesus had announced: 'The time has come, the kingdom of God is near. Repent and believe the good news' (Mk. 1:15), and when at the end of his ministry Pilate asked him whether he was 'the king of the Jews', he did not deny that he was. A very important key to understanding the nature of the kingdom that he came to establish, however, is provided by his answer to Pilate, 'My kingdom is not of this world. If it were, my servants would fight to prevent my arrest by the Jews. But now my kingdom is from another place' (Jn. 18: 36).

Space does not allow a detailed discussion of what Jesus meant by referring to him being 'from another place'. For the purpose of this chapter, suffice it to highlight the following characteristics of this kingdom.

First, *he did not come to establish a national Jewish kingdom* in which, according to current messianic expectations, the glory of David would be restored to Israel. In that sense, his kingdom 'is not from this world'.

Second, *his kingdom is a present reality*. To be sure, it has not yet come in its fullness, but it can already be perceived because it has come in the person and work of Jesus, the king. Jesus' words in response to the question by the Pharisees as to when the kingdom of God would come point to that presence: 'The kingdom of God does not come with your careful observation, nor will people say, "Here it is," or "There it is," because the kingdom of God is *among* you' (Lk. 17:20–21).[7] When Jesus announced the coming of his kingdom, he was not referring to a kingdom which was to come in a distant future, but to an eschatological reality that he himself was inserting into history – a reality that demanded from his listeners an immediate response in terms of repentance and faith.

Third, *the politics of the kingdom of God manifest in Jesus Christ stands in contrast with contemporary political alternatives*. As N. T. Wright has cogently argued in *Jesus and the Victory of God*, no serious attempt to understand Jesus historically is possible without taking into account Jesus' relation to the various religious-political groups in his Jewish context.[8] When that approach is followed, the uniqueness of Jesus' view of how

God intended to fulfil his purpose outlined by the Old Testament prophets becomes clear.

Most of the *Sadducees* were related to the high-priestly families, regarding whom Josephus wrote right at the beginning of his autobiography that, 'As nobility among several people is of a different origin, so with us to be of the sacerdotal dignity is an indication of the splendour of a family.' From their perspective, Israel's future was closely related to its acceptance of the Hellenistic culture and to its diligence not to displease the Roman authorities. They were a sort of 'fifth column' within Judaism, through whom the Hellenistic culture, and later that of the Romans, was allowed to influence the Jews. Jesus warned his disciples against 'the leaven of the Sadducees' (Mt. 16:6).

The *Pharisees*, whose origin could be traced back to the party of the *Hasidim*, who made a name for themselves during the Maccabean Wars, understood their vocation to be the preservation of Israel and Jewish identity through the keeping of the law and tended to be strongly legalistic and ritualistic. They were quite numerous and active in Galilee and everywhere else. A common trait that marked them was their emphasis on purity, coupled with their aversion towards the popular masses, whom they spitefully called *am-haarets* – in John's words, 'This mob that knows nothing of the law' (Jn. 7:49).

The *Zealots* held to a strong Jewish nationalistic position and expected the coming of the Messiah as a political figure who, exalted as king by his followers, would restore theocracy to Israel.

The Qumran sect of the *Essenes* regarded the high-priestly dynasty as usurpers, saw themselves as the true Israel, and retired to the Dead Sea to wait for God's vindication.

Each one of these groups had its own understanding of how Israel was to fulfil its call to be the people of God living under God's rule. Jesus' agenda did not differ from theirs in that his was related to a 'spiritual and internal' kingdom. Rather, it differed in that he understood the kingdom of God as God's power erupting in the midst of oppression, injustice and violence, and bringing freedom, justice and peace through his own person and ministry.

The nature of the kingdom that Jesus proclaimed and embodied is synthetically expressed in his combination of three figures that in the Old Testament appear in isolation from one another: the Messiah of the Remnant, the suffering Servant of the Lord and the Son of Man. Several biblical scholars have found in this very original combination the key to understanding Jesus' own concept of his mission. From this perspective, he came to be the king of the Jews – the descendant of David through whom the glory of Israel would be restored – and the Son of Man, but he would not establish an earthly kingdom by coercion nor would he come 'with the clouds of heaven', with a great display of power. Instead, as the suffering Servant of the Lord, he would establish a heavenly kingdom – a kingdom 'from another place' – by giving his life in love to God and to others. In order to gain a clearer view of this kingdom, we will briefly examine seven gospel pictures of Jesus' earthly life and ministry: his baptism, his programme, his preaching, his concept of power, his entry into Jerusalem, his cleansing of the temple and his crucifixion.

Jesus' baptism

The combination of the figure of the Messiah of the Remnant with that of the suffering Servant of the Lord is already present at the scene of Jesus' baptism by John the Baptist. As Jesus was praying, 'Heaven was opened and the Holy Spirit descended on him in bodily form like a dove. And a voice came from heaven: "You are my Son, whom I love; with you I am well pleased"' (Lk. 3:22; cf. Mt. 3:16–17). The combination of Psalm 2:7 – *'You are my Son'*, God's words addressed to David's descendant as he is installed as 'King of Zion' – with Isaiah 42:1 – 'Here is my servant . . . *in whom I delight*' – by the Father's voice speaking to the Son at the very beginning of his earthly career defines the way in which Jesus is to fulfil his messianic mission. He is the Messiah – David's descendant who comes to sit on Israel's throne – but his messiahship is to be fulfilled in terms of the suffering Servant of the Lord, through suffering, humiliation and death on the cross.

Jesus' programme

In Jesus' earthly ministry, this kingdom politics was the basic motivation for his miracles of healing and exorcism. It was also behind Jesus' Galilean option – the option for marginalized sectors of the population of Galilee in those days – in order to fulfil the programme that he had defined in the synagogue of Nazareth at the beginning of his public career, 'The Spirit of the Lord is on me, because he has anointed me to proclaim good news to the poor. He has sent me to proclaim freedom for the prisoners and recovery of sight to the blind, to release the oppressed, to proclaim the year of the Lord's favour' (Lk. 4:18–19).

Without attempting a detailed analysis of this passage, we will make a few observations on it. First, the opening reference to the Spirit is significant in light of the definition of the mission that follows: *the purpose of the anointing by the Spirit is the realization of the mission of the Messiah, God's anointed one*. For him, anointing and mission are inseparable.

Second, *the mission of the Messiah is to work on behalf of the most vulnerable people in society*: the poor, the captives, the blind, the oppressed. Evidently Jesus thinks that his ministry is going to produce radical changes in the society of his day, sufficiently important as to interpret them as signs of the coming of a new era of justice – the era of God's reign. The Spirit has anointed him as the one who comes to accomplish God's liberation of the oppressed, to realize the work of, 'the God who can disrupt any circumstance of social bondage and exploitation, overthrow ruthless orderings of public life, and authorize new circumstances of dancing freedom, dignity, and justice'.[9]

Third, this passage is a quotation of Isaiah 61:1,2, in which the prophet speaks to a group of disillusioned Jews, some time after the Exile. The quotation, however, appears with an additional phrase taken from Isaiah 58:6, 'to release the oppressed', which in its original context has a social connotation. The oppressed in Israel are those who, finding themselves economically ruined, have sold themselves as slaves. The only hope for them, as for all who are in a position of disadvantage in society, is the cancellation of their debts and the announcement of their liberation on 'the year of the Lord's favour', the year of jubilee (cf. Lev. 25) – a metaphor for the messianic era initiated in history by Jesus Christ. *Right at the beginning of his earthly ministry Jesus stamps an eschatological mark on his ministry by introducing himself as the Servant of the Lord who has been anointed by the Spirit of God to initiate a new order of justice and peace.* He claims that in his person and ministry the messianic prophecies of the Old Testament are being fulfilled there and then, in his hearers' presence, 'Today this scripture is fulfilled in your hearing' (Lk. 4:21). What Jesus proclaims is nothing more or less than the coming of a new era of human history. Anointed by the Spirit of God, the Messiah is the agent of eschatology in the process of realization. According to contemporary Judaism, the Spirit of God had left the world and his return would be the fulfilment of the messianic expectation. According to Jesus' proclamation, the new era of justice and peace has begun in his own person and work: he has come to fulfil the Old Testament prophecies regarding the Servant of the Lord anointed by the Spirit of God to break every form of oppression and to carry out the messianic hope of a new social order of 'freedom, dignity, and justice'.

The actual spelling out of the meaning of the Nazareth manifesto is in the narratives of the life and teaching of Jesus found in the gospels. The portrait that emerges from these narratives is one of a prophet whose proclamation on the kingdom of God centres on the God of the kingdom as a God of love that forgives the sinner and reconciles the enemy, justice that vindicates the oppressed and lifts up the sinned-against, and peacemaking that creates a community of *shalom* – fullness of life for all. It is the portrait of the prophet of 'the upside-down kingdom'.[10] Jesus focuses his ministry on the most needy, not only from the standpoint of physical and economic need, but also from the social and spiritual perspectives. The repeated references that Luke's Gospel makes to Jesus' exorcisms (Lk. 6:18; 7:21; 8:2,29; 9:42; 13:10–12) may lead us to think that the only form of oppression that Jesus deals with is oppression by evil spirits. His exorcisms, however, are frequently associated with his healing of sicknesses, and both exorcisms and healings take place mainly among the poor. They point beyond themselves to the kingdom of God that has become a present reality and is bringing wholeness among people who at that time are at the bottom of the social scale: the blind, the lame, the lepers, the deaf (Lk. 7:22), as well as women, children, Samaritans and tax collectors. The relationship between the kingdom and the Spirit is so close that, in response to the accusation that the restoration of a blind and mute man has been done 'by Beelzebub, the prince of demons', Jesus replies: 'If I drive out demons by the Spirit of God, then the kingdom of God has come upon you' (Mt. 12:28). It is worth taking note that in the parallel passage in Luke, the Spirit is described as 'the finger of God' (11:20).

Jesus' preaching

Jesus' concrete action corroborates his preaching. He rejects a legalistic religion that is used to oppress people who are in a position of social disadvantage and he is criticized because he has table fellowship with people outside the limits of social respectability such as tax collectors and 'sinners' (Mk. 2:16; Mt. 9:11; 11:19; Lk. 5:30; 15:1–2). Although he does not refuse to meet with Jewish leaders who are willing to meet with him, he surrounds himself with ordinary people – the 'little ones', the nobodies (including women and children) who are set aside by the rich and powerful. When John the Baptist, imprisoned by Herod and in the midst of a crisis of faith, sends a delegation to ask Jesus whether he is really the expected Messiah, Jesus cured people who were commonly regarded as under God's curse and said to the messengers, 'Go back and report to John what you have seen and heard: The blind receive sight, the lame walk, those who have leprosy are cured, the deaf hear, the dead are raised, and the good news is preached to the poor. Blessed is the man who does not fall away on account of me' (Lk. 7:22–23). Quite clearly, his restorative action on behalf of the poor authenticates him as God's Messiah because it displays God's power to transform humankind beginning with the marginalized. It is also a sign that God loves justice and intends not merely to 'save souls' and send them to heaven but to restore humankind and the whole of creation according to his love.

The extent to which the politics of love is designed by God himself to accomplish his redemptive purpose is thrown into relief by one of the most radical injunctions in the Sermon on the Mount, 'You have heard that it was said, "Love your neighbour and hate your enemy." But I tell you: Love your enemy and pray for those who persecute you, that you may be the sons of your Father in heaven' (Mt. 5:43–45). According to the politics of the kingdom that Jesus came to establish, no person, not even an enemy, falls outside the orbit of neighbourly love because no person is marginalized from God's love.

Jesus' concept of power

Another scene, this time near the end of Jesus' earthly career, shows the centrality of the figure of the suffering Servant of the Lord in Jesus' understanding of his messianic mission. On the way to Jerusalem, where he is to be crucified, two of his disciples – James and John who, together with Peter, form the core group of disciples closest to Jesus – obviously driven by political ambitions, come to him with a request: 'Let one of us sit at your right [as primary minister!] and the other at your left [as private secretary!] in your glory [the earthly Jewish kingdom that you are to establish]' (Mk. 10:37). Jesus' reply, in which he refers to his death on the cross in terms of the *cup* that he is going to drink and the *baptism* with which he is going to be baptized, makes it clear that there is no participation in his kingdom without participation in his death. When the other ten disciples, driven by the same political ambition that has impelled James and John to make their request, become indignant with them, Jesus spells out his concept of political power and defines his own mission by combining the figure of the suffering Servant of the Lord with that of the Son of Man:

> You know that those who are regarded as rulers of the Gentiles lord it over them, and their high officials exercise authority over them. Not so with you. Instead, whoever wants to become great among you must become your servant, and whoever wants to be first must be slave of all. For even the Son of Man

> did not come to be served, but to serve and to give his life as a ransom for many. (Mk. 10:42–45)

In other words, he is the Son of Man whose coming is announced in Daniel 7, but he does not fulfil his vocation according to what has been called the 'transcendental messianism' of apocalyptic expectations, but in terms of the suffering Servant who, according to Isaiah 53, gives his life as a ransom for many in an act of sacrificial service.

Jesus' entry into Jerusalem

In the third century AD, Rabbi Joshua Joshua ben Levi, according to tradition, said that if Israel was worthy by keeping one Sabbath, as was prescribed, or two Sabbaths, as some rabbis taught, the Messiah would come to them 'with the cloud of heaven' (as in Dan. 7:13). On the other hand, if Israel was not worthy, the Messiah would come 'gentle [lowly] and riding on a donkey, on a colt, the foal of a donkey' (as in Zech. 9:9). In line with the prophetic tradition, Jesus entered into Jerusalem as the humble Messiah, riding an ass that no one had ever ridden (Lk. 19:28–38). A king riding on a donkey! Most likely, the 'crowd of disciples' (v. 37) that followed him and exalted him as 'the king who comes in the name of the Lord' (v. 38, quoting Ps. 118:26) expected him to sit on David's throne to establish a nationalist Jewish kingdom that would deliver them from Rome through military force. The kingdom that he had come to bring, however, was not 'from this world', but 'from another place', and in order to establish it he had to die.

Jesus' cleansing of the temple

N. T. Wright has rightly highlighted the importance of symbols for Jesus' announcement of the kingdom of God within the Judaism of his day.[11] According to him, Jesus engaged in controversies mainly with the Pharisees, not so much about religion, but about eschatology; not so much about morality, but about the kingdom of God. From his perspective, Israel would not preserve its Jewish identity by means of ancestral codes, but by fulfilling its God-given vocation to be 'light of the nations'. In line with this position, he questioned both the revolutionary agenda of the leaders of the Pharisees and the symbols of Jewish culture and aspirations, such as the Sabbath, dietary codes, nation and land, and the temple.

The temple was, in fact, the key symbol of Jewish identity. It was, or had been, God's dwelling, and it continued to be regarded as the place of sacrifice for the sake of forgiveness and the place of fellowship between Israel and its God. Furthermore, it was a symbol of royal power, related to David and Solomon, and the centre of Jewish religious and political life, under the charge of the ruling class made by the chief priests, accompanied by the Herodian dynasty and supervised by the Romans.

Taking as his starting place a different eschatological perspective, Jesus carried out a prophetic act through which he symbolically portrayed God's judgement over the injustice of the religious and political system represented by the temple. By expelling the traders from the temple courts (Lk. 19:45–46), he announced the fulfilment of Jeremiah's prophecy (Jer. 7:2–15) regarding the destruction of the temple, which had become 'a den of robbers' (v. 11) – people who needed to be called to 'really change [their] ways and [their] actions and [to] deal with each other justly', and 'not [to] oppress the alien, the fatherless or the widow' (vv. 5–6). Without the trade, no sacrifices would be possible, and without sacrifices, the temple would lose its meaning as the place where forgiveness and fellowship with God would be possible.

For Jesus, the symbols of Jewish identity, including the temple, had to be changed in light of the fact that the kingdom of God had come in him. The temple of Jerusalem would be destroyed by the Romans. On the other hand, as the Servant of the Lord, he himself was now the place of forgiveness and reconciliation with God open to all.

Jesus' crucifixion

The climax of Jesus' solidarity with the poor and undeserving is his death on the cross, in which God identifies himself with the victims and provides the means for the victims to recover their human dignity as persons created for the glory of God. The politics that he proclaimed and lived out was in Pauline language the politics of *the crucified Messiah* (1 Cor. 1:23; 2:3), the politics of love through which God's justice would be brought to the world.

The paradoxical character of that Pauline description can hardly be exaggerated. How could a person who died hanging on a cross as a subversive be regarded as the one through whom Israel's messianic hope for liberation and the establishment of the kingdom of God could be fulfilled? How could God through him rescue Israel and bring justice to the world?

The answer lies in Jesus' own understanding of his own messiahship not in terms of a glorious king who imposes his authority through violence and coercion, as the majority of Jews expected, but in terms of the Servant of the Lord who in love takes upon himself the sins of the world (Isa. 53) and is exalted as Lord over all things.

The church as the messianic community

For the sake of brevity, we will limit ourselves to listing a few conclusions from the foregoing discussion, which are relevant to the mission of the church as the messianic community.

First, the mission of the church is kingdom mission – the continuation of the mission of Jesus through which God intends to fulfil his purpose for humankind and for all creation. The church is not the kingdom; rather, it exists in the service of the kingdom, to give witness about the kingdom by being, doing and speaking.

Second, the mission of the church takes as its starting point the kingdom that has already entered into history in the person and work of Jesus Christ. The church acknowledges Jesus Christ as the Messiah and Lord and seeks to live out that confession.

Third, the mission of the church is not restricted to the religious sphere of life, but has to do with every aspect of it. From this perspective, there is no secular–sacred divide, no separation between the public and the private or between justification by faith and the struggle for justice.

Fourth, the mission of the church involves not only the proclamation but also the demonstration of the gospel.

Fifth, the mission of the church gives priority to the poor. It seeks the reconstruction of all humankind beginning with the poor, to whom it brings good news.

Sixth, the mission of the church is the mission of the Holy Spirit through the church.

Seventh, the mission of the church replaced the love of power by the power of love – love which is translated into sacrificial service.

The mission of the church is both eschatological and political and always stands in contrast with other alternatives that fail to put love of God and neighbour at the centre of life.

The meaning of the kingdom of God for the mission of the church is highlighted by the following call in the document that emerged out of the Consultation on 'The Church in Response to Human Needs' in 1983:

> The reality of the presence of the kingdom gives us the courage to begin here and now to erect signs of the kingdom by working prayerfully and consistently for greater justice and peace and toward the transformation of individuals and societies. Since one day God will wipe away all tears, it grieves us to see people suffer now. Since one day there will be perfect peace, we are called to be peacemakers now. We humbly yet urgently call upon you, the churches, to stand with us in this ministry of practising love and seeking to restore the dignity of human beings created in the image of God.

7

Isaiah 58: The Fast that God Requires

Tony Campolo

If you are seeking a passage of Scripture that contrasts formal religiosity with God-pleasing spirituality, you need look no further than Isaiah 58. There, in that chapter of the Bible, the prophet called Second Isaiah serves as an intermediary between God and the people of Israel. He declares the people's questions to God, and then delivers God's response to the people.

What the people want to know is why, after they had performed the solemn rituals which the priests had prescribed for them, observed the ordained feasts and kept the commanded Sabbaths which supposedly were to be pleasing to God, they had not received the blessings God had promised. With zeal and sincerity they had kept their part of the covenant, which they had assumed assured them of God's good favour and benefits, and they wanted to know why God had not kept his side of the bargain. Why had there not been a restoration of Jerusalem and a rebuilding of the temple, which they believed should have been forthcoming? Why, they were asking, had there not been a fulfilment of the promise that they thought God had made to those who would be faithful in observing these religious rites?

The people are told what they lacked

The chapter begins with God asking the prophet to tell the people what their worship was lacking and what they had failed to do and be so as to validate their worship. God's admonishment of them was not meant to be a putdown of worship, but their religious observances, in and of themselves, were not enough to please him. The prophet is instructed by God to 'cry aloud' (v. 1). In the original language that phrase meant to scream at the top of your lungs with passion and vehemence. This was ordered by God so that the prophet's message would be delivered with such intensity that the people would be certain to hear it. God wanted the people to know that he was disgusted with them in spite of their religiosity. Acknowledging that they had been personally pious and sticklers when it came to living out their cultic rules and regulations, the message from God goes on to declare that this was not enough to please him. God declared in this chapter that the observance of religious rituals is only meaningful if people live out justice for the poor; work for freedom on behalf of indentured servants; feed the hungry; clothe the naked; and recognize their obligations to meet the needs of those who live around them. In short – they were told that loving service and social justice are more important than the self-denying, sacrificial religious rituals, and that without them God finds no pleasure in their religious observances.

Prosperity theology under attack

What was particularly upsetting to God was the selfishness that lay at the base of the people's worship. It was an ancient version of that 'prosperity theology' that is increasingly common in modern Christendom. There was in their worship the belief that, if they did their part and lived out the religious requirements laid down by their priests, God's promises would be kept and God would give them all that they desired.

In verse 3, the people ask the prophet to relay to God their complaints. They wanted God to take note of the fact that they had kept the religious observances that were designed to remind them of the great calamities that, because of their sins, had befallen them in the past (i.e. the fall of Jerusalem; the Babylonian captivity; and the destruction of the temple).

Therefore, the people wanted to know why God had not poured out his blessings on them in return.

We cannot help but recognize parallels in the religiosity of these ancient Jews and what we often see and hear being promoted by some American preachers and televangelists. Too often, over television, we hear religious hucksters claiming that if those in the listening audience would just do what *they say* the Bible is prescribing as obligations for believers and send in a tithe to support their television programming, then God will make them rich in return.

Perhaps the most blatant distortion of Christianity comes from those prosperity theology preachers who plead with their listeners to practise what they sometimes call 'the reverse tithe'. In simple language, that means that if a listener gives 10 per cent of the money he or she dreams about, that person will receive the other 90 per cent of that amount. For example, if someone gives $1,000 to the ministry, then God will give back to that person $9,000 in return. Reverse tithing, these charlatans claim, is an investment that will bring huge financial returns. Accordingly, they suggest that there is no requirement for Christians to feed the hungry or clothe the naked. There is no need to deliver the oppressed from their suffering or to spend money to meet the needs of widows or orphans. This form of Christianity is not about those sorts of things. Instead, it is about getting rewarded by God through the reverse tithing formulas that these televangelists contrived.

Sadly, it is not just American televangelists who are into these kinds of shenanigans. If you go to Africa, Latin America and Asia, you will find variants of these same distorted interpretations of Scripture. Among the socially disinherited people who live in obscene poverty in these places, you will find similar kinds of preaching. In Africa, there are preachers who are chauffeured around in luxury cars, wearing thousand-dollar suits, and whose fingers are adorned with diamond rings who claim that these are God's rewards for following the prescriptions for prosperity that they say are laid down in Scripture. They tell their followers that the same kind of affluence will be theirs if they just give sacrificially to the ministries of these preachers. The people are promised that

God will pay back faithful worshippers beyond their wildest imagination.

All too often, these manipulated people, after they have given so sacrificially, ask, as did the Jews described in Isaiah 58, why God did not deliver what they were led to believe would be promised miraculous benefits. Their disillusionment with a God that they believed did not keep what they thought was part of the deal, was often intense.

Bronislaw Malinowski, the famous anthropologist, once defined the difference between magic and prayer. Magic, Malinowski contended, is the performance of certain rituals in order to get God to do your will. He said that prayer, on the other hand, is becoming submissive to God so that God's will can be done through you. The televangelists I have described, along with those prosperity theology preachers, are simply modern exaggerations of magic. And it was this kind of religion, in less blatant and more sophisticated forms, which was practised by the ancient Jews we read about in Isaiah 58.

The people described in this chapter of the Bible were good at worship and there is no doubt that there was sincerity in what they did. They humbled themselves (v. 3) and they endeavoured to keep the Sabbath. However, sincerity and humility are not enough. The Lord requires more than that. As it says in Micah 6:8, the Lord requires people to 'do justly, and to love mercy, and to walk humbly with thy God.'

The prophets did not plagiarize from each other's writings, but they were certainly on the same wavelength in their thinking. Here, in Isaiah, we pick up Micah Challenge. Here we have echoes of what we read earlier in Isaiah's writings when he declared that God was offended by the noise of solemn assemblies that were not marked by deeds of loving service for the needy (Isa. 1:13f).

The creative power of worship

When relating Isaiah 58 to our existential situation, it is easy to become cynical about some of what happens in what is called 'contemporary worship'. Typically, we see people with upraised arms singing, 'It's all about you, Lord! It's all about you!' But we are prone to wonder if all of their outpourings of devotion are connected to the kinds of social concerns that we read about in this chapter of Scripture (see vv. 6–7). Do these modern worshippers realize that, if religious enthusiasm is not connected with caring for those in need, it can easily become little more than a sentimental orgy? Do they recognize that religious ecstasy can easily become an escape from social responsibility?

Worship, especially the music employed in worship, can have far-reaching effects. It should be noted that studies made by historians and sociologists provide evidence that the theologies that governed the life of the church were sometimes more conditioned by the music of the church than by the writings of religious scholars. For instance, there are reports that, in the doctrinal arguments that eventually led to the Council of Nicaea, the final decisions of the Council were settled more as the result of hymns that were sung than by the discussions of the ancient church fathers. What was at stake at that Council was the doctrine of the deity of Christ. Athanasius, the church father who taught that Jesus was God incarnate, stood against Arius, who claimed that Jesus was not actually God but only a creation of God. It is said that both Athanasius and Arius had choirs on hand at Nicaea and that each of their choirs went through the streets of the town singing hymns that promoted their respective doctrines. A case can be made that in the end Athanasius won out because the songs that expressed his teachings about the deity of Christ were more catchy than the songs of Arius's choir.

If what we sing at worship can be that influential, we have to ask what the long-term effects will be of much of the contemporary worship music that has become the craze in many of our churches, and especially among young people. Will this new kind of worship music mould our theologies so that our religion in the years that lie ahead will be likened to that of the people of Israel, devoid of social justice concerns and, therefore, unacceptable to God? Will we have worship music that has Christians, like those described in Isaiah 1:15–17, with uplifted hands singing love songs to God, while failing to 'seek justice, correct oppression, defend the fatherless, and plead for the widow'? We need to take a serious look at the lyrics of contemporary worship music and ask what kind of church it will create in the years that lie ahead.

The good potentialities in worship

Isaiah 58 should not be taken as a condemnation of liturgy. It is far too superficial a judgement to declare religious rituals as meaningless and dismiss them in a cavalier manner. The rituals in church liturgy can have a vital role in the lives of those who would be spiritually attuned to God. Emil Durkheim, one of the giants of modern sociology, in his book, *The Elementary Forms of the Religious Life*, outlined some of the most important contributions that rituals can make to faithful believers. Rituals, according to Durkheim, enhance the solidarity of a group, as well as increasing the commitments of its members to the values and beliefs of the group. Furthermore, contended Durkheim, rituals, when properly exercised, bring to consciousness those defining events of the past that gave birth to the faith commitments of believers. He also made the point that such rituals must be maintained if the religious life of the community is to have a future. Rituals remind the participants of what must never be forgotten, and they teach new generations what is essential for their faith.

It was not the rituals in and of themselves that irked God, according to Isaiah. What had led to God's angry frustration was that the fasting of the people was no longer accomplishing the kinds of things that Durkheim defined. The fasting and the other religious observances of the people of Israel had not brought to remembrance the meanings of the events that rituals were supposed to call to mind. Their worship practices were supposed to create remembrance among the Jews that they themselves were once aliens in a strange and distant land, and that there was a time when they too suffered from poverty and oppression. Their rituals were expected to lead them to commitments to care for the poor and minister to the aliens who were living in their midst. Other rituals were supposed to renew in their consciousness the great calamities that came upon Israel because they failed to do justice and disregarded the needs of the widows and orphans. Instead, their rituals had become little more than attempts to manipulate God into pouring out benefits upon the worshippers. The fasts of Israel were supposed to call the people into becoming righteous servants of those in need, but they had become nothing more than attempts to please God to the end of gaining an array of blessings.

The prophet declared to the people that the fast that God really desired was a fast that was connected to loving sacrifices to meet the needs of the homeless, the hungry and the naked. What God sought, according to Isaiah, were efforts to bring deliverance for people who were yoked to exploitative servitude. That had not happened. Even their observance of the Sabbath had become marred in God's eyes. Historians tell us that in the days of the prophet Isaiah observing the Sabbath had become the primary prerogative of the rich elite. The poor were expected to continue on with their assigned labour, even on this holy day. Relegating the poor to work on the Sabbath must have infuriated God in ways that are hard for us to imagine.

As God expressed displeasure and spoke to their failure to meet the economically based needs of the socially disinherited, we learn that he was also upset with the psychologically damaging ways in which the people treated their neighbours. Through Isaiah, God condemned this kind of oppression as the prophet preached against the act of 'pointing of the accusing finger' (v. 9). In Isaiah's day, such behaviour amounted to slandering one's neighbour, or giving one's neighbour 'the evil eye'. God let it be known that diminishing the dignity of another person is still another serious form of oppression, and this too is something that interferes with true worship.

The weeping visionary prophet

The prophet wept over what the people had become. Prophets always weep. There was no standing aloof from them as he pronounced God's judgement. Instead, Isaiah was so empathetic with God that the disappointments of God became his disappointments, and the emotional pathos of Yahweh became his own. Simultaneously, Isaiah was so connected spiritually and emotionally with his people that he also wept because he knew that he too would share in the consequences of their failure to live out love and justice, and that their plight would be his own.

A prophet of God, however, does more than just weep. The true prophet also offers an alternative vision of what the future can be, if only the people would repent of their indifference to the needs of the poor and again commit themselves to seeking justice for the oppressed. Isaiah told the people that if they lived out God's will, God had promised them that a 'new day would dawn' for them (v. 8). He told them that it would be a time wherein God will be ever present with the people. There was no prosperity theology being articulated in these promises of God. Individuals were not promised wealth. There would be, however, the promise of a blessed communal life for the Jews, as well as an outpouring of God's joyful spirit upon them.

Most important, in response for doing the social good that God required of them, the people would once again feel God's presence with them. No longer would they feel that he was far off and distant from their concerns. What is more, they would experience spiritual ecstasy and a renewed fulfilment in their daily lives. All of this is what was meant with the words that God would cause them to 'ride upon high places' (v. 14).

The promises of God to the ancient Jews included not only spiritual blessings, but the assurances of the renewal of the people's community life. The buildings that had been demolished by enemy armies will be restored and the walls of the city, that once provided security for those who lived there, will be rebuilt (v. 12). The renewal of Jerusalem and the rebuilding of the temple on the Holy Mount, so important for the cultic life of the Jews, will then be realized.

The prophet's message in the modern age

These promises to Israel for spiritual renewal were reiterated many years later by the nineteenth-century evangelist, Charles

Finney, in his essays on spiritual revivals. Finney's conviction was that the outpouring of God's Spirit on the people of America was conditioned by the extent of the establishment of social justice in their land. In his day, Finney was convinced that if spiritual renewal, with all of its ecstatic qualities, was to come to America, then the curse of slavery and the injustices related to the subjugation of women must be ended. Finney, following the lead of Isaiah, saw that at best there should be a connection between spiritual ecstasies in worship and social justice. We need that nexus today! Without social justice, contended Finney, worship would not bring about spiritual revival in America.

This message that we can all learn from Isaiah 58 is that spiritual renewal and true worship must always be undergirded by lifestyles marked by commitments to social justice for the oppressed and efforts to meet the needs of the poor. This is a message that in today's world is increasingly being heeded. Consider the good news that the Pentecostal movement, which is just a little more than a hundred years old, is showing marked signs of developing an intense social consciousness. In many sectors of this movement, which puts a strong emphasis on possessing spiritual gifts, having the ability to 'pray in tongues' is no longer sufficient evidence for demonstrating that persons are 'Spirit-filled'. More and more there are requisites that Spirit-filled Christians should also show evidence in their lives of having the 'fruits of the Spirit'. In Galatians 5, we read that at the top of the list of these fruits is the commitment to living out love. Consequently, in many Pentecostal churches, loving poor and oppressed people is especially being emphasized. Ministries to needy people are increasingly evident in their congregations. Today, Pentecostal churches are now among the leaders in providing child sponsorships for boys and girls in developing countries through such parachurch organizations as World Vision and Compassion International. Their churches also are highly visible in ministries to drug addicts and the homeless. These kinds of social concerns represent a major step in the right direction for Pentecostal churches as they strive to embrace a holistic gospel.

There is a reluctance, however, for Pentecostal churches to try to change society by endeavouring to address structural evil through political action. Consequently, they are not too likely to support political efforts to raise the minimum wage or to campaign for a universal health care plan that would help alleviate the fears of those 46 million Americans who have no coverage. Pentecostal preachers tend to support American-sponsored wars that could easily be labelled as unjust. At times they espouse a nationalism that verges on idolatry. There is not much talk in Pentecostal circles concerning such global issues as the cancellation of developing world debts or the ending of trade policies that are hurting people in the global South.

What is true of the Pentecostal movement in respect to working for structural change in society is sadly also true for a good part of the evangelical community. While evangelical churches are heavily involved in charitable ministries that help the poor, there is an evident reluctance for them to work towards changing such social systems as the way public education is funded in America. Generally, public education is dependent on land taxes, which means that wealthy townships with rich tax bases have extensive financial support for their schools, while school districts in urban neighbourhoods with poor tax bases languish with basic needs unmet. Evangelicals are not likely to oppose America's military establishment or question abuses in the capitalistic economy. Challenging such structural evils is not common among evangelicals. They are very committed to ministering to society's victims, but are rarely at work trying to change the social systems and institutions that create these victims.

Lately, there are signs that things may be changing with evangelicals. As a case in point, The National Association of Evangelicals recently took a bold stand advocating public policies to address the problem of global warming. Their leaders have been calling upon government to regulate emissions that cause global warming. Their rather progressive position on this matter has earned them some vitriolic criticism from some sectors of their constituency, but the NAE has not backed down. The NAE especially recognizes the relationship between environmentalism and poverty. Their position paper on the environment claims that environmental degradation most affects the poor because it diminishes food production and access to clean drinking water.

Justice is love in action

Isaiah's prophetic call for social justice is related to living out love. If we stop to think about it, justice is nothing more than love translated into social policies. If we are committed to the justice prescribed by love, we will have to acknowledge that charity is not enough. It is not enough to clothe the poor and feed the hungry. We must also change the social policies that make people poor and hungry.

In summary, the prophet would have strong words for those in our present world who are heavily into worship but, like those in ancient Israel, have done little in working for social justice. Worship, which has become a dominant part of the life of the evangelical and Pentecostal churches, must be coupled with commitments not only to loving charity, but also to justice on behalf of the poorest of the poor of the world. The prophet would declare to the modern Christians that if they fail to do this, their people will be faced with the same judgements made by God and articulated through his prophet thousands of years ago.

The proper response to all of this can only be that when God's people fast and worship it must be done in the context of love and justice for those who are in need. Only then will what they do be pleasing to God, and only then can they expect God to respond to them and bring about spiritual renewal. Any other kind of fasting and worship will incur the silence of God. Jews in Isaiah's day had to learn this, and Christians in today's world must learn this too.

8

Poverty, Sin and Social Structures: A Biblical Perspective

Ronald J. Sider

To think biblically about poverty today, we must be clear about four things: God's special concern for the poor; the multiple causes of poverty; the biblical teaching on unjust social systems; and the reality of structural injustices today.

God and the poor

The Scriptures speak of God's special concern for the poor in at least four different ways.[1]

1. Repeatedly, the Bible says that the Sovereign of history works to lift up the poor and oppressed. Consider the Exodus. Again and again the texts say God intervened because God hated the oppression of the poor Israelites (Ex. 3:7–8; 6:5–7; Deut. 26:6–8). Or consider the Psalms: 'I know the Lord will get justice for the poor and will defend the needy in court' (140:12 RSV; cf. 12:5). God acts in history to lift up the poor and oppressed.
2. Sometimes, the Lord of history tears down rich and powerful people. Mary's song is shocking: 'My soul glorifies the Lord . . . He has filled the hungry with good things but has sent the rich away empty' (Lk. 1:46,53 NIV). James is even

> more blunt: 'Now listen, you rich people, weep and wail because of the misery that is coming upon you' (Jas. 5:1 NIV).

Since God calls us to create wealth and is not biased against the rich, why do the Scriptures warn again and again that God sometimes works in history to destroy the rich? The Bible has a simple answer. It is because the rich sometimes get rich by oppressing the poor. Or because they often have plenty and neglect the needy. In either case, God is furious.

James warned the rich so harshly because they had hoarded wealth and refused to pay their workers (5:2–6). Repeatedly, the prophets said the same thing (Ps. 10; Jer. 22:13–19; Isa. 3:14–25). 'Among my people are wicked men who lie in wait like men who snare birds and like those who set traps to catch men. Like cages full of birds, their houses are full of deceit; they have become rich and powerful and have grown fat and sleek. . . . They do not defend the rights of the poor. Should I not punish them for this?' (Jer. 5:26–29 NIV)

Repeatedly, the prophets warned that God was so outraged that he would destroy the nations of Israel and Judah. Because of the way they 'trample on the heads of the poor . . . and deny justice to the oppressed,' Amos predicted terrible captivity (2:7 NIV; 5:11; 6:4,7; 7:11,17). So did Isaiah and Micah (Isa. 10:1–3; Mic. 2:2; 3:12). And it happened just as they foretold. According to both the Old and New Testaments, God destroys people and societies that get rich by oppressing the poor.

But what if we work hard and create wealth in just ways? That is good – as long as we do not forget to share. No matter how justly we have acquired our wealth, God demands that we act generously toward the poor. When we do not, God treats us in a similar way to those who oppress the poor. There is not a hint in Jesus' story of the rich man and Lazarus that the rich man exploited Lazarus to acquire wealth. He simply neglected to share. So God punished him (Lk. 16:19–31).

Ezekiel's striking explanation for the destruction of Sodom reveals the same point: 'Now this was the sin of your sister Sodom: She and her daughters were arrogant, overfed and unconcerned; they did not help the poor and needy. . . .

Therefore I did away with them' (16:49–50 NIV). Again, the text does not charge them with gaining wealth by oppression. They simply refused to share.

The Bible is clear. If we get rich by oppressing the poor or if we have wealth and do not reach out generously to the needy, the Lord of history moves against us. God judges societies by what they do to the people at the bottom.

3. God identifies with the poor so strongly that caring for them is almost like helping God. 'He who is kind to the poor lends to the Lord' (Prov. 19:17 NIV). On the other hand, one 'who oppresses the poor shows contempt for their Maker'. (14:31 NIV)

Jesus' parable of the sheep and goats is the ultimate commentary on these two proverbs. Jesus surprises those on the right with his insistence that they had fed and clothed him when he was cold and hungry. When they protested that they could not remember ever doing that, Jesus replied: 'Whatever you did for one of the least of these brothers of mine, you did for me' (Matt. 25:40 NIV). If we believe his words, we look on the poor and neglected with entirely new eyes.

4. Finally, God demands that his people share God's special concern for the poor. God commanded Israel not to treat widows, orphans, and foreigners the way the Egyptians had treated them (Ex. 22:21–24). Instead, they should love the poor just as God cared for them at the Exodus (Ex. 22:21–24; Deut. 15:13–15). When Jesus' disciples throw parties, they should especially invite the poor and disabled (Lk. 14:12–14; Heb. 13:1–3). Paul held up Jesus' model of becoming poor to show how generously the Corinthians should contribute to the poor in Jerusalem (2 Cor. 8:9).

The Bible, however, goes one shocking step further. God insists that if we do not imitate God's concern for the poor we are not really God's people – no matter how frequent our worship or how orthodox our creeds. Because Israel failed to correct oppression and defend poor widows, Isaiah insisted that Israel was really the pagan people of Gomorrah (1:10–17). God despised their fasting because they tried to worship God and oppress their workers at the same time (Isa. 58:3–7). Through Amos, the Lord shouted in fury that the very religious festivals God had ordained made God angry and sick. Why? Because the rich and powerful were mixing worship and oppression of the poor (5:21–24). Jesus was even more harsh. At the Last Judgement, some who expect to enter heaven will learn that their failure to feed the hungry condemns them to hell (Matt. 25). If we do not care for the needy brother or sister, God's love does not abide in us (1 Jn. 3:17).

Jeremiah 22:13–19 describes good King Josiah and his wicked son Jehoiakim. When Jehoiakim became king, he built a fabulous palace by oppressing his workers. God sent the prophet Jeremiah to announce a terrible punishment. The most interesting part of the passage, however, is a short aside on this evil king's good father: 'He defended the cause of the poor and needy, and so all went well. *"Is that not what it means to know me?"* declares the Lord' (v. 16; my italics). Knowing God is *inseparable* from caring for the poor. Of course, we dare not reduce knowing God only to a concern for the needy as some radical theologians do. We meet God in prayer, Bible study, worship – in many ways. But if we do not share God's passion to strengthen the poor, we simply do not know God in a biblical way.

All this biblical material clearly demonstrates that God and God's faithful people have a great concern for the poor. God is partial to the poor but not biased. God does not love the poor any more than the rich. God has an equal concern for the well-being of every single person. Most rich and powerful people, however, are genuinely biased; they care a lot more about themselves than about their poor neighbours. By contrast with the genuine bias of most people, God's lack of bias makes God appear biased. God cares equally for everyone.

How then is God 'partial' to the poor? Because in concrete historical situations, equal concern for everyone requires special attention to specific people. In a family, loving parents do not provide equal tutorial time to a son struggling hard to scrape by with 'Ds' and a daughter easily making 'As'. Precisely in order to be 'impartial' and love both equally, they devote extra time to helping the more needy child. In historical situations (e.g. apartheid) where some people oppress others, God's lack of bias does not mean neutrality. Precisely because God loves all equally, God works against oppressors and actively sides with the oppressed – in order to liberate both whom he loves equally!

We see this connection, precisely in the texts that declare God's lack of bias: 'For the Lord your God is God of gods and Lord of lords, the great, the almighty, the terrible God, who is not partial and takes no bribe. He executes justice for the fatherless and the widow, and loves the sojourner, giving him food and clothing' (Deut. 10:17–18 RSV). Justice and love are virtual synonyms in this passage. There is no suggestion that loving the sojourner is a benevolent, voluntary act different from a legal demand to do justice to the fatherless. Furthermore, there is no indication in the text that those needing food and clothing are poor because of some violation of due process such as fraud or robbery. The text simply says they are poor and therefore God who is not biased pays special attention to them.

The multiple causes of poverty[2]

If we want to end poverty, we must be clear about its causes. And there is not just one cause.

Some poverty is caused by sinful personal choices. Laziness, misuse of drugs, alcohol and sex all contribute to poverty. To state that clearly is not 'to blame the victim'. It is to acknowledge honestly what both human experience and biblical teaching (Prov. 6:6–11; 14:23) clearly show.

Misguided worldviews and cultural values also create poverty. For example, Hinduism's caste system clearly contributes to the agonizing poverty of more than 200 million 'untouchables' in India.

Disasters – whether caused by nature or humanity – also produce devastating poverty. Hurricanes, floods, earthquakes and drought all exact a terrible toll.

Lack of technology is another cause. Many people are eager to work but lack the proper tools and knowledge.

And then there are unjust structures: long-standing social and economic systems that contribute a great deal to poverty.

Tragically, many Christians, especially evangelical Christians, do not understand the role of social systems in creating poverty. Therefore we need to devote greater attention to this cause of poverty in two ways. First we need to understand the biblical teaching and then we need to see how present unjust structures actually help produce poverty today.

Biblical teaching about social injustice[3]

Neglect of the biblical teaching on structural injustice or institutionalized evil is one of the most deadly omissions in many parts of the church today. Christians frequently restrict ethics to a narrow class of 'personal' sins. There is an important difference between consciously willed, individual acts (like lying to a friend or committing an act of adultery) and participation in evil social structures. Slavery is an example of the latter. So is the Victorian factory system that had ten-year-old children working twelve to sixteen hours a day. Both slavery and child labour were legal, but they destroyed people by the millions. They were institutionalized, or structural, evils.

In the twentieth century, evangelicals have become imbalanced in their stand against sin, expressing concern and moral outrage about individual sinful acts while ignoring, perhaps even participating in, evil social structures. But the Bible condemns both.

The Old Testament

Speaking through his prophet Amos, the Lord declared, 'For three transgressions of Israel, and for four, I will not revoke the punishment; because they sell the righteous for silver, and the needy for a pair of shoes – they that trample the head of the poor into the dust of the earth, and turn aside the way of the afflicted; a man and his father go in to the same maiden, so that my holy name is profaned' (Amos 2:6–7).

Biblical scholars have shown that some kind of legal fiction or technicality underlies the phrase, 'selling the needy for a pair of shoes'. This mistreatment of the poor was legal! In one breath God condemned two detestable practices: sexual misconduct and the legalized oppression of the poor. Sexual sins and economic injustice are equally displeasing to God.

The prophet Isaiah also condemned both personal and social sin:

> Woe to those who join house to house, who add field to field, until there is no more room, and you are made to dwell alone in the midst of the land. The Lord of hosts has sworn in my hearing: 'Surely many houses shall be desolate, large and beautiful houses, without inhabitant . . . Woe to those who rise early in the morning, that they may run after strong drink, who tarry late into the evening till wine inflames them!' (Isa. 5:8–9,11)

Equally powerful is the succinct, satirical summary in verses 22 and 23 of the same chapter: 'Woe to those who are heroes at drinking wine, and valiant men in mixing strong drink, who acquit the guilty for a bribe, and deprive the innocent of his right!' Here, in one brief denunciation, God condemns both those who amass large landholdings at the expense of the poor and those who are drunkards. Economic injustice is just as abominable to our God as drunkenness.

Some young activists suppose that as long as they fight for the rights of minorities and oppose militarism they are morally righteous, regardless of how often they shack up for the night with a man or woman involved with them in the fight for social morality. Some of their elders, on the other hand, suppose that because they do not sleep around they are morally upright even though they live in segregated communities and own stock in companies that exploit the poor. From a biblical perspective, however, robbing your workers of a fair wage and robbing a bank are both sinful. Voting for a racist because he is a racist and sleeping with your neighbour's wife are both sinful. Silent participation in a company that carelessly pollutes the environment and thus imposes heavy costs on others and destroying your own lungs with tobacco are both sinful.

rly reveals his displeasure at evil institutions prophet Amos (to understand the meaning of this p in mind that Israel's court sessions were held at the city gate), 'They hate him who reproves in the gate . . . I know how many are your transgressions, and how great are your sins, you who . . . take a bribe, and turn aside the needy in the gate . . . Hate evil, and love good, and establish justice in the gate' (5:10–15).

'Let justice roll down like waters' (v. 24) is not abstract verbalization. The prophet is calling for justice in the legal system. He means, get rid of the corrupt legal system that allows the wealthy to buy their way out of trouble but gives the poor long prison terms.

The dishonest and corrupt individuals in the legal system are not the only ones who stand condemned. Laws themselves are sometimes an abomination to God:

> Can wicked rulers be allied with thee, who frame mischief by statute? They band together against the life of the righteous, and condemn the innocent to death. But the Lord has become my stronghold, and my God the rock of my refuge. He will bring back on them their iniquity and wipe them out for their wickedness; the Lord our God will wipe them out. (Ps. 94:20–23)

The Jerusalem Bible has an excellent rendition of verse 20: 'You never consent to that corrupt tribunal that imposes disorder as law.' God wants his people to know that wicked governments 'frame mischief by statute.' Or, as the New English Bible puts it, they contrive evil 'under cover of law'.

It is possible to make oppression legal. Now, as then, legislators devise unjust laws, and bureaucrats implement the injustice. But God shouts a divine woe against rulers who use their official position to write unjust laws and unfair legal decisions. Legalized oppression is an abomination to our God. Therefore, God calls his people to oppose political structures that frame mischief by statute.

God hates evil economic structures and unjust legal systems because they destroy people by the hundreds and thousands and millions. We can be sure that the just Lord of the universe will destroy wicked rulers and unjust social institutions (see 1 Kgs. 21).

Another side to institutionalized evil makes it especially pernicious. Structural evil is so subtle that we become ensnared without fully realizing it. God inspired his prophet Amos to utter some of the harshest words in Scripture against the cultured upper-class women of his day: 'Hear this word, you cows of Bashan . . . who oppress the poor, who crush the needy, who say to [your] husbands, "Bring, that we may drink!" The Lord God has sworn by his holiness that, behold, the days are coming upon you, when they shall take you away with hooks, even the last of you with fishhooks' (4:1–2).

The women involved may have had little direct contact with the impoverished peasants. They may never have fully realized that their gorgeous clothes and spirited parties were possible partly because of the sweat and tears of the poor. In fact, they may even have been kind on occasion to individual peasants. (Perhaps they gave them 'Christmas baskets' once a year.) But God called these privileged women 'cows' because they participated in social evil. Before God they were personally and individually guilty.

If we are members of a privileged group that profits from structural evil, and if we have at least some understanding of the evil yet fail to do what God wants us to do to change things, we stand guilty before God. Social evil is just as displeasing to God as personal evil. And it is more subtle.

It is important to understand that structural evil is morally distinguishable from personal sin. Structures do not have minds and wills in the way individuals do. Evil systems cannot repent of their sins, receive forgiveness through Christ's atonement, receive baptism and be on their way to eternal life, the way sinful persons can. Responsibility is not the same thing as guilt. Every individual in a society has some responsibility to correct the evil around them, whether the evil is individual or corporate, but that does not mean each person is guilty of every sin in their society.

But do we sin personally when we participate in an evil system? That depends on our knowledge and our response. If we have absolutely no understanding of the evil, then our participating does not involve personal sin. If we do understand something of the evil and do all God wants us to do to correct the injustice, then again, we do not sin. Persons sin by participating in evil systems when they understand, at least to some degree, that the system displeases God but fail to act responsibly to change things.

Two additional points, however, are crucial. First, the fact that I have no knowledge of a system's evil and am not personally guilty before God for participating in that system does not change the fact that the system is nonetheless wicked and evil and stands under God's condemnation. God always hates structural evils and works to end their injustice. Whether or not I have any understanding of a system's oppression does not change the objective fact that it is an abomination to our holy God.

Furthermore, most of the time, people living in and benefiting from unjust structures know something – albeit not everything – about their evil. In fact, very often we know enough to choose not to learn more lest we feel guilty. Mafia wives know enough about their husbands' activities to decide not to ask many questions. Rich Christians know enough about the ravages of poverty that we turn off the TV special on poverty in the developing world or inner city. We rush past the bookstore's section on economic justice. Why? Because we know that knowing more will make us morally obligated to change. Are we not guilty, to some extent, for choosing not to know about evils that benefit us and injure others? 'All who do evil hate the light and do not come to the light, so that their deeds may not be exposed' (Jn. 3:20 NRSV).

Unfair systems and oppressive structures are an abomination to God, and 'social sin' is the correct phrase to categorize them. Furthermore, as we understand their evil, we have a moral obligation to do all God wants us to do to change them. If we do not, we sin. That is the clear implication of Amos's harsh attack on the wealthy women of his day. It is also the clear implication of James 4:17: 'Whoever knows what is right to do and fails to do it, for him it is sin.'

The New Testament

In the New Testament, the word 'cosmos' (world) often conveys the idea of structural evil. In Greek thought, the word 'cosmos' referred to the structures of civilized life, especially the patterns of the Greek city-state, which were viewed as essentially good. But the biblical writers knew that sin had invaded and distorted the structures and values of society.

Frequently, therefore, the New Testament uses the word 'cosmos' to refer to human society organized on wrong principles.

Before conversion, Christians follow the values and patterns of a fallen social order, 'You were dead in your transgressions and sins, in which you used to live when you followed the ways of this world' (Eph. 2:1–2 NIV). Paul, in his letter to the Romans (12:1–2), and John, in his gospel, urge Christians not to conform to this world's pattern of evil systems and ideas.

> Do not love the world or the things in the world. The love of the Father is not in those who love the world; for all that is in the world, the desire of the flesh, the desire of the eyes, the pride in riches, comes not from the Father but from the world. And the world and its desires are passing away, but those who do the will of God live forever. (1 Jn. 2:15–17 NRSV)

Behind the distorted social structures of our world, Paul says, are fallen supernatural powers under the control of Satan himself. After Paul said that the Ephesians, before their conversion, had 'followed the ways of this world,' he added, 'and of the ruler of the kingdom of the air, the spirit who is now at work in those who are disobedient' (Eph. 2:2 NIV). Paul warns that 'our struggle is not against flesh and blood, but against the rulers, against the authorities, against the powers of this dark world and against the spiritual forces of evil in the heavenly realms' (Eph. 6:12 NIV).

Both Jews and Greeks in Paul's day believed that good and evil supernatural beings were behind the scenes influencing social and political structures. To modern secular folk, that view of the supernatural belongs to George Lucas and Stephen

King. But when I look at the demonic evil of social systems like Nazism, apartheid and communism, or even the complex mixture of racism, unemployment, sexual promiscuity, substance abuse and police brutality in American inner cities, I have no trouble believing that Satan and his gang are hard at work fostering oppressive structures and thus doing their best to destroy God's good creation.

These fallen supernatural powers twist and distort the social systems that we social beings require for wholeness. By seducing us into wrong choices that create evil systems, by working against attempts to overcome oppressive structures, and sometimes by enticing politicians and other leaders to use the occult, these demonic powers shape our world. Evil is far more complex than the wrong choices of individuals. It also lies outside us in oppressive social systems and in demonic powers that delight in defying God by corrupting the social systems that his human image-bearers need.

Pope John Paul II has rightly insisted that evil social structures are 'rooted in personal sin'. Social evil results from our rebellion against God and our consequent selfishness toward our neighbours. But the accumulation and concentration of many personal sins create 'structures of sin' that are both oppressive and 'difficult to remove'.[4] When we choose to participate in and benefit from evil social systems, we sin against God and our neighbours.

God's response

The prophets bluntly warned people about the way the God of justice responds to oppressive social structures. God cares so much about the poor that he works to destroy social systems that tolerate and foster poverty. Repeatedly God declared that he would destroy the nation of Israel because of two things: its idolatry and its mistreatment of the poor (see, for example, Jer. 7:1–15).

Attention to both of these is crucial. We dare not become so preoccupied with horizontal issues of social injustice that we neglect vertical evils such as idolatry. Modern Christians seem to have an irrepressible urge to fall into one extreme or the other. But the Bible corrects our one-sidedness by making it clear that both lead to destruction. God destroyed Israel and Judah because of both their idolatry and their social injustice.

Here, however, our focus is on the fact that God destroys oppressive social structures. Amos's words, which could be duplicated from many other places in Scripture, make this divine response clear, 'Behold, the eyes of the Lord God are upon the sinful kingdom, and I will destroy it from the surface of the ground' (9:8). Within a generation after Amos, the northern kingdom of Israel was completely wiped out.

Probably the most powerful statement of God's work to destroy evil social structures is in the New Testament, in Mary's Magnificat. Mary glorified the Lord who 'has put down the mighty from their thrones, and exalted those of low degree; [who] has filled the hungry with good things, and the rich he has sent empty away' (Lk. 1:52–53).

The Lord of history is working just as hard today to bring down sinful societies where wealthy classes live by the sweat, toil, and grief of the poor.

An Indian bishop once told me a story that underlines the importance of understanding social sin. A psychiatric institution in his country had a fascinating way of deciding whether patients were well enough to go home. They would take a person over to a water tap, place a large water bucket under the tap and fill the bucket with water. Then, leaving the tap on, they would give the person a spoon and say, 'Please empty the bucket.' If the person started dipping the water out one spoonful at a time and never turned the tap off, they knew he or she was still unwell.

Too often, Christians, like the Indian mental health patients, work at social problems one spoonful at a time. While working feverishly to correct symptoms, they fail to do anything to turn off the tap (e.g. change legal systems and economic policies that hurt people). And they remain confused and frustrated by how little progress they are making.

Understanding the biblical concept of social sin is essential to understanding the seriousness of unfair systems and their contribution to poverty today.

Structural injustice today[5]

Are Western Christians today a part of unjust structures that contribute to world hunger? A discussion of several issues will reveal our involvement: (1) market economies; (2) international trade; (3) natural resources and the environment; (4) food imports from poor nations.

Evaluating market economies

Do market economies help or hurt the poor? Our exploration of the structural causes of poverty must begin with this question. Democratic capitalism has won the most dramatic economic/political debate of the twentieth century. Almost every country in the world praises the ideal of democracy. Most nations are taking steps toward a 'market economy'. Anybody concerned about the poor must struggle with how this momentous global embrace of market economies impacts the poorest.

Communism's state ownership and central planning did not work. They were inefficient and totalitarian. Market economies, on the other hand, have produced enormous wealth, and not only in Western nations. Many Asian countries have adopted market economies. The result has been a dramatic drop in poverty in the world's most populous continent. In 1970, chronic undernourishment plagued 35 per cent of the people in all developing countries. In 2003 – in spite of rapid population growth – only 17 per cent of the people in developing countries were chronically undernourished.[6]

The evidence is clear. Market economies are more successful than centrally owned and centrally planned economies at creating economic growth. China's phenomenal growth rate over the last two decades is clearly the result of its substantial adoption of free-market measures in both agriculture and substantial parts of industrial production. Throughout most of East Asia, including China, Malaysia, Indonesia and Thailand, market economies are producing explosive economic growth.

Central to this growth is the expansion of exports and international trade. The rapid growth of the newer Asian market economies was directly related to their decision to reduce trade barriers and emphasize exports – along with substantial government activity. Scores of careful studies show that greater concentration on goods for export almost always produces economic growth.

The first conclusion to draw, therefore, is that market economies are better at producing economic growth than present alternatives. Furthermore, since poor nations need economic growth in order to provide an adequate standard of living for the world's poorest people, those who care about the poorest should accept markets as an important, useful tool for empowering the poor.

Unfortunately, today's market economies also have fundamental weaknesses. When measured by biblical standards, glaring injustices exist. Precisely as we adopt a market framework as better than known alternatives, we must examine and correct problems that exist in today's market economies. Here I mention only one: the glaring problem that at least a quarter of the world's people lack the capital to participate in any major way in the global market economy. Land is still the basic capital in many agricultural societies. Money and education are far more crucial in modern capital-intensive, knowledge-intensive economies. At least one in four people in our world has almost no land, very little money and virtually no education.

The market's mechanism of supply and demand is blind to the distinction between basic necessities (even minimal food needed to avoid starvation) and luxuries desired by the wealthy. According to the United Nations Development Programme, Human Development Report 2002, the richest 5 per cent of the world's people have incomes 114 times those of the poorest 5 per cent.[7] Left to itself, a market-driven economy will simply supply what the wealthy can pay for – even if millions of poor folk starve.

If we start with the present division of wealth, the outcome of the market will be ghastly injustice. Only if redistribution occurs, through private and/or public measures, will the poorest obtain the capital to earn a decent living in the global market.

International trade

When it works the way it is supposed to, 'free trade' at the global level is good for both poor and rich nations. Trade encourages those places with a comparative advantage (for example, cheap labour or an ideal climate to grow bananas) to produce those things, while other people produce what they can produce most cheaply. That lowers the prices for everyone. It also helps poor nations who often have plenty of people able to perform many tasks far more cheaply than workers in rich countries. Politicians may complain about 'outsourcing' when jobs move from the West to India. But outsourcing helps reduce poverty in India and also lowers prices for everyone.

What, then, is wrong with current patterns of international trade? The industrialized nations have shaped the patterns of international trade for their own economic benefit. One of the most widely used textbooks in economic development says (in the 2003 edition) that 'it is fair to claim that the principal benefits of world trade have been accrued disproportionately to rich nations.'[8]

In colonial days, mother countries regularly made sure that economic affairs were organized to their own advantage. Although colonialism ended decades ago, industrialized nations have continued, over the past several decades, to manipulate international trade by imposing restrictive tariffs and import quotas to keep out many of the goods produced in the less-developed countries. Tariff structures and import quotas affecting the poor nations are in fact one fundamental aspect of systemic injustice today.

In 2003, the World Bank said that the tariffs high-income countries charged on imports from developing countries were four times as high as tariffs charged on imports from other high-income countries.[9] An end to tariff barriers on textile exports from developing to developed nations would provide developing countries with another $9 billion a year in income from textiles alone. Ending tariff barriers on other manufactured goods would add another $22.3 billion in income for developing countries.[10]

Trade barriers cost poor nations dearly – in fact, much more than they receive in foreign aid. In 2001, the United Nations estimated that trade restrictions cost less-developed countries at least $100 billion every year![11] That is almost twice as much as the total foreign aid that developing countries receive from rich nations each year.[12]

High tariffs in rich nations continue to be a problem for poor nations. Most rich nations put high tariffs on agricultural products and simple manufactures: things that developing countries can most easily produce and export. In the 1990s, the average tariff applied by rich nations (OECD) on manufactured products from the developing world were more than four times those placed on manufactures from rich countries. And when poor nations tried to increase their income by exporting processed rather than unprocessed products, rich nations often added additional tariffs.[13]

Especially harmful are the high subsidies that the USA and Western Europe give to their own farmers. According to *The State of Food Insecurity in the World 2003*, direct subsidies to farmers in rich nations in 2002 added up to U.S. $235 billion. That is almost thirty times the amount rich nations give in aid for agricultural development in developing countries![14]

Continuing tariffs, quotas, and other non-tariff barriers (especially huge farm subsidies) in developed nations continue to hurt the poor. They deprive poor countries of millions of jobs and billions of dollars from increased exports.

Destroying the environment and the poor

Our present behaviour threatens the well-being of our grandchildren. Economic life today, especially in industrialized societies, is producing such severe environmental pollution and degradation that the future for everyone – rich and poor alike – is endangered. We are destroying our air, forests, lands and water so rapidly that we face disastrous problems in the next hundred years unless we make major changes. The poor are on the front lines when it comes to the harmful impacts of pollution and environmental degradation. In many instances they are the first to suffer, and they absorb the brunt of the destructive consequences due to their poverty and vulnerability.

We pollute our air, contribute to global warming, exhaust our supplies of fresh water, overfish our seas, and destroy precious topsoil, forests and unique species lovingly shaped by the Creator. In many countries, chemicals, pesticides, oil spills and industrial emissions degrade air, water and soil. 'Is it not enough for you to feed on the good pasture?' the Creator asks. 'Must you also trample the rest of your pasture with your feet? Is it not enough for you to drink clear water? Must you also muddy the rest with your feet?' (Ezek. 34:18 NIV)

Always, of course, the poor suffer the most. This is true in two ways. They already suffer from reduced food production, unproductive land, polluted rivers and toxic wastes that the rich do not want in their backyards. Furthermore, unless we can redirect economic life in a way that dramatically reduces environmental decay, it will be impossible to expand economic growth enough in poor nations to enable them to enjoy a decent standard of living.

The poor also damage the environment. Developing nations often use less-sophisticated technology and consequently consume fossil fuels less efficiently. Desperately poor people also try to farm marginal land and destroy tropical forests. Unless poverty is dramatically reduced around the world, we cannot win the war against environmental destruction.

One of the most astonishing examples of the connection between poverty and environmental destruction comes from anthropologist Sheldon Annis, who describes a scene in Guatemala:

> I recall watching in horrified fascination as an Indian farmer and his son planted their plot of corn on a forested slope. The land was so steep that the son had to be held in place with a rope looped around his waist. As he hopped from furrow to furrow, his father let out the slack from around a tree stump. When I returned to the spot recently, I was not surprised to find that the farmer and his son were no longer there. And neither was the hillside. What remained was a reddish eroded nub – which looked like the next and the next and the next former hillside.[15]

We face a painful choice. To maintain and expand our material abundance, we are polluting our air and water and destroying our lands and forests. We simply cannot continue these present economic patterns, reduce global poverty and preserve a liveable planet all at the same time. We could choose both justice for the poor and a liveable planet – but only if we give up rampant materialism and make hard choices to reverse environmental destruction.

Eating food from hungry nations

Why do countries ravaged by famine export food? Why do poor nations today sell vast quantities of food to rich nations while many of their own people are malnourished or starving?

In recent decades, developing nations with large numbers of malnourished and even starving people nevertheless have exported substantial amounts of food to wealthy nations. The reason that countries with many hungry people willingly export food to wealthy nations is that the poor people in those nations do not have the money to pay for the food, and we do. And the powerful people in poor nations pay for their imports of high technology, oil and luxury goods with the revenue from their exports.

Hungry people prefer food to feed their families. But they have no power, almost no money, little employment and no land to grow food for themselves. Wealthy elites in poor nations have more in common with the rich in high-income nations than the poor in their own. So they sell the food that the poor need but cannot afford.

Sometimes, the origins of this problem go back to the colonial era, when colonial rulers encouraged plantations to grow export crops even to the detriment of food production for local consumption. Local people frequently lost their land and became slaves or poorly paid agricultural workers. Those who managed to keep some land were 'encouraged' to produce foodstuffs desired in the mother countries. Growing food for the 'mother' country was seen as the colony's highest priority.

Colonial days have ended, but some of the effects remain. The plantations have not been returned to the descendants of their original owners. New owners (whether local elites or multinational corporations) of the same large holdings still look to the industrialized countries as their trading partners – the poor, after all, have little purchasing power.

Owners of large landholdings could, of course, choose to grow beans, corn or rice for the local population, but the local people cannot pay much because they have very little capital to produce anything marketable. Landholders can make more money by growing crops for export. So the owners look to rich countries for their markets. They send us cotton, beef, coffee, bananas or other agricultural products, and we send them the goods they desire in return. The system favours the wealthy, and the poor suffer.

None of the above information leads to the conclusion that we ought to scrap international trade in food products or reject market economies in favour of Marxism. What it does mean is that the jubilee principle of Leviticus 25 is enormously important.

God wants society's pool of productive assets to be distributed so that everyone has the resources to earn his or her own way. When members of a society lose their assets, by whatever means, it is difficult for them to participate in economic activity. People with no assets simply starve.

In most of today's poor nations, the displacement of people from the land began many years ago and continues. Seldom has anything like the jubilee occurred. So the problems persist. That is why rich people eat food from nations where poor people starve.

Conclusion

In numerous complicated ways, Western Christians are involved in one way or another with unjust global structures. The mechanism of the market is a useful tool for organizing a great deal of economic life, but today's market economies also produce serious injustices that we must correct. International trade patterns contain injustice. Some current patterns of economic life threaten the global environment and the long-term economic opportunities of the developing world. The life of every person in developed countries is touched in some way by these structural injustices. Unless you have retreated to some isolated valley and grow or make everything you use, you participate in unjust structures that contribute directly to the desperate poverty of some of our billion suffering neighbours.

We should not, of course, conclude that international trade or investment by multinational corporations in poor countries is in itself harmful. Done right, both help the poor. Nor would the economies of the developed world be destroyed if present injustices in today's global economic system were corrected. The proper conclusion is that injustice has become deeply embedded in some of our fundamental economic institutions. Biblical Christians, precisely to the extent that they are faithful to Scripture, will dare to call such structures sinful – and work hard to change them.

9

Justice and Approaches to Social Change

Melba Padilla Maggay

The concern for the poor has always been at the heart of the missional sense of the church. There may be times when it is obscured by attenuated theologies abstracted out of contexts of relative affluence. Still, wherever bearers of the gospel have been confronted by need, acts of compassion have issued. Modern missionary movements, mostly pietistic and quiescent in their theologies, have nevertheless spawned hospitals, schools, feeding programmes and other such concrete responses to situations of need.

Today, particularly in the Majority World, there has been a remarkable recovery of the social dimensions of the gospel. Partly because of the poverty that stares us in the face, those of us who live in these places are pressed to account for the hope that is in us in a way that has the poor at the centre of its vision. In my own country, the Philippines, during the last 30 years, there has been a mushrooming of faith-based NGOs and a decisive movement towards making a difference for the poor even among conservative churches.

However, there is also a decided drift towards merely technical or spiritualistic solutions to poverty. Faith-based NGOs have yet to recognize that the paradigm that undergirds their social involvement is mostly borrowed from modernization theories and its language of 'development'. Some concerned churches, on the other hand, tend to labour under the notion that 'spiritual warfare' is enough to dislodge entrenched structures of ancient wrongs.

In the following, we discuss the need for some 'ideological suspicion' in the way we go about helping the poor. We shall revisit biblical ideas of justice as it relates to governance and processes of social change. In the course of it, we hope to gain clarity in some of the issues we face as people of the kingdom, wanting to make a difference in the many difficult places where we have been called to be disciples.

The paradox of our poverty

Without being conscious of it, many development practitioners operate from the assumption that poverty is caused by 'underdevelopment' of some kind. The theory is that people and countries are poor because of certain 'deficits': lack of capital, natural resources, technology or an underdeveloped human resource. The solution is a package of interventions that gives the poor access to capital (microfinance), renews environmental resource (sustainable development), closes the technological gap (infrastructure and communications technologies) and invests in capability-building (education).

There are countries like mine, however, with none of these deficits. Yet we continue to see a great proportion of our people getting poorer. The paradox of our poverty, and I suppose, also that of many countries, is that it exists side by side with immense wealth. We have tremendous agri-marine resources; our people are educated and cross-culturally agile; there is no great lack of technical know-how; and there is lots of money stashed away in Swiss banks or invested in China and elsewhere.

What seems to be wrong is the ancient structure of inequality which allows the elite to perpetuate privilege and corner much of the resources. Since the time of Spanish colonialism, which began in the sixteenth century, the elite have benefited from the largesse made possible by cooperation with those with power. This historical reality has become further ingrained by the unbroken symbiosis between politics and economics. With the advent of globalization and the digital divide, the poor have been swept to the sidelines even more significantly.

Given some variations in detail, this is a story shared by many decolonized countries, particularly those in Latin America. For a while, dependency theories offered a plausible explanation for the continuing poverty. A 'core' was viewed as siphoning off resources from the 'periphery,' within and among nations. This neocolonial element has intensified, it is said, with globalization, where the global centres, or at least those countries with the power to project themselves beyond their borders, overrun and weaken nation states. Societies implode from external and internal pressures brought about by porous borders and the rise of primal identities, now ethnically or religiously defined.

With the failure of socialist experiments and the resurgence of neocapitalism, dependency theories have gone somewhat out of date, leaving the Majority World with a crisis of paradigm. Left with the pieces, faith-based organizations in these parts of the world tend to take on the question of poverty reduction piecemeal, mixing empowerment strategies with tools that allow the poor access to the market, like microfinance. Even before the collapse of the welfare state, and knowing that there is no such thing as a free lunch, these organizations mostly help the poor to adapt to the market and make it there.

Meanwhile, governments clamber up the fast train to becoming a 'newly industrialized country', or 'NIC-hood' as it used to be called in East Asia. Under the old theme of 'enlarging the pie', there is a great deal of optimism that if we play 'catch up' with the leading growth centres, the benefits will 'trickle down' to the rest of the population.

This line of thinking has been with us in the 'developing' world for some time, unaware that much of what works within this paradigm is embedded in the historical development of the West and may not at all be transferable elsewhere. It assumes that development is unilinear, that the experience of the West can be universalized. As articulated by the likes of Walt Rostow, development is a uniform pattern of growth that evolves by stages; traditional societies pass from being feudal agrarian economies to modern industrial states. 'Undeveloped' countries will need to more or less follow the same path to modernization that the 'advanced' economies have trod in order to 'take off' at some point.

This development narrative has been around for half a century, yet many countries are still reeling from spiralling poverty in spite of infusions of capital from the World Bank Group and International Monetary Fund. It is a path characterized by an over-reliance on market forces and the over-exploitation of resources to feed the insatiable engines of growth. It has also reduced people into corporate automatons, and societies into lonely crowds. It is a wonder why the rest of the world seeks to follow the same path.

It is not within the purpose of this essay to go into a detailed critique of this narrative. It is necessary only to point out that the tools and strategies that have worked under its regime may be of doubtful efficacy in contexts where there is an absence of the conditions under which Western economies flourished.

In the first place, many poor countries today suffer from the historical disadvantage of economic lag due to the shock of colonialism and its consequent psychological and social dislocations. The corrosive effects on governance brought about by the breakdown of the old indigenous institutions have been irreversible.

In the second place, studies by people like Gunnar Myrdal, writing from his experiences in South Asia, have long ago discovered the difficulty of lifting the plight of the poor in situations where there are entrenched structures of inequality, like the caste system. This calls for something more than merely technical solutions to the problem of poverty.

Given all this, what has Scripture to say about confronting poverty and transforming unequal worlds into just societies?

Justice as minimum requirement

It needs pointing out that the one purpose mentioned for the existence of the state as an institution is 'to punish those who do wrong and to commend those who do right.' Rulers, says Paul, are not meant to be 'a terror to good conduct but to bad' (1 Pet. 2:13; Rom. 13:3).

The state has been given authority to wield the sword to secure justice. The coercive power of the state is mainly to ensure that crime is punished and the pursuit of the common good encouraged. It is not primarily to serve as a cradle-to-the-grave Big Brother, as has happened in failed welfare states. It is also not there as an instrument for safeguarding society's morals, inducing religiosity in the citizenry by legislating such pieties as prayer in the schools. Scripture's purpose for the state is minimalist, as is also characteristic of societies where there are no great expectations from government and all that is being asked is that governance be just.

Justice is important for all, to be applied to both rich and poor. 'Justice, and only justice, you shall follow' (Deut. 16:20), Israel was told. Kings are to judge fairly, to use their power to maintain the rights of those who are usually unable to defend themselves: the poor and the needy (Prov. 31:8–9).

The prophets served constant reminders of the priority of justice in governance. 'Let justice roll down like waters,' thundered Amos. From the wilderness and remote villages they would, from time to time, address the powerful rulers of the country. For unlike other nations, Israel was meant to be ruled, not by monarchical institutions, but by the Law. They were to be governed primarily by a set of laws, which were given to them long before they were given a land and clamoured for a king. Israel was unique in that they were ruled by a Law higher than the often arbitrary and absolutist reign of royal dynasties of the time. The Israelite kings were subject to this Law, as articulated by their prophets, priests and wise men. Most likely, this is the origin, in Judaeo-Christian cultures, of what in time evolved into the modern idea of the 'rule of law'.

It is not an accident that countries that have difficulty adhering to this principle, governed largely by the sort of justice cynically defined as 'the interest of the stronger', also tend to have unstable institutions. The failure to enforce the rule of law, particularly on those in high places, makes for what Myrdal calls a 'soft state'. Corruption in governance goes rampant, and rule-keeping buckles down before pressures from the powerful.

A 'strong state', biblically defined, is not a state ruled by the iron fist of a strongman or a military clique, nor an elaborate welfare state that has its hands on everything, including business and market mechanisms. Instead, it is a state where justice is done, such that the public trusts its institutions to the degree that there is fear and anxiety about wrongdoing, and a sense of stability and security when one is obeying the rules. There is no need for government to arrogate to itself extraordinary powers, nor to overload it with too many expectations. The enforcement of justice is enough to secure public order and social wellness (Prov. 21:15).

Justice and righteousness: our twin mandate

How then do we bring forth justice, particularly in those places where law and governance are subject to the informal pressures of kinship, political dynasties and other power holders?

First of all, it is important to grasp that in the Old Testament, the words 'justice', *mispat*, and 'righteousness', *sedeqa*, are used interchangeably: to do justice to someone is to 'declare one right' (2 Sam. 15:4; Ps. 82:3; Ex. 23:6–8). Our twin biblical mandate is 'justice and righteousness,' so often put together as in Amos's famous denunciation of Israel's empty ritualism: 'I hate, I despise your feasts . . . But let justice roll down like waters, and righteousness like an overflowing stream' (Amos 5:21–24).

Unlike today's culture wars, there is no divide here between issues of public justice and issues of private morals. Scripture sees no separation between structural inequality and the need for personal fairness. There is no divorce between justice and morality, good governance and compassionate giving, the struggle for liberation and the small kindnesses of doing acts of mercy.

While 'justice' is properly an attribute of the state, 'righteousness' ought to be characteristic of the whole society.

Government can at best provide an enabling environment for social compassion and public morals to flourish. It cannot legislate morality, nor the kind of civic virtue that will tenderly care for the elderly, the needy or the rights of the unborn.

This brings me to my second point – that the 'justice' that is properly the task of the state is in truth made possible by 'righteousness' in the larger society. Objective, structural conditions need a correlative subjective consciousness for the system to work. As Mao Zedong has said a long time ago, an egg will hatch into a chicken by applying a certain degree of heat. But no amount of temperature will turn a stone into a chicken; the internal condition for it just does not exist.

Similarly, just governance requires a civil society whose values fit the system. Institutions need to be buttressed by corresponding values, an infraculture as it were. Unfortunately, many of the structures that have been transplanted under the rubric of 'democracy' in post-colonial times have no culture-fit with the old indigenous patterns of governance and accountability. Modern and impersonal systems of bureaucracy have difficulty thriving in traditional, personalistic cultures where kinship and other such connections play a major role in getting things done. Where the system is soft and slippery, this may be largely accounted to the lack of supportive norms. Laws do not get implemented, or are ignored, because people have yet to be socialized and habituated into the new norms necessary to make them conform.

This is not to say that pre-modern societies should necessarily adapt to modern systems of governance. It is simply to point out that such systems are dysfunctional, not because of something very wrong with these cultures, but because of the internal dissonance experienced by the people in acculturating to alien ways of social organization. It took the West five centuries to make the transition from despotic monarchies and tribal conflicts to democratic and peaceful ways of leadership succession and conflict resolution. Yet, we expect decolonized countries to behave in similar ways within 50 years of independence.

It is important to note at this point that societies readily adapt only to trivial artefacts of foreign influences, but are rarely changed in the deep structures of their cultures. On the surface, there may be shifts in such things as food patterns, clothing, architecture and building technologies. However, this is not replicated in matters like worldview or religious orientation, as seen in the resistance shown by village people when development personnel introduce new health care or agricultural practices. The impact of innovations run aground before a culture's metanarratives, those stories that make sense of a people's primal history and lend meaning to their collective experience.

For substantial change to happen, the Christian story must engage these metanarratives. We are to come, not as mere agents of modernization, but as servants of the Most High bringing a story that affirms people's stories from the shadowy past, and like the writer to the Hebrews, lend to these foreshadowings clarity and meaning within the larger light of Christ.

Missiologists estimate that only about 5 per cent of the elements of a culture need changing, but these are usually central structures rooted in the religious imagination, like the caste system in India, voodoo cults and female circumcision in Africa or familism in East Asia. Most cultures are elaborations of a faith tradition; at their base is a religion that once served as centre of integration, no matter how eroded by secularization.

This means that the resources of our faith – the Word and the Spirit – continue to be our primary means for change. It is not, at first instance, development tools and resources; we are barely scratching the surface if we think that these, coupled with 'evangelism 'as usually practiced, are what 'wholism' is about. Engaging the deep structures of our cultures is what turns nations around and brings them decisively towards Christ. Failure to do this merely domesticates Christianity, reducing it into a pet religion that has little to do with everyday life and the 'weightier matters of the law'.

When Hispanic Christianity came to our shores for instance, the interface with the indigenous religious consciousness was mostly an exchange of statues: we exchanged dark, wooden *anitos*, carvings of our ancestral spirits, for ceramic saints with

Caucasian features. The native religious imagination remained the same, such that to this day, it has retained its preoccupation with the spirit world. The indigenous religion is quite adept in its transactions with supernatural powers, but profoundly uninterested in philosophical speculations about the 'ground of being' as with Hinduism, and without much introspective curiosity about the problem of pain as with Buddhism. Its concerns are pragmatic – how to access potency and spiritual power and ward off evil. Sensitivity to horizontal relationships matter, not as an ethical interest, as in Taoism or Confucianism, but as a strategy for social maintenance.

On the whole, the culture has mostly adapted but not converted. By its accommodative plasticity, it has gained the reputation of being the 'only Christian nation in the Far East'. Yet, in the places where it matters, it has remained unchanged, untouched by the ethic of Christ. In a cross-cultural study some time back, the Philippines figured as the 'most religious'; yet in perception surveys of firms doing business in Asia, it has been consistently listed as one of the most corrupt countries in the region.

This phenomenon was not unknown in ancient Israel. The prophets spoke in contexts where intense religiosity coexisted with rife injustice and unrighteousness. In the end, Israel was judged and banished from the land because of idolatry and oppression, the twin failure to love God and neighbour.

Similarly, nations continue to fail because of false gods and the consequent fallout on public order. No society can survive without a minimum moral sense.

Ultimately, a nation's level of public justice and righteousness is determined by the depth at which it changes as a result of its people's encounter with the one true God.

Strategies for social change

Does the foregoing mean then that evangelism is our best hope for transforming a nation, or that change in individuals automatically means change in society, as is so often supposed by well-meaning Christians?

The simple answer is 'no'. There are larger, much more complex forces at work in human society than the volitional agency of men and women of goodwill. There is a great deal of talk in my country about 'political will', meaning the determined use of power towards particular ends. This sometimes works, but is more often subject to the limits imposed by popular opinion, a recalcitrant bureaucracy, oligarchs and other militant defenders of the status quo, available resources, a fractious civil society or competing political and other interests.

Also, church renewal or revival does not necessarily mean it will issue in justice and righteousness. For decades now there has been considerable church growth in many Two-Thirds World countries, but this has yet to impact the level of corruption in governance. There was a time when the Philippines ranked next to Korea and Brazil in terms of church growth. But the new-found rise in status and numbers among our burgeoning megachurches has yet to influence decisively the plight of our poor.

Certainly, there are stirrings in the churches towards lifting the poor. There are many small and promising initiatives, particularly the fairly large microfinance industry. But these mostly manage to merely keep the heads of the poor above water. While micro-lending and other such acts of mercy are always good in themselves, these cannot substitute for hard social analysis and confronting the power structures that hold so many hostage to poverty.

Evangelicals are unfortunately stuck in merely providing discrete services to the poor, without addressing the larger context of why people are poor. There is a reluctance to engage in advocacy, to create a public voice and insert the cause of the poor into political space. The mandate to 'Speak up for those who cannot speak for themselves, for the rights of all who are destitute' is clear. Yet this remains unheeded for fear of getting 'too political' and stepping out of the boundary lines artificially set between church and state by secular society (Prov. 31:8).

We need to confront the fact that sin can be institutionalized, embedded in unjust structures and entrenched systems of oppression. Often, power is on the side of the oppressor, and the system crushes those who seek to change the order of things. There is a hardness, a mystery to evil that defies and taunts all attempts at social engineering: 'What is crooked can not be made straight' (Ecc. 4:1; 10:8–9; 1:15).

Consciousness of the tragic nature of sin in human life does not mean, however, that we lie supine before the overwhelming forces of systemic evil. It is precisely because we live in a fallen order that we work for structural safeguards against concentration of wealth and perpetual poverty. Scripture itself has a host of social legislation providing safety nets and the chance of being able to start again for those who have fallen on the wayside. Prominent among these is the jubilee principle in Leviticus 25, which provides for a periodic rearrangement of power relations and the equalizing of access to resources.

Every 50 years, the playing field is levelled: families return to their ancestral lands, debts are cancelled, slaves are freed and there is a Sabbath rest for all. The jubilee restores original ownership of lands to those who, by some misfortune, have lost their inheritance and hence find themselves bereft of their means of production and livelihood. Slaves and debtors walk away in freedom. All this breaks the poverty cycle and allows the people to start again.

In giving rest to both land and people, meaning and enjoyment are also restored, something that is missing in the frenetic life system of many in the workplace today. Scholars say that the jubilee was never implemented in Israel. Still, it remains as a compelling paradigm of what a just society looks like.

How then do we move towards this kind of society?

Studies tell us that there are at least three general approaches to effecting social change:

1. The *empirical–rational* approach. This is knowledge-based. It is the application of 'people' or 'thing' technologies to effect change. The premise here is that information, or educating people into awareness, causes them to get liberated, or at least modify behaviour. It also facilitates problem-solving, as with systems analysis or operations research.

However, this does not take into account the fact that knowledge is rarely decisive in motivating changed behaviour.

Everybody knows that smoking causes cancer, but this does not deter those who smoke and refuse to quit. Our fallen nature dooms us to the tragic condition described by Paul: 'I do not do what I want, but I do the very thing I hate . . . I can will what is right, but I can not do it.' (Rom. 7:15–18)

2. The *normative–re-educative* approach. This is educating people into new norms, patterns and systems as internal support for planned change. As people clarify their values, it leads to a measure of control, since self-awareness means greater self-mastery. Included in this are such interventions as creativity enhancement and capacity-building for problem-solving.

'Value formation' has been the standard response whenever the political behaviour of the masses is seen as problematic, or micro-creditors lag behind in their repayments, or farmers need some collective sense to get a cooperative going. In truth, however, a science has yet to evolve out of this process; no one really knows how conviction begins in one and cynicism in another, or what moves people to shift from individualism to a sense of community, to hope instead of despair. The work of the Spirit is intractable. In a postmodern world, it is acknowledged that it is spiritual traditions who know best the business of forming values. This is where the church can best contribute – creating new norms out of its faith perspectives. It is here that the resources of faith communities should be mustered in full force.

3. The *power–coercive* approach. This is the use of power, whatever its nature, to ensure compliance and enforce planned change. It is usual to think that this is the sole preserve of politics; but power can be both formal and informal. There is the *formal power* of government and other institutions, where contestations on policy, and the recomposing of the political elite and other power holders happen. There is also the *non-formal power* of social movements, whether traditional (church, labour unions, cooperatives, electoral blocs) or non-traditional ('civil society' or NGOs centred on gender, ethnicity, environmental and other concerns).

In societies where the prevailing systems are merely borrowed from outside and circumvented by the local culture, non-formal powers tend to wield hidden but considerable influence. Our country's experience of the 'conjugal dictatorship' of Ferdinand and Imelda Marcos is one patent example, and so was the late Cardinal Sin's magisterial presence in the events leading to the overthrow of the regime. The nation formally subscribes to the 'separation of the church and the state', yet the church exercises an almost medieval power, reminiscent of the friocracy of the Spanish colonial period. This is partly a consequence of history and partly a function of native spirituality.

In countries that have yet to secularize, spiritual traditions are a vital element in public life. The rise of 'fundamentalism' or 'political religions' in recent times is witness to this fact. In many such places, an authentic church has tremendous opportunity to serve as a guiding light if it remains true to its calling. There is no need to make use of the coercive powers of the state to advance its own ends and persuade people of the cogency of its values. Simply by its faithfulness, a church authenticates itself and gains authority and power in the eyes of those longing for the reality of a transcendent goodness.

Having considered such approaches in the wider marketplace, I would like to suggest some strategic areas for action specific to us as people of the kingdom:

1. *Constructively engage the powers.* The parable of the wheat and the weeds tells us that the evil and the good are inextricably entangled together. The mystery of human solidarity is such that we share in the general contamination inherent in our condition. This means that we learn to move things and make a difference in places that are far from ideal. This is not an easy task, for as Walter Wink reminds us, there are subhuman powers at work in social institutions.

The language of Paul in Ephesians 6 – thrones, dominions, principalities and powers – indicates that even in politics we are not dealing with mere sociology but spiritual forces that have lodged and embedded themselves in structures and life systems. This is why institutions, when left to their own inertia, tend to drift and eventually run away with a logic of their own. They develop internal contradictions and end up becoming the very opposite of what they set out to be. Churches, NGOs, revolutionary movements and other such idealistic do-gooders at some point come face to face with their own shadows. Once unmasked, they either seize this as opportunity to reform and turn the organization around or lash back at those who have served as mirrors to the monster that stares them in the face.

But then there is beauty even in the beast, and it takes the eye of faith to believe that it can be tamed. By sheer endurance and the willingness to suffer, genuine movements for change emerge out of the depths of the most unlikely places: 'Can anything good come out of Nazareth?'

The missiologist Andrew Walls once noted that Christianity throughout history has shifted centres: churches like Antioch emerged from the 'periphery' and eventually eclipsed the originating 'core' of the faith, the older Jerusalem church. Then it moved to the barbaric hordes of the North – what is now Europe – then to the Americas and now in Africa and pockets of Asia.

As with geography, so with power relations: part of the movement of the kingdom is 'the overthrowing of the mighty and the lifting up of the lowly'. A reversal – *peripeteia* – happens on the ground, in our objective social and economic relations, not just in our soul. It does not matter that it starts small, like a mustard seed, for inevitably, it soon grows into a very large tree, where all kinds of strange birds and bedfellows take shelter under its shade.

The early church was powerless to fight slavery frontally as an institution, but there was a new spirit in the way they related to each other as slave and master. The social vision of Galatians 3:28 – where rich and poor, male and female, slave and free stand equally in Christ – eventually eroded the social fabric of the Roman Empire and contributed to its final collapse.

Christianity transforms structures from within; it does not, at first instance, tear down things so it can build again. It is not so much revolutionary as subversive. Like the yeast, it works mysteriously yet is visible in its results. Quietly, it penetrates society and alters it at its centre, at that place where things begin to turn and move towards a vision of 'the better country' we only see dimly from afar.

2. *Think contextual, act local*. Part of the mystery of our faith is that the God of the universe was a Jew; he had a nationality, a history, a hometown where he walked the dusty streets and was so embedded in its village life that the people could not believe he could be other than the carpenter's son. Jesus was not a free-floating global citizen with no permanent address. He was rooted where he was. No other religion talks of God in this way; you have mythical avatars that make fleeting appearances or an Allah so high he is beyond touching or imagining. In contrast, Jesus is 'that which we have heard, which we have seen with our eyes, which we have looked upon and touched with our hands,' says John with awe and amazement. He, who was from the beginning, entered human history and became like us.

Quite the reverse, in an age of mass migrations, we are tempted instead to escape our histories and seek other identities. For economic and other reasons, people are forced to forsake home and rootedness. We are told that God cares for our geography; he has allotted territories for our habitation and defined their boundaries. The violation of these spaces by imperialism is now being paid for by both victim and aggressor. Migrants mostly become wraithlike shadows inhabiting the dark underside of global cities, strangers vulnerable to loss of rights and, more tragically, identity and significance. The theologian Walter Brueggemann once said that 'to be in history is to be in a place somewhere and answer for it.'[1] We have yet to understand the dislocation, the toll on the human sense of home, purpose and identity by this global diaspora.

The incarnation as a pattern of engagement means that all our interventions in communities must be rooted and shaped by the local context. The trouble with organizations with a singular focus – whether health, children at risk, microfinance, environment, etc. – is that interventions tend to get fixed into a template, without regard to the peculiar contexts of communities. Similarly, international NGOs tend to skew the work of local organizations towards their preferred agenda, simply by funding only those concerns that interest them. There is a subtle cultural imperialism in tying grants to compliance with systems, tools and procedures that they have unduly universalized, on the assumption that they are generic and can be applied in other cultures with the same degree of usefulness. The tension between respecting local norms and measures of performance on one hand, and accountability in a way that makes sense to donors on the other hand, needs to be negotiated with a great deal of cultural sensitivity.

Being contextual also means that we take seriously the indigenous human and material resources. Communities have stories, myths and legends that inspire and help them to survive all sorts of vicissitudes. Elders, opinion leaders, gatekeepers need to be engaged, but also the local gambling lord, faith healer and shaman. There is a great deal of indigenous technical knowledge among farmers, fishermen, craftsmen and the herbal doctor. These should not be bypassed but carefully listened to as important resources, and enlisted in the work of transforming cultures.

3. *Nurture a strategic minority*. Changes begin with a small but determined minority of creative deviants. Social historians say that it only takes 5 per cent of a community or nation to turn it around. We need to empower and nurture strategic minorities into a critical mass that turns into tidal change. Churches must begin to intentionally grow those among us who, like Daniel and Joseph, can interpret the times, articulate an alternative vision, and administer a planned response.

Of special concern to us in this day and age is the shaping of a cognitive environment that will serve as a foil to global media. We live in a time of what the sociologist Jacques Ellul calls 'shadows' – a secondary environment of myths and narratives constructed for us by media. More than our own primary experiences, we tend to believe those anonymous, saturnine authorities that churn out those images and column inches of doom and gloom. Many societies hobble and are continually disempowered by 'strongholds in the mind', those subtle and pernicious lies just below the threshold of our consciousness, telling us we shall forever be basket cases. What the Germans call 'Zeitgeist' or the 'spirit of the times' are usually influences emanating from the 'prince of the power of the air'. Along with their technological savvy, the new generation must be equipped to discern the seductions of this power, to smell the hidden rot and name the ways by which evil 'comes up softly like a flower' as the poet Baudelaire says.

This means that artists, writers, journalists, social scientists and others with similar gifts for analysis and articulation must be inspired with a vision that will challenge and give them a missional sense of their significance in a postmodern world. It is now through the imagination rather than through reason that the Word breaks through to people. It is time to anoint these underutilized gifts in the Body of Christ and release them to the wider world.

To sum up, justice is the primary reason for the existence of the state. Biblically, the doing of justice and righteousness go together. To survive, all societies need a minimum moral sense; acts of mercy are best done by the citizenry and not by an impersonal welfare state. Education, value formation and the use of power are approaches to changing social behaviour; but even more important than these is the ability to constructively engage structures, help communities to resource their own needs within their own context, and nurture a strategic minority that will create a presence and a voice in public space on behalf of the poor.

10

The Tipping Point: Faith and Global Poverty[1]

Jim Wallis

For the first time in history we have the information, knowledge, technology and resources to bring the worst of global poverty to an end. What we don't have is the moral and political will to do so. And it is becoming clear that it will take a new moral energy to create that political will. I believe the religious communities of the world could provide the 'tipping point' in the struggle to eliminate the world's most extreme poverty. Faith communities could provide the crucial social leadership the world desperately needs, and I don't see where else that prophetic leadership might come from.

Malcolm Gladwell, in his best-selling book, *The Tipping Point*, talks of how an idea, product or behaviour moves from the edges of a society to broad acceptance, consumption or practice, often suddenly and unexpectedly. Along the way there is a 'tipping point' that transforms a minority perception to a majority embrace. Today, a sizeable and growing number of individuals and institutions have identified the deep chasm of global poverty as their central moral concern and have made significant commitments to overcoming the global apathy that leads to massive suffering and death. But we have not yet reached the tipping point – when the world demands solutions.

The most astute observers of the issue now realize that only a new moral, spiritual and even religious sensibility, in relation to the problems of global poverty, will enable us to reach that critical tipping point. Even some of the world's political leaders who are focused on this question (whether they themselves are religious or not) are coming to realize the need for a moral imperative. And it is clear that the moral imperative must now focus on the interrelated issues of debt, aid, trade and AIDS. This will be the 'template' for real solutions. None of these elements will be enough in themselves; only all four essential ingredients in combination will produce lasting results in overcoming global poverty.

In a 2004 speech to a conference of mostly faith-based development agencies in the United Kingdom, the then Chancellor of the Exchequer, Gordon Brown, gave a sobering report on how the world was failing to keep the promises of the Millennium Development Goals in the crucial areas of education, health, and targeted poverty reduction.[2] Despite the commitments made by 147 nations to cut extreme poverty in half by the year 2015, global progress was significantly behind schedule. As to the causes of the 30,000 infant deaths that still occur each day in the poorest parts of the world, Brown pointed to our moral apathy: 'And let us be clear: it is not that the knowledge to avoid these infant deaths does not exist; it is not that the drugs to avoid infant deaths do not exist; it is not that the expertise does not exist; it is not that the means to achieve our goals do not exist. It is that the political will does not exist. In the nineteenth century you could say that it was inadequate science, technology and knowledge that prevented us saving lives. Now, with the science, technology and knowledge available, we must face the truth that the real barrier is indifference.'

Point by point, the Chancellor went through the alarming facts and statistics showing how these once hopeful goals had already fallen far short. 'If we let things slip,' he predicted, 'the Millennium Goals will become just another dream we once had and we will indeed be sitting back on our sofas and switching on our TVs and – I am afraid – watching people die on our screens for the rest of our lives. We will be the generation that betrayed its own heart.' He ended his speech with a passionate appeal to the non-governmental organizations

(NGOs) and the faith communities in particular, quoting the prophet Isaiah,

> I appeal to NGOs and faith groups: to hold us accountable, to be the conscience of the world, to be the voice that guides us at this crucial crossroads, to work together with no one ever subordinating their own objectives but recognizing that each of our objectives can be better realized if we can agree on the financing to underpin them. In 2015 we cannot look back and say: 'It was not us who acted, it had to be left to the next generation. It was not now, but some other distant time in the future.' That is not good enough. When the need is urgent and our responsibilities clear; and even when the path ahead is difficult, hard, and long, let us not lose hope but have the courage in our shared resolve to find the will to act. And let us say to each other in the words of Isaiah 'though you were wearied by the length of your way, you did not say it was hopeless – you found new life in your strength.' The strength together to fight poverty, remove destitution, end illiteracy, cure disease. The challenge for our time and for our generation. And let us achieve it together.

On an earlier occasion, Gordon Brown said to me, 'The most important social movement in Britain since Wilberforce was Jubilee 2000. Without that campaign, led by your church people, our government simply would not have cancelled the debts of the poorest countries.' William Wilberforce, the eighteenth-century British parliamentarian who was converted in the Wesleyan revival, became the political leader of the historic anti-slavery campaign, which was sparked by spiritual renewal. Brown led the Labour government of Tony Blair in their decision in 2000 to cancel the bilateral debts to Britain of the world's most impoverished nations, and Jubilee 2000 was the church-initiated movement for debt cancellation. 'It's obviously only a start to completing this process of debt relief and poverty reduction,' Brown said, 'but it is the important start that I think everyone is looking for.' And it serves as perhaps the best modern case study of what a faith-based initiative can do.

Jubilee: Cancel the debt

On a trip to London in 1999, I was amazed when I saw the words Jubilee 2000 emblazoned high atop the millennial countdown clock at Piccadilly Circus – the closest thing central London has to Times Square. I knew the grassroots campaign begun by religious and secular poverty activists in Britain to cancel the debt of the world's poorest nations had been having remarkable success, but I didn't expect to see its name in London's lights on the way to a theatre in early January.

Over an Indian meal with our friends Peter and Dee Price, Joy and I discussed the extraordinary success of Jubilee 2000. Peter had just become a bishop in the Church of England and was a staunch supporter of the campaign. He told us about the humble beginnings of the effort. Too radical a pipe dream, said most. Sure, forgiving the crushing debt of the world's poorest nations would, more than anything else, begin to make poverty reduction possible. But how could you ever convince the world's wealthiest countries, their banks and the World Bank and International Monetary Fund (IMF) ever to forgive those debts? Even the biggest international aid and development groups were sceptical of the idea at first.

But at the beginning of the new millennium, Jubilee 2000 reported enormous progress in moving the world toward a cancellation of the poorest nations' debts. In Britain, where the movement began, Gordon Brown and then Prime Minister Tony Blair had already announced their goal to end the debt of the world's poorest countries by the end of the year and called upon other nations to follow suit. Former President Bill Clinton also announced his desire to cancel the debt owed to the United States, and bipartisan support was growing in Congress. The G7 countries had begun to take some positive steps toward debt relief, and even the World Bank and the IMF were exploring how the crushing debt of the world's most impoverished nations might indeed be relieved, using the savings to reduce poverty in those countries.

It was extraordinary that the biblical principles of jubilee had become part of the international economic discussion. World Bank president James Wolfensohn and the leaders of the IMF now knew that Leviticus 25 proclaims the biblical jubilee: a periodic economic redistribution in which slaves are set free, land is returned and debts are forgiven. Jubilee is a call for a regular 'levelling' of things, necessary because of the human tendency toward over accumulation by some while others lose ground. The Bible doesn't propose any blueprint for an economic system, but rather insists that all human economic arrangements be subject to the demands of God's justice, that great gaps be avoided or rectified, and that the poor are not left behind. The World Bank and the IMF have been discussing the implications of such biblical texts with religious leaders and must cope with an international grassroots campaign that has enlisted a variety of supporters, from U2's Bono to the Pope. Did anybody really think that Bill Clinton and Tony Blair would have been calling for debt cancellation without such international pressure from a movement that began with religious imperatives?

While there is much left to do to definitively cancel all that debt (especially the multilateral debts held by international bodies like the World Bank and the IMF), an enormous amount of progress has already been made. Jubilee 2000 was up in lights! Just shows you what a grassroots campaign can do.

Jubilee 2000 stands as an example of how a movement of concerned and active people, grounded in moral and religious beliefs, can 'change the wind' to accomplish what only a few short years ago seemed impossible.

At the annual meetings of the IMF and World Bank, supporters of debt relief are now always present – both in the suites and in the streets. Partly because of that pressure, the World Bank now argues that economic growth alone is not sufficient to overcome poverty as long as existing political and economic systems favour the rich over the poor. The director of one World Bank study noted, 'In order to increase poor people's share of this growth, we're going to have to address inequalities.' In the USA, Jubilee 2000 is now the Jubilee Network, and its supporters still call on the World Bank and IMF to cancel 100 per cent of the debt owed to them. Along with street demonstrations, there are also meetings with top officials of the institutions and even public dialogues between critics from a variety of NGOs and financial leaders.

At one World Bank/IMF meeting, Wolfensohn noted the demonstrations in his speech: 'Outside these walls, young people are demonstrating against globalization. I believe deeply that many of them are asking legitimate questions, and I embrace the commitment of a new generation to fight poverty. I share their passion and their questioning.'[3] That continual questioning must go on because the full debt cancellation needed has yet to be accomplished at the World Bank and the IMF. Congresswoman Maxine Waters, a supporter of the effort, noted especially the role played by Jubilee 2000, 'This [debt cancellation] is really a spiritual movement. And I want you to know it could not have been, had it not been for Jubilee 2000. They have been able to organize religious organizations all over the world to come together with NGOs and to really move this issue forward. It would not have happened without them.'

Since the historic protests in Seattle against unjust globalization, and since the Jubilee 2000 movement, no G8 meeting of the world's leading industrial nations will escape moral scrutiny and public accountability. It's been only ten years since 70,000 people formed a human chain around the G8 meeting in Birmingham, England, marking the first major appearance of the Jubilee movement. Much has been accomplished in the years since then. The network of faith communities, NGOs, celebrities and millions of people around the world has brought a moral spotlight to the unsustainable indebtedness and the systemic poverty of the world's poorest countries. And the world has begun to address the problem.

The limited debt relief provided to these poor countries has made some significant changes in living conditions. Jubilee USA reports for example that in Uganda, debt savings were used to double elementary school enrolment. In Mozambique, half a million people were vaccinated against deadly diseases. Tanzania used debt savings to eliminate school fees, and 1.5 million children will be able to return to school this year, while in Honduras, the savings went toward access to junior high school for all young people.

Yet major problems remain with the Heavily Indebted Poor Countries (HIPC) Initiative – as the current World Bank programme is called. At the end of 2003, after seven years of the initiative, a report by the British New Economics Foundation found that of the 42 countries considered to be 'heavily indebted poor', only 8 had passed the 'completion point' where debts were cancelled, rather than the 21 the original timetable called for. Only 19 others had qualified for some debt relief.[4]

It also provides too little relief. The HIPC Initiative defines 'debt sustainability' as countries whose outstanding debt is 150 per cent more than its annual exports. Only those countries are eligible for relief. But that definition is already outdated. As prices drop for exports, the relief will end up being too small to reduce the debt for many countries to even that 'sustainable' level of 150 per cent of exports. Uganda, for example, has completed the programme but still has an 'unsustainable' debt projected by the World Bank at 250 per cent of exports. Jubilee notes that half of the countries in Africa pay more on debt service than on health care while 6,000 people a day are dying from AIDS. Estimates are that stopping the epidemic would cost $7–10 billion annually, while Africa pays $13.5 billion annually on debt service. It is past time to label such policies for what they are: illogical and unconscionable.

Fair trade

More equitable trade practices are also crucial for seriously reducing poverty. Countries that rely on the export of raw materials to the industrialized world are at the mercy of market forces that lead to further indebtedness. Simply providing more debt relief and aid without changing the rules of the game is not the solution to global poverty. Justice and sustainability are better long-term solutions than benevolence. A worldwide movement of protest against unfair 'free trade' administered by the World Trade Organization (WTO) is now under way. The current wave of protests aimed at unjust globalization policies began in Seattle in December 1999.

On a Sunday night, just before the week of scheduled protests that would rock the WTO meeting and the world, I preached in Seattle's St James Cathedral. From the pulpit, I looked out over the standing-room-only crowd and could feel the electric excitement. We were all gathered for a religious service organized by Jubilee 2000.

Just before I preached, the text was read from Leviticus 25. As I listened to the prophetic Scripture being read, I marvelled at how it was being used that night: as a relevant contribution to a public discussion on the rules for global economics!

The official World Trade Organization meetings planned for Seattle were never meant to be public. Quiet and private WTO proceedings of a very elite group had been scheduled to determine the rules of the global economy. But the events of the next several days would shout a message heard around the globe: that discussions about how to conduct international trade would no longer be private conversations. Instead of a small, behind-the-scenes meeting to determine the rules of global trade, a very noisy public debate ensued, asking who makes those rules, who benefits and who suffers.

The issue in Seattle was not whether there should be global trade. There is, and there will be. The question is, what will the rules of trade be? There are and will be rules, and somebody will make them. But who will profit from those rules, and who will be left behind? The street prophets in Seattle said that the rules should protect the lives of workers, the environment and human rights.

Until now, the definition of free trade preferred by the world's largest corporations has paid little or no attention to workers' rights, environmental threats and political oppression. Within developed countries, there are rules that companies must abide by. In the United States, for example, you can't legally pour sewage into rivers, foul the air or produce your goods in exploitative and unsafe sweatshops. There are rules. How do we construct fair rules for a global economy?

In the past decade, a series of regional free trade agreements have exacerbated these realities – from NAFTA (North American Free Trade Association) to FTAA (Free Trade Association of the Americas) to CAFTA (Central America Free Trade Association) – agreements that benefit the largest corporations and wealthiest countries without adequately protecting workers, human rights and the environment. Such agreements have helped to fuel the growing anti-globalization movement, which protests these realities.

While it is good to protest, having an alternative is better. And there are alternatives. The anti-globalization movement sums it up with its slogan, 'Another world is possible.' Fair trade or trade justice, rather than mere free trade, is the objective. Achieving this requires fundamentally changing the underlying principles of the world trading system so that they also benefit poor countries and people, not just the wealthiest.

One of the keys is who gets to sell what in whose market. Agreements that force poor countries to open their markets to the wealthy countries, while their protectionist policies block exports from developing nations, simply perpetuate and exacerbate the rich–poor gap. And the failure to require policies from corporations that protect labour rights and the environment means that poor workers and farmers are further harmed.

In developing new policies, poor countries must become active participants – able to choose and help shape the policies that will work best to reduce poverty. And poverty reduction, rather than simply profit maximization, must be a primary criterion by which to judge any trade policy. Only with that clear focus will the lives of the majority of people in the poor countries genuinely improve.

Trade policies should be determined with the active involvement of the people who will be affected: poor people themselves, NGOs that work with them and, increasingly, faith-based organizations. Rather than the closed-door meetings in resort hotels that still characterize trade summits today, they should be open debates with high public participation and reporting. Civil society groups must then be involved in monitoring and evaluating trade agreements.

For poverty reduction to succeed, however, the development of democratic governance and transparency in poor countries must also continue. Aid and trade that simply line the Swiss bank accounts of already wealthy and oppressive despots in poor nations will change nothing. Endemic corruption in the developing world is also an important cause of poverty, along with the oppressive structures and rules of the global economy that keep some poor and others rich. And, of course, the expansion of fair and just trade improves living conditions, which will also provide an incentive for greater democracy. People who are educated and no longer hungry are also more able to freely participate in their society. The biblical prophet Micah proclaims that this will make us more secure.

Along with advocacy for fair trade policies, we all have the opportunity to buy fair trade products through a growing network of non-profit organizations that deal directly with producers, eliminating the middlemen and paying a fair, above-market price. Such fair trade products now being marketed throughout the developed world include coffee, tea, cocoa, chocolate, clothing and crafts.

One of the major products in the growing fair trade movement is, of course, coffee. Although a very heavily traded commodity, most coffee farmers living in the poorest countries of the world receive little. Coffee prices in the market fluctuate widely, and there are many steps between the farmer and the supermarket. Fair trade coffee is giving these farmers the alternative to deal directly with organizations that distribute the coffee in the United States and elsewhere. The prices they receive are above the market rate, enabling them to better support their families. Equal Exchange, an active fair trade coffee distributor in the United States, was founded in 1986 and is now the largest Fairtrade-certified coffee company in North America, with seventeen trading partners in ten countries in Latin America, Africa and Asia. Although not faith-based, Equal Exchange has partnered with national church organizations in a growing 'Interfaith Coffee Programme' to market coffee for fellowship hours after worship. In 2004, these partnerships included Lutheran World Relief, Catholic Relief Services, the American Friends Service Committee, the Presbyterian Church (USA), the Unitarian Universalist Service Committee, the United Church of Christ, the United Methodist Committee on Relief and Brethren Witness. The organization notes, 'Equal Exchange's fair trade practices help build pride, independence and community empowerment for small farmers and their families. A coffee processing plant in El Salvador, community stores in Colombia, the training of doctors and nurses in Mexico, reforestation programmes in Costa Rica, new schools in Peru – these are all examples of the initiatives that co-ops have taken in their own communities with the income from fair trade.'[5]

There is also a growing market for handicrafts. Ten Thousand Villages was founded in 1946 as a non-profit programme of the Mennonite Central Committee (MCC), the relief and development agency of Mennonite and Brethren in Christ churches in North America. It now operates over 180 stores across North America staffed by thousands of volunteers. Products from more than thirty countries are sold, including everything from textiles to ceramics to art, toys and games.[6]

MCC operates under the guidelines of the International Fair Trade Association, which notes that 'fair trade is better than aid – it builds a sustainable future on artisans' own abilities. Artisans receive a fair price for their goods, enabling them to improve their quality of life. And, cultural exchange and understanding is facilitated as consumers are told about the people who made the handicraft they bought.[7]

The fair trade consumer movement is much further along in Europe than in the United States, but it is growing steadily here too. In London supermarkets, one can find a whole array of fair trade products now. People would rather buy something they know was traded fairly, where the proceeds go to the producers themselves and where the environment is also protected. That kind of shopping just feels better and concretely contributes to a more just world.

A New Marshall Plan

Definitive debt cancellation, wise aid programmes and trade justice are all crucial for addressing global economic inequality and improving the lives of millions of the poorest of the poor around the world. Debt, aid and trade are the pillars of global poverty reduction, and they are becoming the moral imperatives of a growing popular movement that has strong support in the faith community.

Diverse Christian groups are now mobilizing around the issues of international debt, aid and trade. At one such event in London, I preached a sermon on this movement in the historic Wesley Chapel and from the revivalist John Wesley's pulpit. I couldn't escape the feelings of excitement as I wondered if a new movement to overcome global poverty might be rising up, born of spiritual renewal just like the anti-slavery campaign more than two hundred years ago.

After the service, I met again with some of the British government leaders who are most involved in the issues of debt, aid and trade. America's leading ally in the world today is utterly convinced that terrorism will not be defeated without a new initiative for the economic development of the world's poorest nations. And the United Nations' stated goals to dramatically reduce global poverty are now helping to shape British foreign policy. The United Nations' Millennium Summit, held in the fall of 2000, made a commitment to cut global poverty in half, reduce infant mortality by two-thirds and make primary education available to all children – all by 2015. These Millennium Development Goals (MDGs) and their 2015 commitments are a part of every discussion of international affairs I have with the UK leaders of both church and state.

The MDGs are indeed an important and urgent commitment. Today, some 800 million people around the world are malnourished. According to UNICEF and the World Health Organization, 30,500 children die every day in the developing world from hunger and preventable diseases. Almost 3 billion people, nearly half the world's population, live on less than $2 a day, 1.2 billion of them on less than $1 a day.

In 1970, the United Nations estimated that commitments to significantly reduce global poverty could be met by increasing development aid to poor countries by $50 billion per year, and it set a goal to accomplish this with developed countries spending 0.7 per cent of their GNP. They haven't even come close – the current average is between 0.2 and 0.3 per cent.

In several speeches over the past few years, Chancellor of the Exchequer (and now Prime Minister) Gordon Brown has called for a new 'Marshall Plan' of aid to developing countries in order to accomplish the ambitious Millennium Development Goals. In a speech on 17 December 2001, at the National Press Club in Washington, Brown recalled how US Secretary of State George Marshall had committed the resources needed to rebuild Europe after the Second World War, believing that a true victory in that war would require a global fight against 'hunger, poverty, desperation, and chaos'. 'Today', said Brown, 'there cannot be a solution to the urgent problems of poverty the poorest countries face without a . . . substantial increase in development funds for investment in the very least developed countries . . . We must move from providing short-term aid just to compensate for poverty to a higher and more sustainable purpose, that of aid as long-term investment to tackle the causes of poverty by promoting growth.'

Brown is right – an international war against terrorism that doesn't target global poverty is doomed to failure. The US government's 44 per cent increase in the military budget since September 11 (from $306 billion in financial year 2001 to $441 billion in financial year 2004) will do little to eradicate the conditions of poverty, injustice and lack of democracy, which breed terrorism.

Clare Short, former British Secretary of State for International Development, put it this way when I interviewed her in the fall of 2003:

> I do think one of the greatest dangers to the future security and safety of the world is the level of poverty and inequality in a world of great riches, of technology, capital, and knowledge, and now with the speed of communications that means we both have the capacity to spread basic development and the basic decencies of life across the globe – that could be easily done, it's a matter of will. It's not a matter of affordability, and it's a grave injustice when people can see each other and some fifth of humanity are living in abject poverty, the sort of conditions that were in Britain at the time of the Industrial Revolution – child labour, illiteracy, the lack of clean water, curable diseases killing people, women dying in childbirth – all that is the condition of a fifth of humanity. With a bit of effort, those people could be given the chance to improve their lives,

> get their kids to school, have some basic healthcare, be able to work – fairer trade rules so they could export their products, etc. The world wouldn't be equal, but it would start to be decent and there would be no one living in those abject conditions. So, I think this is the biggest moral issue we face.[8]

I've often met with Brown, Short and several other members of the British Parliament. All of them are convinced that churches and faith-based organizations could play a decisive role in convincing the people and governments in the West of the political and moral imperatives of dramatically reducing global poverty. The British leaders believe that unless the United States and the United Kingdom can be persuaded to lead in this effort, it cannot really succeed, and that the churches must help their governments to act.

Together the churches and the faith-based development agencies must create transatlantic and international alliances aimed at mobilizing our own people and pushing our governments toward effective moral and political leadership in seriously reducing global poverty. The Millennium Development Goals are not at all out of reach, but their achievement requires the creation of a new political will. They are indeed possible, but not without a spiritual engine to drive them forward. That is indeed what the religious community can best provide. Together, we can commit to work to make the possible . . . possible.

The moral crisis of HIV/AIDS

Today we must aim our moral energy at the developing world in places like AIDS-affected sub-Saharan Africa and in response to the urgent moral call to dramatically reduce global poverty. Our churches must convince our political leaders that such a moral and political initiative aimed at the root causes of global injustice will enable the war against terrorism to succeed far better than dropping more bombs on more countries. This may not be the kind of faith-based initiative that our political leaders had in mind, but it may be the kind of witness that many churches may now be ready to offer.

There are many signs that the churches may be ready to take just such an initiative. One very powerful sign is how a growing number of church-based organizations and leaders are being drawn to respond to the crisis of HIV/AIDS. After many years of reluctance to engage the issue, many surprising people and groups (including many conservative evangelical leaders and organizations) are joining the fight against AIDS.

Today, 9,000 people will die of HIV/AIDS. And almost all of them will be poor; they simply can't afford the drug treatments that prolong life. World Vision says it well, 'For the majority of patients in poor countries, AIDS is a death sentence – not a chronic, manageable condition.[9]

Today, 14,000 new people will be infected with the disease, most of them in poor countries. Forty-two million already have it, 22 million have already died and the World Health Organization puts the number of new infections at 5 million per year. The world has never seen a public health crisis like this. Given the numbers, one could say it is a crisis of biblical proportions.

Former UN Secretary General Kofi Annan has said prophetically,

> For me it's not just statistics. . . . I've seen the human suffering and the pain, and what is even more difficult is when you see somebody lying there dying who knows that there is medication and medicine somewhere else in the world that can save her. But she can't have it, because she is poor and lives in a poor country. Where is our common humanity? How do you explain it to her, that in certain parts of the world AIDS is a disease that can be treated and one can live with and function? But in her particular situation, it's a death sentence.[10]

People dying of AIDS, who know that elsewhere medication is saving the lives of others, know that they are dying because they are poor. That, indeed, is a biblical matter.

The only good news is that the churches are changing. We must admit that the churches have been slow to respond. AIDS has carried a sexual stigma for the churches, and we didn't want to deal with it. The early perceptions of the disease were mostly associated with homosexuality – and the church didn't want to deal with that either.

But most victims of HIV/AIDS today are women and children – infected by the promiscuity of men and exacerbated by their poverty. An entire generation of children – 13 million worldwide – have been orphaned by AIDS and face a bleak future without our immediate support.

We are finally seeing new church leadership and, perhaps most significantly, new evangelical leadership. We can now point to strong and unequivocal statements of commitment from groups like World Vision, World Relief and the National Association of Evangelicals, along with the Catholic bishops and the mainline Protestant Church World Service. HIV/AIDS is awakening the conscience of the churches.

Some have likened AIDS to a modern-day leprosy – the terrible scourge of Jesus' day. The gospels note that Jesus went out of his way to embrace the lepers who were isolated and abandoned by the society and the religious people of his day. He instructed his followers to heed his example. Today, Christians are starting to follow Jesus, who said, 'I was sick and you took care of me.' Against a health crisis unlike anything the world has ever seen, the faith community is beginning to raise up a prophetic voice and undertake a new faith-based initiative on HIV/AIDS. To take such an initiative that will help in both the prevention and treatment of AIDS is now quite simply a matter of good faith – and of making good on faith. More than 12 million orphaned children in Africa alone demand our response. There can be no excuses. It is a moral imperative, as well as a political necessity. For all of us, it is a matter of faith.

In his State of the Union address in 2003, President Bush outlined a bold role for the United States by pledging $15 billion over five years to fight HIV/AIDS in Africa and the Caribbean. The initiative promises to provide life-prolonging treatment to 2 million people and to prevent 7 million new infections. In addition to this desperately needed new money, the president stated a principle that activists and people of faith have embraced in the fight against HIV/AIDS. 'In an age of miraculous medicines,' Bush said, 'no person should have to hear "You've got AIDS. We can't help you. Go home and die."' But that bold plan has yet to be fully funded or implemented.

Adam Taylor, Sojourners' senior political director, has said this

> With Bush's plan the devil lies in the details. The political landscape around HIV/AIDS will be defined by how this new commitment is implemented. The advocacy battle must turn to getting the details right. While the details may not generate the same degree of outrage, they will determine how many lives are lost or saved. In the AIDS initiative, Bush exacerbates an ongoing streak of the United States going it alone in addressing global crises. In the first year, only 10% – $200 million – of the new money will go through the Global Fund for HIV/AIDS, Malaria, and Tuberculosis. The Global Fund represents a new multilateral mechanism designed to pool money from wealthy nations and deliver it to scientifically sound and fiscally accountable programmes in countries most heavily impacted by HIV/AIDS. The fund represents one of our best hopes, because it significantly depoliticizes aid and gives both the donor and recipient country a say in how money is used. A pledge of only $200 million would mean a significant step backward in U.S. leadership toward the fund and could cripple the fund in the future. And the World Health Organization conservatively estimates that a fair U.S. share of AIDS assistance would be at least $3.5 billion a year, while the Bush initiative includes less than $2 billion in its first year.[11]

At the time, Taylor was the executive director of Global Justice, a very hopeful network of students and young people in the United States and around the world who are coming together over the AIDS crisis, much as student movements have done in the past around great social issues. He likens their activism to the role of students in the civil rights movement, which was led by groups such as the Student Non-violent Coordinating Committee, which trained, educated and mobilized a generation of students to fight for freedom. Taylor and the young activists who currently make up the Global Justice network make the moral and political connections of HIV/AIDS to global poverty.

Says Taylor, 'The longer our nation waits to address the crisis with the urgency and priority it deserves, the more lives will be lost and the more costly it becomes to turn back the course of the epidemic. The war against HIV/AIDS must be wrapped around underlying issues of poverty, inequality, and marginalization. HIV disproportionately impacts "the least of these" in relation to both colour and class. And along with aid, the administration should support full debt cancellation for poor nations in order to free up desperately needed resources for health.[12]

I stood outside the US Treasury Building on World AIDS Day 2004 at a religious vigil that the young people had organized. Adam Taylor said that we stand at a 'crossroads' in the fight against HIV/AIDS and he likened the solutions to the battle against global poverty: 'We have the tools of prevention, treatment, and care to stop this deadly epidemic. What is needed most is the personal, societal, and political will. To paraphrase Rabbi Hillel: If not now, when? If not people of faith, who?'

His words at the US Treasury bring us all the way back around to the beginning of this chapter. Success in the fight to overcome global poverty is more a battle for the necessary moral and political will, rather than a problem of resources, information or technology. It is a battle of the spirit – and therefore a task for the community of faith.

11

Poverty: What Does It Look Like and Can We Rise to the Challenge?

Malcolm Duncan

There was once a rich man, expensively dressed in the latest fashions, wasting his days in conspicuous consumption. A poor man named Lazarus [literally means 'without help'], covered with sores, had been dumped on his doorstep. All he lived for was to get a meal from scraps off the rich man's table. His best friends were the dogs who came and licked his sores. (Luke 16:19ff, The Message)

At the heart of my politics has always been the value of community, the belief that we are not merely individuals struggling in isolation from each other, but members of a community who depend on each other, who benefit from each other's help, who owe obligations to each other. From that everything stems: solidarity, social justice, equality, freedom. We are what we are, in part, because of the other. (Tony Blair, Faithworks Lecture, March 2005)

These goals – clean water for all; school for every child; medicine for the afflicted; an end to extreme and senseless poverty – these are not just any goals; they are the Millennium Development goals . . . And they are more than that. They are the Beatitudes for a Globalized World. (Bono, National Prayer Breakfast, Washington DC, 2 February 2006)

A North/South divide

One of the shining achievements of the United Nations is the articulation of the Millennium Development Goals. These eight aspirational commitments demonstrate that global leaders, with the United Nations as a catalyst, can actually put their heads above the parapet of mediocrity and banality and paint a vision of the future that is both inspiring and challenging. That being said, current trajectories make it impossible to see how the achievement of the MDGs is even remotely possible. Yet, if the strength of a nation's 'citizenship' and 'humanity' is measured by the attitude of that nation to the most marginalized and the poorest then surely so called 'developed' nations are by and large failing miserably. Given the struggles to even reach 0.7 per cent of GDP on development and relief spending by nations such as the USA, there is a long way to go if the Northern Hemisphere nations are to claim in any way that we are serious about tackling issues of poverty and deprivation. Nations of the North can have as many security plans and military interventions as we like in the name of 'freedom' and the so-called 'war on terror' but until they also recognize that poverty and deprivation are the swamp beds in which the mosquitoes of terror thrive,[1] they appear to be tilting at windmills. In the United Kingdom, there is a real hunger to make a lasting humanitarian difference on issues of poverty. Campaigns have come and gone, and have undoubtedly been successful. From the Jubilee Debt Campaign to Make Poverty History through to Live 8, each campaign shows that there is a consciousness and awareness of poverty in 'Joe Public' in the UK, the depth of which has yet to be plumbed. It seems that the people of the UK desperately want to see our national politicians rise to the challenge of an authentically compassionate and just foreign policy. Few have done more for this 'ethical' foreign policy than Gordon Brown, yet the war on Iraq (whether one agrees with it or not) is a spectre that casts a long shadow over anything that claims to be ethical. That being said, there is a real opportunity in the UK to 'catch the wind' for tackling international poverty – and there is no doubt that local churches should be at the heart of this movement. It remains to be seen whether or not the church generally, or congregations locally can rise to that challenge.

Dives and Lazarus: an indictment of the church in the Northern Hemisphere?

One of the saddest indictments of many aspects of the church in the Northern Hemisphere – particularly in North America and in the UK – is that we have become the 'rich man' in Jesus' parable recorded in Luke 16. We have become a church that is obsessed with ourselves. If the churches of the North are the 'rich man', then the churches of the South are often the poor man at the door. The same is true of our societies. It would seem that what is true internationally is also true nationally. The resources available to local congregations in the UK vary vastly. The 'fashionable' churches have healthy bank balances, the struggling do not. The former do not help the latter enough. Poverty walks our neighbourhoods, our streets and our workplaces as well as the soils of other continents. This reality is often uncomfortable for churches and yet it is an *integral* part of a local church's mission to address issues of poverty. However, many find it easier to focus on straightforward evangelism at the expense of integral mission. (After all, for many church leaders *integral mission* is just a trendy phrase for evangelism anyway!)

In Jesus' parable, the rich man goes unnamed, and the poor man is named Lazarus, which literally translated means 'someone without help'. The church in the UK could be accused of leaving the poor without help, at home and abroad, far too often. But we have gone further. In a cruel twist of irony we have made sure that our names are known – and have often taken the very names of poor people away from them. Luke often reverses social situations to make a point and he has done the same here. The tragedy is we still do it! Too often our work *with* the poor has become our work *for* the poor. We have too often robbed poor people of their dignity and their voice and in doing so we have compounded their poverty and taken their name from them.

At the heart of Micah Challenge, there are two key objectives. One focuses on tackling the issues of poverty globally and the other on tackling the issues of poverty in our own neighbourhoods. Local churches must not address one at the expense of the other.

We ignore what we do not understand – or fear it

So why do churches so often pay lip service to the issue of poverty at home or abroad? The absence of the poor from our churches and our lack of understanding of mission and advocacy are problems that are easier to ignore than face. Internationally, we can salve our consciences by assuring ourselves that we give a monthly amount to help 'poor people in Africa' or some other part of the world. Yet, that can hardly be described as 'spending ourselves on behalf of the hungry', as we are called to in Isaiah 58. It seems, when it comes to poverty, that we are determined to make a little go a very long way. When William Booth was asked in the nineteenth century why he had founded the Salvation Army, he replied that he had done so because there was no church for the poor. In 2006, where is the church for the poor – nationally or internationally? We have too often adopted the principles of market forces in place of moral obligation. It may be uncomfortable for us as Christians to be confronted with the biblical call to serve the poor and to adopt a different approach to mammon. However, it is an important exercise that shows us the level to which many of us have gone in pretending that there isn't an issue to be faced.

The challenge for us is to do something about poverty. To that end, local churches can support the Millennium Development Goals. The MDGs cannot be the full expression of how we address poverty, because they do not connect directly with issues of whole life spirituality. That being said, the MDGs provide a framework for the alleviation of material poverty that fits closely within a biblical worldview:

1. God sides with the poor.[2]
2. The love of money is the root of all evil.[3]

3. The church cannot serve God and lust after money, power and influence simultaneously.[4]
4. Every person bears the image of God.[5]
5. We have a moral obligation to the poor and not to show favouritism.[6]
6. We should show compassion to those who are poor.[7]
7. What we have is not ours, but entrusted to us that we might use it wisely.[8]
8. The gospel is for the poor.[9]
9. Poverty will be eradicated because of the promise of the kingdom, which was inaugurated in Christ's first advent and will be consummated in his return.[10]
10. Christians engaged in the eradication of poverty do so from the perspective of hope, not despair.[11]

Faces of poverty?[12]

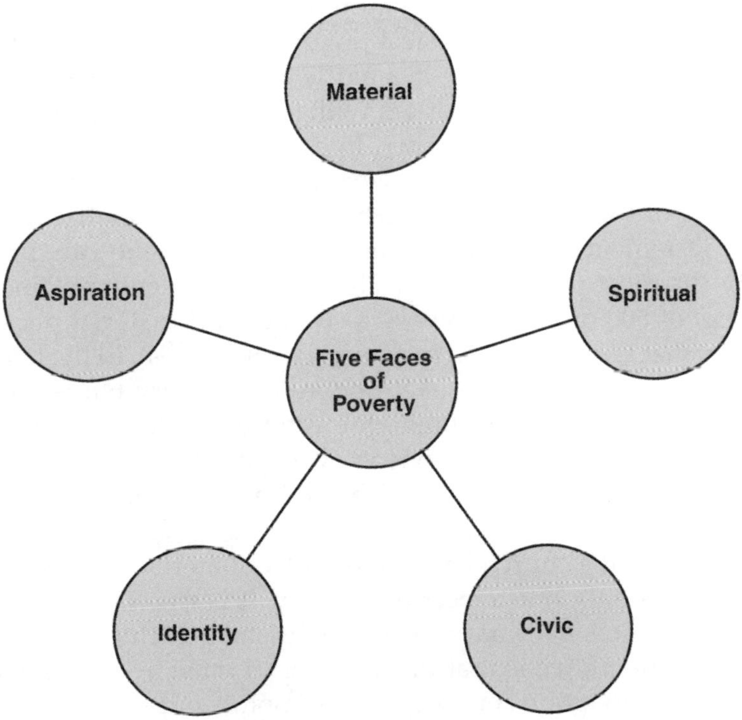

The challenges around a definition of poverty are well known. When we address poverty as Christians, we cannot only address material poverty. Indeed, at the heart of an integrated approach to both mission and alleviation of poverty there is a demand to think about the interconnectedness of the differing facets of poverty. One impacts on the other, like wheels within wheels.

1. Material poverty

It is important to make sure that we do not reduce material poverty to one aspect of poverty *like any other*. There is no doubt that there is an emphasis on physical and material poverty within the Bible. Material poverty is anything that deprives a human being of the physical requirements for living a fulfilled life as God intended.

Physical poverty and social change have long been championed by the church, from Roman Catholicism to Methodism. Many in the church who are more socially progressive would see the eradication of physical poverty as their utmost imperative. They would engage in a battle to see the materially poor served, supported and worked with in order to bring an end to the injustice of poverty in their lives.

Physical poverty and/or wealth are some of the central themes of the Bible, particularly as related to idolatry. In the Old Testament, idolatry and the handling of money are probably the most present issues. The New Testament contains in excess of 500 direct references to wealth and material possessions (that is one mention in every sixteen verses). In the books of Matthew, Mark and Luke, one verse in every ten is about poverty and wealth. In Luke, the ratio drops to one verse in every seven. In James, it is one in every five. Jesus talked about money and wealth more than he did about almost anything else.[13]

Too often the church has downgraded material and physical poverty as only one aspect of poverty. It is true that it is one aspect, but it is a primary focus of Christian teaching. And the biblical imperative is that the good news must be shared with the materially poor. As Albert Nolan points out:

> The option for the poor is not a choice about the recipients of the Gospel message, to whom we must preach the Gospel. It is a matter of what Gospel we preach to anyone at all. It is concerned with the Gospel message itself. The sign that Jesus gives is not that the Gospel is proclaimed to all peoples: it is that the Gospel is proclaimed to the poor.[14]

It is worth noting that somehow the presence of material poverty in the world challenges the church about the effectiveness of our gospel. Fr Mathew Kariapuram, a research scholar at Madras University, India, has noted that 'Poverty is a dehumanizing situation and when it is rampant God's image can never be made perfect in human beings.'[15]

The reality of material poverty cries out at us. It is impossible to ignore it. The travesty of life is that it has become almost as impossible for a poor man to live on earth as for a rich man to enter heaven. Rich people are always finding new friends, but the poor cannot keep the few they have. In such a situation, theologizing cannot but force us to take sides and show where our priorities lie.[16]

Perhaps one of the reasons that we have shied away from the material face of poverty so much is because of the challenge of obeying the teachings of Christ on the subject of wealth. After all, many of us are deeply challenged by the call of Luke 14:33: 'So therefore, whoever of you does not renounce all that he has cannot be my disciple.'

The international challenges around material poverty are clear. The fact that a child dies every three seconds from a preventable illness is nothing short of a scandal for the church and for society as a whole. In effect, we repeat the death toll of the 2004 Boxing Day Tsunami every few weeks. But there are also challenges around the UK context which we cannot ignore.[17] Bartolomé de las Casas, a Dominican missionary from the sixteenth century, said: 'Of the least and most forgotten people, God has a very fresh and vivid memory.'[18]

In fact, we would do well to remember some Roman Catholic doctrine when it comes to material poverty. The 1938 Catechism reads:

> Excessive economic and social disparity between individuals and peoples of the one human race is a source of scandal and militates against social justice, equity and human dignity . . .
>
> In economic matters, respect for human dignity requires the practice of the virtue of temperance, so as to moderate attachment to this world's goods; the practice of the virtue of justice, to preserve our neighbour's rights and render him what is his due; and the practice of solidarity . . .' (Catechism, 2407)

St John Chrysostom made it clear that he believed Christians had an obligation to overcome material disparity: 'Not to enable the poor to share in our goods is to steal from them and deprive them of life. The goods we possess are not ours, but theirs.'

The Salvation Army have made their commitment to the materially poor clear too.[19] Having recognized their responsibility to the poor, the task force from the Lotus Notes and Internet conference on poverty concluded:

> The group operated with full acceptance of the Army's sixth doctrine, noting also that '. . . any Gospel which is truly universal – or, as Salvationists would say, "for the whosoever" – must clearly identify the poor and oppressed as the first ones to be addressed and invited to enter the new Kingdom. The easiest ones to exclude must be the first ones included. Otherwise, the Gospel's whosoever is in jeopardy.'[20]

Albert Nolan was right. If we have not engaged with the materially poor, we have not shared the gospel.

2. *Spiritual poverty*

There is a sense in which all of us are poor without the knowledge of God and his commitment and love to us. This is spiritual poverty. It is clearly outlined within the context of both theology and Scripture. It is perhaps this poverty that evangelicals and pietists have focused on most. For them, the precedence has been given to helping those who are spiritually poor understand that they need a relationship with God as their Creator and their Redeemer in order to thrive and prosper.

Oscar Romero put it this way:

> In our preaching to rich and poor, it is not that we pander to the sins of the poor and ignore the virtues of the rich. Both have sins and both need conversion. But the poor, in their condition of need, are disposed to conversion. They are more conscious of their need of God. All of us, if we really want to know the meaning of conversion and of faith and confidence in another, must become poor, or at least make the cause of the poor our own inner motivation. That is when one begins to experience faith and conversion: when one has the heart of the poor, when one knows that financial capital, political influence, and power are worthless, and that without God we are nothing. To feel that need of God is faith and conversion.[21]

For all Christians, there is a deep connection between the physical and the spiritual. Physical poverty cannot be overcome for the Christian without also addressing the pressing need to eradicate spiritual poverty. Change works best from the inside out. Too often, we have viewed the material as containing the spiritual, but actually within a biblical worldview, the physical is contained within the spiritual.

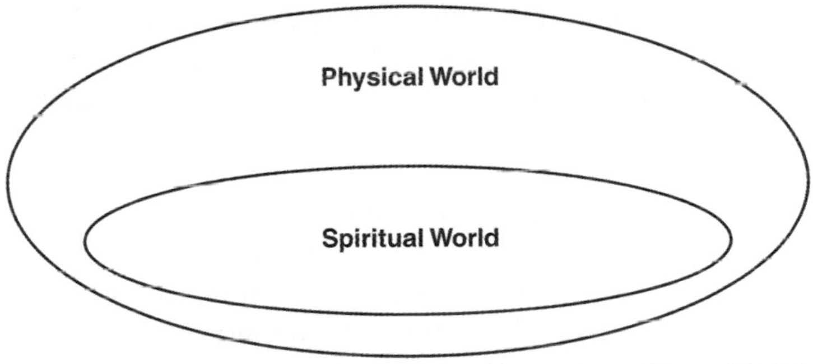

Wrong Model

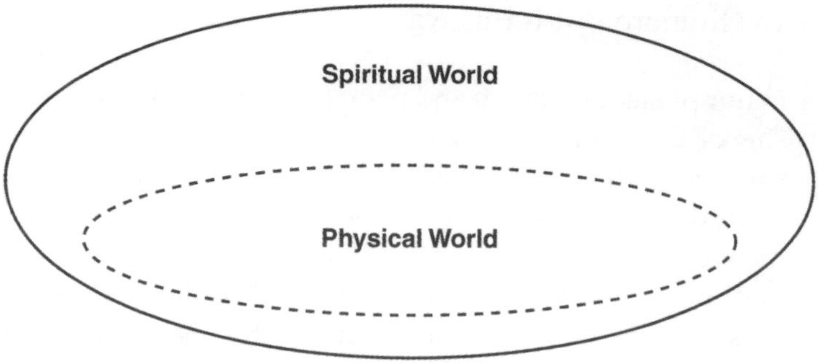

Right Model

3. Civic poverty

Dom Helder Camara, a liberation theologian and priest, once commented that when he asked why the poor had no food, people called him a communist. Yet, he struggled because he knew that it was not enough to feed the poor, although they need to eat; it is important to ask why they are hungry in the first place. Why is it that they have been excluded and marginalized? This is civic poverty. Pope Pius XI called this struggle against civic poverty a 'struggle for justice'. Civic poverty is the lack of opportunity for the excluded and poor to shape their own future and have a role in their own community and society. It is disempowerment of the poor. Why is it that when we ask why the poor are hungry we are communists, yet when we feed them we are saints? We are struggling against an unjust system.

In addressing civic poverty, we must begin to ask hard questions of our society and of ourselves: questions about the very understanding of poverty and sin,[22] questions about the connection between personal responsibility for poverty and societal responsibility. We cannot eradicate poverty by working only with individuals. Nor can we eradicate poverty by working only on the challenges of society. The two are connected. There is strength in both models. We need both. There has been a tendency for churches to fall into 'one camp' or the 'other' when addressing the issues and challenges of poverty. However, if we are to see long lasting solutions rather than sticking plaster answers, we must move beyond extremes and learn from one another's approaches in addressing poverty and ensuring its eradication.

4. Identity poverty

This is a poverty that is deeply embedded in the psyche of individuals, even whole communities throughout their history. It is a poverty that springs from being undervalued persistently. It is a sense that the community you are part of is worthless, or that you yourself are worthless. It springs from bad parenting, inappropriate educational techniques or poor mentoring for individuals. It is the constant voice in the mind of a person, which may sound like an angry father or a neglectful mother or an overly harsh teacher. The sentiment of being stupid, or worthless, or hopeless or from 'bad stock' lies behind this poverty of identity. It is a belief that the past is more important than the present and the future and that, because of where you have come from or what you have been told about yourself, you are worthless. It is the most debilitating poverty imaginable because it holds its victims in a vice of self-doubt and degradation. It is also a lie.

It can be perpetuated about a community by constantly reporting the history of the community and its troubles, rather than focusing on the positive things that also take place within it. It is often most employed by an 'outsider' as they view the community from a distance. By labelling an individual or a community because of its past, we actually perpetuate the impoverishment of that community.

5. Aspirational poverty

Closely tied to the identity poverty of the past is aspirational poverty for the future. This poverty exhibits itself in the conviction that an individual or a community cannot change – that change itself is impossible. The very dreams and ambitions of a person or the community that they belong to can be stolen from them by an attitude of hopelessness and despair. This can spring from past failure, from lack of understanding of a way forward or from a sense of being overwhelmed by the challenge and possibility of change, renewal and transformation. It is perhaps the most harrowing thing to witness because it is the witnessing of the slow and steady death of a person's or a community's hope.

This sense of powerlessness and inability to shape our lives or our world is a far cry from Gordon Brown's sentiments, expressed when he addressed the National Council for Voluntary Organizations in 2004: 'I certainly grew up influenced by the idea that one individual, however young, small, poor or weak, could make a difference.'

Yet, the sense that change is *impossible* permeates so much of the thinking of a vast number of individuals and communities both within the UK and beyond. There is a sense in which a community of geography or interest can become convinced that things *will never change*, and that leads to a sense of hopelessness and apathy about life and about the future.

Conclusions

We, as Christians, must understand that to engage with the poor is to engage with God. As we fight not just the symptoms but the causes of material, spiritual, civic, identity and aspirational poverty, we are doing what God has called us to do. As we work with people and stand alongside them, we are following the example and model of Christ. The heart of Christian unity is living out the good news to the poor – this is our mission. We must also recognize that words and essays and debates are never enough. For poverty to be tackled we must do something – as individuals, as local churches and as the Christian church. Lastly, hope is our greatest gift. Things do not always have to be the way they have always been. As Christians we are harbingers of hope, we are convinced that the world for individuals and communities will be a better place. But we are also convinced that change is only possible as we learn from one another, and as we each play our part.

Long after social services, government funding and other programmes will have left a community, the church (in the truest sense of the word) should still be there. Long after the Millennium Development Goals are forgotten and the names of the international poverty campaigns have changed again, the church will still be here – part of God's inaugurated kingdom. A kingdom of God without space for the poor is both a theological impossibility and a spiritual offence. Our commitment is not determined by funding, approval or support from a hierarchy or a government or a programme. We move beyond programmes because we recognize that deeply embedded within every single human being is the image of God. We weep and laugh with them. We stand with them. For in following Jesus, we follow the One who leads us to the poor. Wherever there is good work, wherever there is a stand for justice and against injustice, wherever the poor are cared for, whatever the name of the person or group helping, God smiles. We must stand with those who stand with the poor for in so doing we stand with God.

In the tradition of St Francis, we must hold on to the conviction that when we touch the poor, or are touched by them, we are touching God himself.

> God is in the slums, in the cardboard boxes where the poor play house. God is in the silence of a mother who has infected her child with a virus that will end both their lives. God is in the cries heard under the rubble of war. God is in the debris of wasted opportunity and lives, and God is with us if we are with them. (Bono, National Prayer Breakfast, Washington DC, 2 February 2006)

12

'This Stuff Works': Specific Action to Combat Poverty

Andrew Bradstock

Working through this book, with its challenge to look afresh at global poverty and the reasons why, as Christians, we should be involved in tackling it, one question may have constantly dogged you: 'What difference can I or my church really make?'[1]

When confronted by the number of people living in dire poverty and perhaps also with HIV/AIDS, or by the pace of global warming which will lead to even more suffering in the developing world, it is easy to despair of things ever improving. And our pessimism and sense of inadequacy can become even greater when we add in factors holding back progressive and just solutions, like inactivity or dissemblance on the part of some governments, the self-interestedness of some multinationals, corruption and malfeasance in high places, what St Paul calls 'the principalities and powers of this present darkness' (Eph. 6.12). Well might we cry, in the words of one recent book looking at tackling global poverty, 'What can one person do?'[2]

Changing the wind

Yet these are actually exciting times to be pursuing social change. It has often been said that we are the first generation who really can 'make poverty history', and that is not mere rhetoric, because we know what is needed to achieve 'a better world' and it is within our capability.

What do I mean? Well, when we listen to senior politicians talking about how the Millennium Development Goals can be achieved or how the threat of climate change overcome, they all admit that the key factor is not cost or resources but 'political will', by which they mean a commitment by world leaders actually to make change happen. No one doubts that the Goals *are* achievable. The United Nations has said that they are feasible, both financially and technologically, and senior British politicians affirm that they will not require unimaginable sums of money to come to pass. No, what it will take to see them realized is a change of heart by those with the power to make the big decisions, the 'political will' to make it happen. As Bob Geldof once perceptively put it: people in Africa are not dying of drought, they are dying of politics.[3]

Look at it another way. Whenever governments decide to engage in or prepare for war, or pursue any other cause they deem serious enough, money and person-power can be found, even at very short notice. The challenge for us is to persuade governments that they should demonstrate the same level of commitment – indeed, *a much higher level of commitment* – to overcoming hunger and protecting the environment as they do to military endeavours. On one level this sounds a tall order, given that more than a million people opposing the invasion of Iraq did not convince former Prime Minister Tony Blair to change his decision. But the key is to commit to the 'long haul', to work at what Jim Wallis has called 'changing the wind', so that eventually politicians can no longer ignore the force of our argument.[4]

I do think this is very important. Wallis often talks about how politicians fear to act unless they know they have popular backing, how they always need to discern the way the wind is blowing and then move in that direction. We should of course expect a degree of responsiveness to public opinion on the part of elected representatives in democratic states, but the degree to which legislators follow the public mind is quite surprising. Hence political change can be achieved as we work to raise public awareness and shift public opinion, as we change the culture in which our political leaders operate. And the reason I see our present moment as one of great opportunity is because we in the churches are good at helping to 'change the wind' and have an impressive track record to prove it.

Take the issue of developing-world debt. At the beginning of the 1990s few people were aware how significant debt was as a factor in perpetuating poverty in developing countries, yet by the year 2000 – thanks to a movement founded by two people with the genius to link the issue to the 'jubilee' principle in the Hebrew scriptures – a massive, unstoppable campaign was capturing the imagination of millions throughout Europe and beyond, demanding all outstanding debts be 'dropped'. Sources close to the G8 leaders who met at Birmingham (1998), Cologne (1999) and Genoa (2001) speak of the profound effect that the Jubilee 2000 and 'Drop the Debt' rallies in those cities had, particularly because the protesters were people who would not normally engage in street action of this kind, including local church congregations.

Our hard work has also brought development into the mainstream. Experts talk about the increasing influence that charities and NGOs are having on issues such as trade and the environment at the global level. On one level, no political party can now afford to ignore the evil of global poverty, and on another a whole new constituency has been radicalized into action much broader than 'traditional' debt and trade campaigners. A survey for Oxfam's 'Generation Why' website found that 84 per cent of 16- to 25-year-olds considered the Make Poverty History campaign and 'Live8' concert had had the biggest impact on them in 2005, ahead of London's Olympic bid and the general election. Some eight million people in the UK wore white wristbands that year, with half a million writing to the Prime Minister and a quarter of a million attending the march and rally in Edinburgh. Churches had no small hand in this development, an external evaluation commissioned by Make Poverty History revealing that they and faith communities generally had created an important bridge between traditional activists and younger first-time campaigners. Church and faith groups had been 'the unsung heroes' of the 2005 campaign, the report concluded.[5]

Mountains *do* still move

We need to remember that revolutions *do* still happen, and that church people are often at the centre of them. However impossible the odds against overturning injustice can appear to be, with patience, resolution and *faith*, huge mountains can be moved and radical and lasting change achieved. So while it may be tempting to think that our one little postcard to the Chancellor or article in the church newsletter or stint on the fair trade stall may not count for much, put together with the tens of thousands of other such actions across the world it counts for *a lot*. In fact, it is potentially world changing! No one person or church or organization can do everything needed to tackle global injustice, but as we work together through agencies and networks, and see our action within the context of wider national and even global movements, so we will resist the temptation to give up in despair. As the archbishops of York and Canterbury said at the launch of the Church of England's Lent initiative for 2007, which encouraged church members to undertake small actions to help 'spread generosity and happiness in their community', 'It's all too easy to feel we are powerless to make a difference, but the truth is, with God's help we can change the world a little bit each day.' Or, as Bob Geldof said, reflecting on the achievements of 'Live8' and the G8 lobby in 2005, 'the individual is not powerless in the face of either political indifference or monstrous human tragedy . . . You can change the world. And millions of you did that this year. This stuff works. Sometimes.'[6]

We can also be encouraged by stories of individuals or small groups who have started something in a humble way and seen it grow in ways they could never have imagined. In the mid 1990s, for example, a group of women with no educational background and very little money founded (after a hard-fought struggle to secure a licence) a bank in their region of India with the aim of helping other Indian women to develop small-scale enterprises. In its first ten years the Mann Deshi Mahila Sahakari Bank (MDMSB) created 17,000 women entrepreneurs in the region around Mhaswad and transformed the lives of many thousands more women, children and men. In the UK, in the 1980s a group of people at St Ives Free Church in the Fens began selling fairly traded goods from a trestle table at the back of the church, an initiative which, within ten years, had led to the church converting some of its space into a shop open six days a week, employing the equivalent of two paid staff and turning over £55,000 per year. Not only has this venture helped transform the lives of many producers in the developing world and raised awareness about fair trade in the local community, any surpluses made have been used to benefit other projects in parts of Africa.

Setting manageable targets

So if our contribution *does* count for something, what could that contribution be? We might not be able to do everything, but what 'something' can we do?

In terms of tackling global poverty, it seems sensible to focus our campaigning on specific issues and intermediate or short-term realizable targets: the awesome challenge of 'defeating global poverty' becomes immediately more realistic once we narrow our focus to a clearly defined and 'manageable' strategy, such as working through a coalition or network like the Trade Justice Campaign, Jubilee Debt Campaign, Stamp Out Poverty or StopAIDS, or lobbying our government to increase the percentage of our gross domestic product we spend on overseas aid.[7]

Increasing aid

To take the last point first, it has been estimated that if the UK had met the internationally agreed target of 0.7 per cent of national income in aid by 2008, an extra 1.5 million people could have beaten poverty that year. What the government in fact committed to doing by 2008 was raising that percentage to

0.47 per cent, some way short of the agreed target and 0.04 per cent less than we were spending in 1979. Looked at in context, these figures show that much progress has been made in recent years: in the six years of Clare Short's tenure at the then newly created Department for International Development, 1997–2003, the UK doubled its aid spending and has continued to increase it since. But we must push our leaders to do more and do it faster. Again, we are not talking huge sums: while the UK devotes £3.6 billion to aid, it spends some £30 billion on defence, £90 billion on health, £90 billion on education and £110 billion on social security, and those who are most informed suggest that we can afford to give more aid without reducing these other very necessary budgets.[8] We must therefore continue to press our case, for, as Professor Jeffrey Sachs, one of the world's leading experts on fighting poverty has said, 'the effort required of the rich is so slight that to do less is to announce brazenly to a large part of the world: "You count for nothing."'[9] In God's eyes, no one counts for nothing, and we need to say so.

Trade justice

We must also continue to campaign for radical change to the rules governing multilateral trade, arguably the biggest single key to eliminating poverty. The Trade Justice Movement has estimated that current world trade rules rob poor countries of £1.3 billion per day: 14 times the amount they receive in aid. On a trip to Mali with Christian Aid in 2002, I saw for myself the effect these rules can have, allowing rich Western nations to subsidize their cotton farmers and in consequence flood the market and drive down prices, leaving farmers in poorer countries, unable even to cover their costs due to falling world prices, to compete with cheap foreign imports. It was heart-wrenching to see in Mali the previous year's harvest still stacked on its pallets, marooned because it would cost more to transport it than would be generated by export income, and then to find in the markets in Bamako not a single item of Malian cloth for sale. Similar stories can be told in respect of producers of other crops across sub-Saharan Africa, all of whom are on a steady downward spiral towards destitution and death as a consequence of the current trade rules and the failure of global institutions to rewrite them in the interests of the poor. The campaign for trade justice has to be one of the most important of our time, and we in the churches need to be passionate and sacrificial in our support of it.

Drop the debt

No less do we need to keep the pressure on politicians to fulfil their promises with respect to debt cancellation. Jubilee 2000 achieved an enormous amount, but still 90 per cent of the debt owed by the South to the North remains outstanding. While AIDS rampages throughout the continent and millions of adults and children remain unable to read or write, there are countries in Africa, Latin America and elsewhere forced to spend more on servicing their debt than on health care or schooling for their people. Some countries have already paid back in interest more than they received in loans many years before (and for which their present governments can hardly be held responsible) and find that they still owe more than they originally received.

The travesty of this situation should impel us to continue to campaign on debt – through the successor to Jubilee 2000, the Jubilee Debt Campaign – aware of the real difference that has been made to people's lives in those countries whose debt burden has been lifted. One practical way for churches to support Jubilee Debt Campaign is to become 'Jubilee Congregations', which means that they agree to take at least one action on debt each year and receive, in return, up-to-date news of the campaign as well as worship and other resources. (The scheme also extends to schools.) As well as maintaining the pressure for debts to be cancelled we need also to call for a new process for dealing with debts that will treat poor nations justly, prevent debt relief being used as a weapon of economic and political control, and avert a new debt crisis in the future.

Defeating HIV/AIDS

Campaigning for action on AIDS is also vital in the struggle against poverty, for the disease creates a vicious downward spiral, leaving families without parents, schools without teachers, hospitals without nurses and businesses without a skilled workforce, all serving to weaken already unstable economies. To take one example, South Africa could face complete economic collapse by the middle of this century unless concerted action is taken to halt the spread of AIDS. Lobbying our government to follow through on Millennium Goal 6, to commit to seeing that HIV treatment is more readily available in the developing world is integral to the struggle to see poverty overcome.

Local church action

There is much else that churches can do to advance the struggle against poverty. Along with agencies and NGOs we can continue to raise public awareness about the situation and seek to persuade those in our churches and elsewhere who are, at present, uncommitted to the cause. Introducing a motion at a church or district business meeting, encouraging a church to support the work of a development agency, and inviting a representative from an agency to speak or preach at a service are all ways of spreading the word. In this context we need also to think more ambitiously than hitherto. For example, many local churches, and all of our main denominations, have a 'social justice' or 'church and society' department, and many support a development agency or overseas project – but is this not in many cases little more than an 'optional add-on'?

In many churches, 'Tearfund' or 'Christian Aid' or 'SCIAF' is something that a small group of particularly committed people in the church 'do', and 'social justice' issues often find themselves way down the agenda at church business meetings and hurried through once more important business like the colour of the new manse carpets has been thoroughly deliberated upon. Perhaps the time has come to challenge our churches to prove how serious they are about wanting the evil of global poverty defeated, and to do more than simply allocate a few minutes at the end of meetings or a 'special Sunday' to considering these issues. How about suggesting to our churches that they devote most of the agenda at their next annual conference or assembly to discussing what they can do to tackle poverty, and only then, if there is any time left over, consider matters relating to their committee structure, restoration projects or leadership patterns? It would not only stimulate a renewed commitment by the church taking this bold and risky step, but relay a powerful message to those outside about our priorities in a world riven by injustice and destitution.

Fair trade

Another important and increasingly influential way in which churches are fighting poverty and injustice is by promoting 'fair trade'. The 'Fairtrade' mark on a product gives us, as buyers, a guarantee that the people in the developing world who have produced or grown it have had a fair deal, specifically a price that covers the cost of sustainable production and an extra premium that is invested in social or economic development projects.

In many areas church people have taken the lead in lobbying supermarkets to stock fairly traded goods and encouraging local towns and cities to achieve 'Fairtrade' status. That the UK fair trade sector is currently growing by 40 per cent a year is also no small credit to churches. Coordinating lobbying of supermarket chains has brought significant results, with the majority now stocking a range of fairly traded goods, and popular pressure on seemingly less-likely companies like Starbucks, McDonalds and even Nestlé has borne fruit. In addition to using fair trade goods ourselves we can press for them to be used at church and synod events, run a fair trade stall on church premises, and encourage members of the congregation to get the fair trade habit. Astonishingly some 18 per cent of the UK roast and ground coffee market is now certified as Fairtrade, and there are more than 1,000 products available in the UK with the Fairtrade mark including fruit, wine, cut flowers and jewellery in addition to beverages, chocolate, snack bars and biscuits. Clearly, if we can afford to buy these products regularly it is good news for producers in the developing world, though we should not mistake 'fair trade' for 'trade justice' and forget the need to focus on the structural reasons why poor farmers so rarely get a fair deal.

Asking difficult questions

Finally, churches should be among those asking the difficult questions and making the problematic connections with respect to poverty reduction. We need to be among those challenging the terms in which the debt issue is framed, asking who is really in the debt of whom given that we in the rich North have prospered for years at the expense of the poor thanks to the inequities of global economic system. We need to be among those calling for joined-up thinking by governments in terms of how our treatment of the environment impacts on the lives of poor people in the developing world. Tearfund and more recently Christian Aid have spelt out how poverty and climate change are 'inextricably linked' and how it is the most vulnerable communities in the world who are suffering – and will continue to suffer – disproportionately from the effects of global warming.[10]

Fighting on

After 2005, when so much was invested in trying to convince world leaders to 'make poverty history' through action on debt, trade and aid, it was perhaps to be expected that campaigning would be less intense. Lobbying by agencies has continued apace, but poverty has dropped out of the headlines and it may be some time before we witness again mass action on the scale we saw around the Gleneagles summit. Yet the challenge for us as Christians is to keep going when the issue is no longer fashionable (during the 'sometimes' to which Bob Geldof refers when this stuff isn't working), fighting on because the cause is just, because we believe change to be possible and because of our unshakeable belief in a God who sides with and vindicates the poor. At all times we shall need to be sustained by prayer, Bible study and fellowship with others of like mind, but particularly when results seem few or when we really feel ourselves to be wrestling with the 'principalities and powers'.

In spite of all that has been achieved, much still remains to be done. Despite increases in aid and debt relief in recent years more money still flows out of Africa to the UK than goes the other way. Trade rules are still grossly unfair to poor countries across the globe. Debt cancellation still comes with 'strings attached' in the form of requirements to privatize services and cut public spending. More than 60 countries still need debt cancellation to be able to meet their people's basic needs. AIDS continues to ravage the continent of Africa. Millions still die of hunger – or should we say, of politics. God forbid that we ever lose our passion to see all people know 'life in all its fullness', or our belief in our potential to influence the people with power to work for justice.

13

The Practice Of Compassion

Dave Andrews

The pathos of compassion

Jesus does not talk of God as *Yahweh* or *Adonai* – but as *Abba* – or *Papa*. Some of us may have been abused by an earthly *Papa* and so struggle to relate to God as *Papa*. But, whatever our term of endearment might be, Jesus invites us all to know God, not as an *apathetic deity* but as a *sympathetic parent* – passionately committed to the welfare of the human family – protective and supportive – utterly compassionate.

If all humans relate to God as their parent, that makes us all brothers and sisters with the intrinsic connections that siblings have with one another. All-inclusive love – even for our enemies – is not only very shocking, but also very scary. According to evangelical spiritual director David Benner,

> When we live in fear we effectively insulate ourselves from life itself – because sorrow, illness, injury and death are unavoidable ingredients in life. Fearful people live within restrictive boundaries. They tend to be quite cautious and conservative. They also tend to be highly vigilant, ever guarding against moving out of the bounds within which they feel most comfortable. People who live in fear feel compelled to remain in control. They attempt to control themselves and they attempt to control their world. Often, despite their best intentions, this spills over into efforts to control others. The fearful person may

> appear deeply loving, but fear always interferes with the impulse to love. Fear blocks responsiveness to others. Energy invested in maintaining safety always depletes energy available for others.[1]

John says that only the 'perfect love' of God can cast out all of the fears that dominate our lives.[2] While human love can never bear the weight of our need *for* divine love, it can teach us *about* divine love. Human love can communicate divine love. Experiences of human love make the idea of God's love believable. The relative constancy of the love of family and friends makes the absolute faithfulness of divine love at least conceivable. However, there is 'no substitute for learning what love really is by coming back to the source. God's love is the original that shows up the limitations of all copies. Only God's love is capable of making us into great lovers.'[3]

Psychotherapist Wayne Muller says, 'It is not the fact of being loved that is life changing. It is the experience of allowing (ourselves) to be loved.'[4] This experiential knowing of ourselves, as deeply loved by God, deepens our thoughts with new data about our world and deepens our feelings with new attitudes towards our world. In the light of our knowledge of God's love we can trust God, take risks and embrace the world that we live in courageously and compassionately.

We may be frightened and be tempted to 'hide behind locked doors'. But Jesus comes to us as he did to his frightened disciples shortly after his crucifixion. 'On the evening of that first day of the week, the disciples were together, hiding behind locked doors because they were afraid. And Jesus came and stood among them and said, *"Peace be with you! Be not afraid!"* The disciples were overjoyed when they saw the Lord. And again Jesus said, *"Peace be with you!" And then he said to them, "Receive my Spirit. As the Father has sent me, so send I you."*'[5]

It would seem that Jesus knows where to find us at times like these. He seeks us out wherever we are hiding 'behind our locked doors'. I don't know how he does it, but somehow or other he manages to walk through the walls we have built around about us and he speaks to us: *'Be not afraid,'* a saying that is repeated over 300 times in the Scriptures.

Being a disciple is to live in sympathy with the *pathos* of God as Jesus did; feeling the throb of God's heartbeat, and teaching our hearts to learn to beat in sync with the love that sustains the universe. It means developing our capacity to intuitively sense what causes love pleasure, and what causes love pain and doing everything we can to enhance the pleasure and to diminish the pain. God is agonized whenever we forget to remember to love one another and neglect our responsibility to do justice to one another; but God is overjoyed whenever love becomes a reality in our lives and we seek to do justice to one another, in spirit and in truth.

The logos of compassion

Our word '*compassion*' comes from '*com*' meaning 'with', and '*passion*' meaning 'suffering'; so to practise '*com-passion*' actually means 'being willing to share in the suffering of others with others.' Paul writes:

> You should have exactly the same attitude as Christ: For he who had always been God by nature, did not cling to his prerogatives as God's equal, but he stripped himself of all privilege, emptied himself, and made himself nothing, in order to be born by nature as a mortal. And, having become a human being, he humbled himself, living the life of a slave, a life of obedience, even unto death. And the death he died, on the cross, was the death of a common criminal.[6]

Christ did not stay in heaven. He moved to earth, into our community, and 'dwelt among us', as one of us. He lived the same life that other people lived, experiencing the same hassles and the same hardships as everybody else. He wasn't full of himself. But 'emptied himself', immersing himself in the lives of others and allowing their concerns to fill his consciousness. In their common struggles, he made himself available to the people as their servant, seeking to do all he could to help them live their lives to the full. When it came to the crunch, he did not cut and run. He was prepared to 'lay down his life for his friends'.

Step 1: Let's select a place to live

All communities are located in a place. For 30 out of the 33 years of his life, Christ lived in a place called Nazareth. For us to practise compassion in a community as he did, we need to live in the place where our community is located. People who expect to move in five years are 25 per cent less likely to actually get involved in their community. So if we really want to get more involved, we will need to live in that community for more than five years.[7] It will also help us to get more involved in a community if we not only reduce the times we move, but also the amount we commute. Every 10 minutes not spent in commuting increases the likelihood of community involvement by 10 per cent – for both the commuters and their families.[8]

We may feel called to be involved in all kinds of communities – an extended family, a friendship network, an apartment block, a nearby suburb, a country town, a city slum, a neighbourhood centre, a church group, a theological seminary, a mission agency, a workers co-op, a trade union, a professional association, a social enterprise, a small business, a big company, a sports club, a local school, a heath clinic, a government department, a reading circle, a theatre troupe, an arts collective, a welfare agency, or a political party – but whatever kind of community it may be, we will need to find a way to be really, truly, continually present to the people in that place.

The easiest way for most people to find more time and energy to be present in a place is to switch off the TV. There are three reasons for this. Firstly, TV takes time. On average people now watch television four hours per day. Secondly, TV induces passivity. The more people watch TV, the more likely they are to want to rest and/or sleep. Thirdly, TV provides a sense of pseudo-community through soap operas like *Coronation Street*. Consequently, each extra hour a day of watching TV reduces community involvement by 10 per cent. If we stop watching *Friends*, chances are that we will find we will have time and the energy to make more friends.[9]

Step 2: Let's connect with the people in that place

Many followers of Christ focus on the last three years of his life and forget the first thirty. After all, they say, it was only in the last three years that he *did* anything. However I would like to suggest that it was his experiences in the first thirty years that provided Christ with the options that he pursued in the last three years. During the last three years he addressed the needs of the community, but it was the first thirty – when he developed relationships, was taught the language, learned the culture, picked up the stories circulating around town and deeply heard the people who were hurting – that gave him the right to speak about the issues that affected the community.

We must not try to be different from the people around us; but discover the similarities we share in the humanity that runs as blood through our veins. We all get sick. We all get tired. We all grow old. Nevertheless, we all want to love and be loved. And we all want to live life to the full before we die. We can enter into these common struggles with people in our community just as Christ did. We need to *bond* with a few people and *bridge* to a lot of people. *Bonds* are strong inward-looking connections, like marriage, that of necessity are exclusive. *Bonds* produce deep, 'thick trust' and are essential for nurturing and supporting one another, for 'getting by'. *Bridges* are weak outward-looking connections, like movements that of necessity are inclusive. *Bridges* produce broad, 'thin trust', and are crucial for cooperating and campaigning with others – for 'getting on'. We need to *bond* with people in our friendship circles, and *bridge* to strangers outside our circles of friends.[10]

Now, there are two traditional ways of building bridges to strangers outside our circle of friends that the Jews refer to in Yiddish as *'schmoozing'* and *'maching'*. 'Schmoozers' take an *informal* approach to bridging. 'Schmoozers' like to visit family, drop in on friends, invite newcomers over for a barbecue or take old-timers out on a picnic. 'Machers' tend to take a more *formal* approach to bridging. 'Machers' are more likely to attend a workshop on community, start a community group and implement a community project. To connect with a wide range of people we need both 'schmoozers' and 'machers', and we need to be both 'schmoozers' and 'machers'. Interestingly, Robert Putnam, the social researcher, says, '"*Schmoozing*" peaks among young adults, enters a long decline as family and community obligations press in, then rises again with retirement; while "*maching*" is relatively modest early in life, peaks in late middle age, and declines with retirement.' So most of us will do more 'schmoozing' when we are younger, more 'maching' in middle age and more 'schmoozing' as we get older.[11] But all the way through our lives we need to make sure we make a priority of 'schmoozing' – as it enables us to connect with people much more personally.

Step 3: Let's choose to empty ourselves for others

If we really want to be there for others, we will need to choose to 'empty' ourselves of our own thoughts and feelings so that we can actually create the psychic space within ourselves to respond compassionately to the joy and anguish of others. Some of us will need to 'empty' ourselves of *the games that we play* – silly games, like 'the piety game'. The object of this game is to convince ourselves and others of our virtue. It is not concerned about meeting people at their point of need. It is about using their needs to make them look bad, and/or make us look good, by comparison. It prevents any genuine encounter with others in which we can come together on the basis of our basic needs.

Others of us will need to 'empty' ourselves of *the goals that we aspire to* – serious goals, like 'proselytization'. Some of us have misinterpreted Christ's call to 'evangelization' as a call to 'proselytization', in which we treat people as faceless targets or 'potential trophies' for *us* to 'win'. In doing this, we do not treat people as people, but focus on our need to win, rather than their need for love. Christ advocated 'evangelization' – sharing the good news of God's radical commitment to a sacrificial concern for the welfare of the other – but Christ repudiated the kind of 'proselytization' that puts us instead of the other at the centre (Mt. 23:15). So, if we are to practise real compassion, like Christ did, we will need to 'empty' ourselves of any propensity we have to use others as a means to an end in accomplishing our self-interested goals.

All of us will need to 'empty' ourselves of *the images we have of ourselves* in relation to others. Paul says that Christ humbled himself and emptied himself in coming to earth. Many of us will need to empty ourselves of the image we have of ourselves as 'big' people who are more important than the 'little' people. As long as we are obsessed with the secret ambition of becoming a 'great' man or woman of God – the next Doctor King or Mother Theresa – we will never be able to respond compassionately to the ordinary men and women around us. Consequently, if we are to practise real compassion, like Christ did, we need to 'empty' ourselves of any 'big' ideas about ourselves, so that we can simply be there for others as their 'little' brother or sister.

Step 4: Let's not expect to be served, but to serve

Christ said, *'I have come not to be served, but to serve,'* to give my life to bring life to others. Thus Christ became a *'servant'* of the people. The word *'servant'* used to describe Christ is not a *'paid public servant'* but *'unpaid personal servant'*. So if we are to serve the people as Christ did, we need to be *'amateur'* servants of the people. The notion of an amateur comes from the Latin word *amator*, which in English means 'love' or, in this context, 'someone who does something for the love of it'. Hence, anyone who serves others for the love of it is an *amateur* at heart because their heart is on fire with a desire to help people meet their needs in any way they can. The amateur may be a professional, but is never a mercenary. An amateur will never sell their services to those who can pay the most. Rather, they provide their services – like Christ did – to those in most need, the people whom he referred to as the 'least of these'.

Step 5: Let's embrace the inevitable suffering involved

If we are going to have any hope of bringing life to people in our community, we too must be willing to pay the price by dying to ourselves in the midst of the inevitable frustrations, tensions, difficulties and conflicts that work in the community always entails. There is no easy option. If there were, Christ would have taken it. He was a Messiah, not a masochist. Christ took the hard path because it was the only path he could take that would lead to the practice of compassion. For those of us who would follow in his footsteps, there is no other way than to open our heart and risk suffering the heartache and the heartbreak of real involvement in peoples' lives.

But we need to monitor our capacity to give ourselves sacrificially to others, 'gladly', so that we do not do it simply out of a sense of duty. If our sole motivation is duty then our service may turn into bitterness with the passing of years in tears.

The ethos of compassion

Most attempts to bring about change in society have not come unstuck because the groups involved lacked the funds or the numbers; most came unstuck because of power struggles that caused the groups to self-destruct. The people involved lacked the power to change themselves, let alone their society. Hence, Christ taught that the most important single issue in bringing about change was for groups to discover an *ethos* that enabled them to transcend their selfishness, resolve their conflicts and deal with their issues in a way that did justice to everybody involved. Without that strong but gentle power, Christ said we should not even try to start working for change, lest we end up destroying the world that we are trying to create (Lk. 24:49). However, with that strong but gentle power, Christ said nothing on earth can stop us from building a better world – neither lack of funds, nor lack of numbers, nothing (Mt. 17:20). So when Christ sent his disciples out to build a better world, he imparted to them 'the power of the Spirit' (Jn. 20:21–22). This Spirit was 'not a spirit of timidity, but of power, characterized by discipline of self and compassion for others' (2 Tim. 1:7). So, as they opened themselves to this Spirit, it produced in them the strong but gentle power to control themselves and to love others as they loved themselves.

There are two ways of understanding power. Traditionally our dominant notion of power has been defined as *the ability to control other people*; it emphasizes the possibility of *bringing about change through coercion* – an approach that tries to make others change according to our agendas. While the traditional dominant notion of power means *taking control of our lives by taking control of others,* Jesus advocated a radical alternative – *taking control of our lives, not by taking control of others, but by taking control of ourselves.* This alternative emphasizes *bringing change by conversion* – an approach that does not try to make others change but tries to change ourselves, individually and collectively, in the light of a glorious agenda for justice. It breaks the control that others have over us and liberates us from our desire to control others. The dominant notion of power is popular because it often brings quick, dramatic results; however, it is characterized by short-term gains for some, and long-term losses for everyone else. Every violent revolution has sooner or later betrayed the people in whose name it fought its bloody war of liberation. The alternative notion of power is unpopular because it is usually a slow, unspectacular process but it is the only way for groups to effect real change.

Self-management is described as the 'fruit of the Spirit' (Gal. 5:22). The capacity to manage ourselves develops quite unobtrusively – indeed, as quietly as fruit growing on a tree – but it is far more significant than we might ordinarily imagine. Like a tiny seed, so small we can scarcely see it, the 'power of the Spirit' seems embarrassingly insignificant to begin with, yet grows into a capacity that is of tremendous significance in the end (Mt. 13:31–32). The capacity to control our own lives does not develop without opposition, but like a plant growing in the midst of weeds it grows strong in an environment that could easily destroy it (Mt. 13:24–30). How the seeds of transformation that bear the 'fruit of the Spirit' grow in a community is a mystery (Mk. 4:26–29). However, it is no secret that the seeds that bear the 'fruit of the Spirit' will not grow if we, whose lives constitute those seeds, do not give of ourselves for our community. 'Unless a seed falls into the ground and dies it produces nothing, but if it dies it will produce much fruit, that brings much life to others' (Jn. 12:24).

When Ange and I started to get involved in the West End, we began by trying as a couple to find at least one other person whom we could link up with so the three of us, as a group, could have the *personal and relational resources* that we needed. As it turned out, we found not one person but two, a couple who had moved into the area with the intention of getting involved in developing community in the locality themselves. We had *no external resources*, only the *internal resources* of our time, energy, knowledge, skills and love and the hope that we might be able to find a way of developing a Christlike life in the community. We sought a lifestyle that was characterized by the radical, non-violent, sacrificial compassion of Christ, and that was distinguished by commitment to love and to justice. We wanted to work from the bottom up to empower people, particularly the marginalized and disadvantaged so as to enable them to realize their potential, as men and women, made in the image of God. It sounds like a grand vision, but it was more a passion than a vision – because we didn't have a clue what to do.

We met regularly for prayer, asking that God would fill us with the strong but gentle 'power of the Spirit', so that we could respond to the plight of the people around us appropriately. Slowly but surely, the dream began to emerge and, as we discussed it with others, a few friends gathered round in the hope that together we could make this dream come true. We decided to call ourselves the West End 'Waiters Union' because we wanted to be 'waiters' in the West End. We didn't want to set agendas for people. We just wanted to be available, like 'waiters', to take people's orders, and to do what we could to help them. We particularly wanted to help to develop a sense of hospitality in the locality, so that all people, especially those who are usually displaced in areas like ours, could really begin to feel at home in the community.

There have never been many people in the Waiters Union. We started with two households 15 years ago and there aren't more than twenty households associated with us now. The Waiters Union is not a high profile group. None of the activities that we are involved in carry our name. They all carry the names of the groups that organize those activities which we contribute to – but do not control. As a result, a lot of people in our area may know us well as people, but may not even know that the group we are part of exists. This is fine, because the group exists to promote the community, not the group; and the group can function more effectively as a catalyst in the community if it is prepared to be more or less invisible, rather than attract attention to itself at the expense of others. However, we are not secretive. We welcome enquiries and answer questions as freely and as fully as we can. And we are inclusive. We invite anyone who is interested in our work to work with us, as partners together.

Through one group, we seek to promote the aspirations of the original inhabitants of our neighbourhood, for whom Musgrave Park, in the middle of the neighbourhood, is still 'sacred ground'. Through another group, we seek to support refugees by sponsoring their settlement and the settlement of their families, working through the anguish they go through as 'strangers in a strange land'. Last, but not least – though they are often considered 'last', and treated as 'least' by the powers that be – through a whole range of groups we seek to relate to the people in our community who are physically, intellectually and emotionally disabled – not as 'clients', nor as 'consumers', still less as 'users' but as 'our friends'!

None of the things we are doing seem that great. However, we constantly encourage one another to remember that true greatness is *not* in doing *big* things, but in doing *little* things with a *lot* of love over the *long* haul. And that, after all, is what the practice of compassion is all about.

Suggestions for reflection and action

Pray this prayer: 'Jesus, Saviour, may I know your love and make it known.' Ask the Spirit to put you in touch with the Spirit of Jesus. As you breathe in, say 'Jesus', and imagine taking in the love of Jesus. As you breathe out, say 'Saviour', and let go of all that is contrary to his love. Then, breathe in again, saying 'May I know your love,' and sense his love for you. And then, breathe out, saying 'May I make it known,' and sense his love for others. Take the prayer into your heart. And pray it by heart as much as you can.

Sit in silence and ask yourself the following questions. Take the time to write down your answers.

1. What community do I feel called to live in more (faith)fully?
2. How can I connect with the people in my community more effectively?
3. What do I need to empty myself of to make more time and space for others?
4. How can I best use my knowledge and skills to serve people in my community?
5. What can I gladly sacrifice today to show compassion to people in my community, that won't make me bitter if it is not reciprocated, appreciated or acknowledged?

Find a friend in your community you can talk to and share with them what you have been reading. Over a cup of tea have a chat and try to answer as many of the following questions as you can:

1. What is the difference between internal and external sources of power?
2. What are the predominant kinds of external power we usually rely on?
3. What are the problems associated with reliance upon external power?
4. What is the kind of internal power that Jesus says we should rely on?
5. What are the principles linked to the practice of the power of the Spirit?
6. What do you think it means to have power within us? Give examples.
7. What does it mean to have power with, rather than power over, people?
8. How can we encourage people to change without trying to control them?
9. How can we encourage people to learn to take control of their own lives?

14

How Can We Bring This Book to Life?

Jon Kuhrt

> The time is coming when matters will not be measured by the talent, or the ability, or by fine clothes, or by power to speak, or by being on platforms, or by listening to those upon platforms; but the time is coming when matters will be measured by those who have the truest faith, the deepest love, and the most sincere acts of obedience to their Lord and Saviour, and most devoted and strong imitation of his blessed example. (Lord Shaftesbury, 1867)[1]

The chapters in this book have been written by some of the best and most experienced people available in the area of integral mission. For me personally, many of the contributors of this book have been hugely influential. We hope you too have found the book stimulating, inspiring and challenging.

But all the effort that has gone into this book, the thinking and experience of the writers, the skill of the editors, the creativity of the publishing and production, will ultimately count for nothing – unless it contributes to action that makes a difference in our unjust and fractured world. The message of this book needs to come to life – for books, theology and social theory are not an end in themselves, and neither are MAs and PhDs, conferences and websites. These are all simply means that should equip us for the transforming mission that God calls each of us to.

Don't get me wrong, books and learning are important: to be carriers of God's message of love we have to understand the message and what it means for today. Strong roots are vital for a healthy tree. But they are not the tree itself. Theological learning and discussion have value, but only in terms of what they contribute to the mission of God in the world. This is why Christian knowledge should never puff us up, make us proud and give us delusions of grandeur. For knowledge must simply oil the works of love, equipping us to live and work for God's purposes in a world dying for transformation.

This closing chapter focuses on how we can bring the message of this book to life. How can we integrate our words and deeds and be about God's purposes in our communities, workplaces and churches? After looking briefly at what it means to be great in God's eyes and the Bible's emphasis on action, we will explore some practical pointers for our daily lives.

Jesus and the greatness of service

Jesus' life, his teaching and message will always be challenging for the religious. Why? Because all religion has an in-built tendency to be sidetracked by the peripheral aspects of God's message to humanity: the rules and rituals, the religious culture, liturgy and music, the politics and the platforms, the status of those who speak and teach. Those things that may have been established to carry the message end up overtaking the original intentions. Maintenance begins to dominate mission. Human *preferences* dominate God's *purposes*.

This is why Jesus attacked so strongly the religious leaders and scholars of his day, and exposed the hypocrisy of those who claimed to speak for God. Their great learning enabled them to claim status within the community, but their lives and the institutions they served did not reflect God's mission of love and redemption. Despite their claims, they simply did not reflect who God is. Of course, status was not just a problem for the religious elite. Even after all the teaching and example Jesus had shared with his ragamuffin bunch of disciples over the previous three years, at their very last meal together they still managed to have an argument over who was the greatest. Jesus said to them:

> The kings of the Gentiles lord it over them; and those who exercise authority over them call themselves Benefactors. But you are not to be like that. Instead, the greatest among you should be like the youngest, and the one who rules like the one who serves . . . I am among you as one who serves (Lk. 22:25–27).

In our culture today, the lure and love of status is as deep and as strong as ever, and this can be just as true in the church as it is in the world. This is a constant danger for Christian leaders, especially those who write books and speak at conferences, because the desire for recognition and status is corrosive; it's the opposite of the self-sacrifice and wholeness found in the kingdom of God.

Jesus could not be clearer: in God's eyes true greatness is found in the service of others.[2] Moreover, as James explicitly states, the kind of 'religion that God our Father accepts as pure and faultless' is 'to look after widows and orphans in their distress and to keep oneself from being polluted by the world' (1:27).

This is the way of Jesus: the way of service. And it was Jesus' faithfulness to this way that meant, 'God exalted him to the highest place and gave him the name that is above all other names' (Phil. 2:9).

Integrating words and actions

Micah's famous challenge to Israel in the eighth century BC was for the people not to indulge in meaningless sacrifices and offerings to God but to, 'act justly, and to love mercy and to walk humbly with your God' (6:8). Micah was talking to religious people but he wanted to strip off the religious baggage of ritualism and return to the core of what God wanted.

- To *act* justly
- To *love* mercy
- To *walk* humbly with God

All of these are intentional actions. God wants to change what we do.

The gap between rhetoric and action is a major theme throughout the Bible. As well as Micah, other prophets such as Isaiah, Jeremiah and Amos condemn religious activity that fails to change the way people act.[3] In the New Testament, there is a constant emphasis on producing 'fruit' in the teachings of John the Baptist, Jesus, Paul and John. After teaching that his true followers would be recognized by the fruit their lives produced, Jesus said, 'Not everyone who says to me "Lord, Lord", will enter the kingdom of heaven, but only he who does the will of my father who is in heaven' (Mt. 7:21). And as James bluntly puts it: 'Do not merely listen to the word and so deceive yourselves. Do what it says' (Jas. 1:22).

So the challenge of Jesus calls us to be people of action: activists for the kingdom of God. As we have seen in this book, he calls our church communities to be places of love and compassion, which publicly embody a different way of life and invite others to join. When our words and actions are integrated it produces a powerful witness. Thus it will be through activism for compassion and justice that an unbelieving world can most clearly hear our message.

It's time we got practical. How do we go about putting God's heart for justice and compassion into action?

Getting practical

We should be sceptical about books and programmes that tell us what to do, or give blueprints for success. There is no guide that is going to give us all the answers. Your response to the challenge of this book will be unique, based on your experiences, passion, skills and the context in which you live and work, and crucially the perspective of the local church that you are part of. But as you embark on the journey, we would recommend you think about the following . . .

Start where you are

Look at where God has put you day to day. Cherish the friends and contacts and opportunities that you already have. Explore what mission you live out in the places you know best and among the people you know. If you are busy at work, think about the opportunities that you have to make your workplace a more just place – for example, could you introduce fair trade coffee and explain why? If you are busy with young children, how can you demonstrate to your friends the compassion and love of God – could you offer support to another parent who is struggling? Wherever you are, the important thing is to start from there.

Remember the power of the ordinary

It is important to remember that it's ordinary people who get things started. So many of the best initiatives have emerged from humble beginnings where one or two people came together to start something to make the world a better place. As someone once said, 'Never believe that a small group of dedicated people can't change the world. It's the only thing that ever has.'

Some of my heroes are ordinary people, like Paul Burson, a bank manager who left his job to become a community worker for Shaftesbury on a tough estate on the South Coast. He recently retired after 12 years' work on the estate where his life has touched thousands and made a huge difference to that community. Paul is an ordinary Christian who has achieved the extraordinary for God.[4]

Journey with others

God calls us to his mission but he does not want us to be Lone Rangers. We are built for interdependence and community and it is so important to have friends with whom you can explore these issues and commit to pray, act and reflect together. If you are part of a small group at your church, could you run some sessions to discuss social justice? Or could you establish a group specifically to look at these issues for a set period? If you do not have these options, think about who would be a good person to ask to meet with regularly, to learn, pray and reflect together. It will make a huge difference to journey with others.

Grow strong roots

Too often, Christian social activism can depend on the overuse of certain popular passages in the Bible (like the Good Samaritan or the Sheep and the Goats). However, it's important to root our activism in strong theology, to see how social justice is at the core of the biblical message rather than confined to a few isolated stories. Like the root of a tree, good theology will nourish and sustain our activism, especially when winds of opposition blow. We need to remember that responding to the challenge of poverty and injustice is about being more biblical and more faithful, not less so.

Try to take your church with you

Often, if you are fired up with a passion for social justice, it is easy and understandable to get frustrated with those who do not share your passion. Disputes and debates will always be part of church life and this is good because we are talking about things that matter. But obviously it is not good when disputes lead to bitterness and broken relationships. It is important to try to communicate your passion in a way that others can grasp and engage with. Even if others are not in the same place as you now, they might be in the future and they might be your allies.

Wise tactics can often help others hear what you are saying and understand your passion. Framing your church's engagement in a national event such as Make Poverty History or Micah Challenge can sometimes help people connect with the message. Remember that action is a vital part of the reflection process so the best time to reflect theologically is often following attendance at a rally or a community project. Getting involved personally is often the best way that people become convinced of the importance of social justice.

Find common cause with other Christians and congregations

Activism for social justice is a great way to unite church congregations around a common purpose because it focuses outward on an issue or on the local community, rather than looking inward. So it's good to ask what justice groups or community projects are already operating in your local area. Is there an opportunity for you to collaborate with them rather than starting up something new?

Use the resources available!

Always remember that organizations like Shaftesbury, Tearfund, Faithworks and many others exist to help the church respond and engage with issues of justice and compassion; they can provide a number of resources to help small groups, Sunday services or youth groups, many of which are free. And, of course, the Micah Challenge website has numerous resources, which can be downloaded, and links to many other organizations that are committed to working for justice.

Just People? The Micah course

One such resource that Shaftesbury and Tearfund have recently developed is *Just People?* This is an accessible six-session course that is designed to help take churches on a journey of biblical reflection, action and learning. It is ideal for a church that wants to go deeper on these issues and can be adapted for different churches in different contexts. In an understandable and positive way, the course covers key areas of theology and mission and explores how the church can respond to issues of local community need but also wider issues of injustice. It also raises questions about how this kind of mission challenges the church and each of us. Using a range of methods, including teaching from the front, exercises and discussion, as well as homework and an integral 'day of action' the course aims to take people on a learning experience which equips them for integral mission.

Some great stories are already emerging from those who have completed the *Just People?* course. We have seen churches engage with campaigning for the first time, establish community projects, and get young people fired up for social action in their local communities. Individuals have decided to change jobs so they can better express the mission and values they want to live out. One attendee, who is from Zimbabwe, has set up a trust fund to support impoverished children in his home country. Another wrote to us saying:

> I was really keen to get stuck in to the *Just People?* course mainly because I'm really aware of my tendency to feel deeply moved, and yet in reality do hardly anything . . . What I loved most about the course was the way it's brought my faith alive at work. Across from me sits a feisty eco-warrior type who makes no secret of the fact she is "diametrically opposed" to my faith, which has sort of put a cap on any God-talk at work. But mentioning I was going to a course about social justice at church caught her interest in a different way. It opened up all sorts of conversations about how my faith impacts on the way I act and the choices I make, and about how church should try to model the radical character of Jesus. Following a chat where I mentioned about a Columbian guy whose uncle had just sold his entire coffee crop for a measly fiver, she ended up emailing the managing director of the entire company and asking why we don't make the switch to fair-trade where we can. He was actually really receptive to this, and agreed we could trial it in our part of the company, so all the tea and coffee is switching over, and we're looking into eco cleaning products too. It feels like the climate in the studio has changed, and there has been a bit of an awakening. It's made me realize that often it's as simple as choosing to speak up that can create a catalyst for change. I'm feeling more convinced that since God gave me hands and a voice and not just a mind, maybe I should start connecting them all more often.[5]

That is the challenge, responsibility and privilege of us all.

Appendix

African Monitor

African Monitor is an independent African body, which acts as a catalyst to monitor development funding commitments, delivery and impact on the grassroots, and to bring strong additional African voices to the development agenda. This pan-African not-for-profit body harnesses the voice of the continent's civil society in monitoring and promoting the effective implementation of promises made by the international community, and Africa's own governments, for the continent's development.
www.africanmonitor.org

Global Call to Action against Poverty (GCAP)

The Global Call to Action against Poverty is a global alliance of trade unions, community groups, faith groups and campaigners working together across more than a hundred national platforms, calling for action from the world's leaders to meet their promises to end poverty and inequality. Micah Challenge is a member of GCAP.
www.whiteband.org

Just People? The Micah course

As part of Micah Challenge UK, Tearfund and Shaftesbury have developed a course for churches to help them discover

how tackling poverty and pursuing justice, both locally and globally, are at the heart of Christian mission. This accessible six-session course can be adapted in different contexts.
www.micahchallenge.org.uk

Micahmorphosis

This Micah Challenge youth site describes 'Micahmorphosis' as an event by which one is transformed from within into an ardent advocate for justice and mercy; an internal transformation creating a new being which routinely acts and evolves with the goal of ending poverty and injustice in our world.
www.micahmorphosis.org

Micah Network

Micah Network is a group of 300 Christian relief, development and justice organizations from 75 countries. These organizations appreciate the opportunity that Micah Network provides for Northern and Southern based agencies to join together as equals. Micah Network was formed in 1999 with the aims to:

1. strengthen the capacity of participating agencies to make a biblically shaped response to the needs of the poor and oppressed;
2. speak strongly and effectively regarding the nature of the mission of the church to proclaim and demonstrate the love of Christ to a world in need;
3. prophetically call upon and influence the leaders and decision-makers of societies to 'maintain the rights of the poor and oppressed and rescue the weak and needy'.

www.micahnetwork.org

The Millennium Declaration

The Millennium Development Goals are derived from the broader 'Millennium Declaration' that was signed in 2000 by all UN member states. This Declaration reaffirms values including equality, mutual respect and shared responsibility for the condition of all peoples. It relates the Millennium Development Goals to an even broader context, including peace and human rights.
www.un.org/millennium/declaration/ares552e.htm

The Millennium Development Goals (MDGs)

During the Millennium Summit held in New York in September 2000, all 189 UN Member States adopted the Millennium Declaration, which contained a group of goals and targets that have since become known as the Millennium Development Goals. These goals, working together, aim to halve poverty by 2015. The Goals include measurable, time-bound targets addressing poverty and hunger, education, maternal and child health, the prevalence of diseases including HIV/AIDS, gender equality, the environment, debt, trade justice and aid.
www.un.org/millenniumgoals/

Goal 1: Eradicate extreme poverty and hunger

- Halve, between 1990 and 2015, the proportion of people whose income is less than one dollar a day.
- Halve, between 1990 and 2015, the proportion of people who suffer from hunger.

Goal 2: Achieve universal primary education

- Ensure that, by 2015, children everywhere, boys and girls alike, will be able to complete a full course of primary schooling.

Goal 3: Promote gender equality and empower women

- Eliminate gender disparity in primary and secondary education, preferably by 2005, and to all levels of education no later than 2015.

Goal 4: Reduce child mortality

- Reduce by two-thirds, between 1990 and 2015, the number of children 5 years old or younger who die from preventable illnesses.

Goal 5: Improve maternal health

- Reduce by three-quarters, between 1990 and 2015, the number of women who die giving birth.

Goal 6: Combat HIV/AIDS, malaria and other diseases

- Have halted by 2015 and begun to reverse the spread of HIV/AIDS.
- Have halted by 2015 and begun to reverse the incidence of malaria and other major diseases.

Goal 7: Ensure environmental sustainability

- Integrate the principles of sustainable development into country policies and programmes and reverse the loss of environmental resources.
- Halve, by 2015, the proportion of people without sustainable access to safe drinking water and basic sanitation.
- By 2020, to have achieved a significant improvement in the lives of at least 100 million slum dwellers.

Goal 8: Develop a global partnership for development (trade/aid/debt)

- Develop further an open, rule-based, predictable, non-discriminatory trading and financial system.

- Address the Special Needs of the Least Developed Countries (LDC) [Includes: tariff and quota free access for LDC exports; enhanced programme of debt relief for HIPC and cancellation of official bilateral debt; and more generous ODA (Overseas Development Assistance) for countries committed to poverty reduction].
- Address the Special Needs of landlocked countries and small island developing States (through the Programme of Action for the Sustainable Development of Small Island Developing States and the outcome of the 22nd special session of the General Assembly).
- Deal comprehensively with the debt problems of developing countries through national and international measures in order to make debt sustainable in the long term.
- In cooperation with developing countries, develop and implement strategies for decent and productive work for youth.
- In cooperation with pharmaceutical companies, provide access to affordable, essential drugs in developing countries.
- In cooperation with the private sector, make available the benefits of new technologies, especially information and communications.

Endnotes

1. Micah Challenge: The Story So Far

[1] Address at Micah Challenge Launch, 15 October 2004.
[2] Isobel was Tearfund staff and co-founder of J2000.
[3] Gordon Brown, address to the J2000 final rally, 2 December 2000 at Emmanuel Evangelical Centre.
[4] Letter from Joel Edwards to Gordon Brown, 11 January 2001.
[5] Resolution of the Assembly of the World Evangelical Fellowship, Kuala Lumpur, 10 May 2001.
[6] Micah Declaration on Integral Mission, 27 September 2001.
[7] Micah Declaration, Oxford, 27 September 2001.
[8] Letter from Joel Edwards to Stephen Rand, 18 January 2002; Correspondence WEA and Tearfund UK April 2002.
[9] 'Releasing the global strength of evangelicalism on behalf of the poor', Stephen Rand, 5 March 2002.
[10] Meeting, High Leigh Conference Centre, 2–4 May 2001.
[11] At this meeting Gary Edmonds was appointed as the WEA International Secretary.
[12] Letter to Micah Network from Steve Bradbury, 8 October 2002.
[13] Shalom 20–15 organizational structure, Doug Balfour, December 2002.
[14] Minutes, First Global Poverty Campaign, Seattle 24–25 February 2003.
[15] Ibid.
[16] Ibid.
[17] Steve Bradbury CEO Tear Oz represented Micah Network and Gary Edmonds international director WEA.
[18] Summary of agreements and actions arising from Global Poverty Campaign meeting, Seattle, February 24–25 2003.
[19] Ibid.
[20] Introducing the Micah Network, November 2001.

21 Amos 5:24.
22 Mic. 6:8.
23 Report on discussions at the Micah Challenge Council Meeting, Queretaro, September 27–28 2003.
24 Micah Challenge, 'Mobilizing Christians Against Poverty' information sheet 2005.
25 Both drafts submitted by Joel Edwards Evangelical Alliance UK and Gustavo Crocker, World Relief, USA.
26 Email from Vinoth Ramachandra, 28h October 2003.
27 One of the earliest guidelines for establishing national campaigns was produced 29 April 2004.
28 On 10 May four representatives from Tearfund UK and Evangelical Alliance received a positive hearing.
29 Tearfund Australia & UK have done a great deal in supporting Micah Challenge with support from other charitable bodies.
30 The current understanding is that each national campaign should contribute a third of their income to the secretariat costs.
31 Micah Challenge Council, 27–28 May 2003.
32 Micah Sunday takes place mid October and promotes the work of Micah Challenge in local churches and communities.
33 Meeting with Sylvia Mwichuli, Deputy director UNDP, 3 December 2006.
34 Isa. 58:10.

3. Walk Humbly with Your God

1 Cited in Duncan B. Forrester, *On Human Worth*, p. 115.
2 George Barna, *Growing True Disciples*, pp. 67–68, 77.
3 C. S. Lewis, *The Screwtape Letters*, pp. 71–72.
4 Ibid., pp. 72–73.
5 John Owen, *Overcoming Sin and Temptation*, p. 282.
6 Leslie C. Allen, *The Books of Joel, Obadiah, Jonah and Micah*, p. 371.
7 Matthew Henry, *An Exposition of the Old and New Testament*, comment on Ex. 3:11–15.
8 Thomas Watson, *A Body of Practical Divinity*, p. 16.
9 C. J. Mahaney, *Humility*, p. 80.
10 Cited in Ibid., 66.
11 John Stott, *The Message of Galatians*, p. 179.
12 See Emil Brunner, *The Mediator*, p. 435.
13 See Tim Chester and Steve Timmis, *Total Church*, chapter 4.
14 See Tim Chester, *Good News to the Poor*, chapters 5–6.

4. New Heavens and New Earth

1 Edward Donnelly, *Heaven and Hell*, p. 112.
2 John Colwell, *Called to One Hope*, p. xi.
3 An important point to be considered by all those enamoured with the *Left Behind* series of novels.
4 Incidentally, this is not to deny the omnipresence of God, but it is to say that though God is present everywhere, he is not present everywhere in unveiled fashion. His presence is cloaked, as it were. The *presence* or *shekinah* that brings God's blessing, is a presence without hindrance.
5 richarddawkins.net/article,1212,Richard-Dawkins-and-Alister-McGrath,Root-of-All-Evil-Uncut-Interviews.
6 N. T. Wright, *The Challenge of Jesus*, p. 21.
7 Steve Chalke and Alan Mann, *The Lost Message of Jesus*, pp. 28, 29.
8 Wright, *Challenge*, pp. 23, 24.
9 The transfiguration is the exception to this, and see also Jn. 17:5.
10 Wright, *Challenge*, p. 34.
11 Karl Martin of Morningside Baptist Church, Edinburgh.
12 I expand on this theme in my book, *Postmodernism and the Ethics of Theological Knowledge*.
13 Adrio Konig, *The Eclipse of Christ in Eschatology*, p. 241.
14 NB the references in Rev. 7:16 to hunger, thirst and destitution may strengthen this point.

5. Divine Power in Human Weakness

1 M. Welker, *God the Spirit*, p. 333; C. H. Pinnock, *Flame of Love*, p. 147.
2 D. A. Black, *Paul, Apostle of Weakness*, pp. 163–181.
3 N. T. Wright, 'Coming home to St Paul?'.
4 N. T. Wright, 'Paul's Gospel and Caesar's Empire'; S. R. F. Price, *Rituals and Power*, pp. 233–248; J. R. Harrison, 'Paul, Eschatology and the Augustan Age of Grace'.
5 M. E. Clark, 'Images and Concepts of Hope in the Imperial Cult', p. 42.
6 B. Winter, 'Roman Law and Society in Romans 12–15', pp. 78–79.
7 P. Oakes, *Philippians*, p. 73.
8 N. Elliott, 'The Anti-Imperial Message of the Cross', p. 182.
9 Rom. 5:12–21. D. Georgi, 'God Turned Upside Down', p. 153.
10 Harrison, 'Paul, Eschatology and the Augustan Age of Grace'.

11 Oakes, *Philippians*, pp. 149–150.
12 C. H. Pinnock, *Most Moved Mover*, p. 131.
13 Isa. 24:1–13, Hos. 4:1–3.
14 Philo, *Op.* 26:79–80. Other Jewish authors: e.g. *Jub.* 23:9–25, *T.Jud.* 23:3, *Sib.Or.* 3:265–280.
15 Deut. 28:38–42; Lev. 26:34f,43f; Isa. 24:4–6; Hos. 4:1–3.
16 C. Uehlinger, 'The Cry of the Earth?'; S. C. Keesmaat, *Paul and his Story*, pp. 103–106.
17 e.g. Ps. 38:9; Job 23:2.
18 Ps. 12:5; cf. Ex. 2:24.
19 Welker, *God the Spirit*, pp. 52–65.
20 N. Wolterstorff, *Lament for a Son*, pp. 85–86.
21 W. Brueggemann, *The Prophetic Imagination*, p. 57.
22 Welker, *God the Spirit*, pp. 166–171; e.g. Jer. 31:33; Isa. 32.
23 Pinnock, *Flame of Love*, p. 179. Similarly, R. B. Hays, *The Moral Vision of the New Testament*, p. 26.
24 S. C. Keesmaat, 'Exodus and the Intertextual Transformation of Tradition in Romans 8:14–30', p. 44.
25 Pinnock, *Most Moved Mover*, p. 178; Welker, *God the Spirit*, pp. 262–263; J. Moltmann, *The Church in the Power of the Spirit*, pp. 60–65.
26 B. Byrne, 'Interpreting Romans', p. 241.
27 R. Aasgaard, '"Role Ethics" in Paul', p. 529. Cf. P. F. Esler, *Conflict and Identity in Romans*, p. 248.
28 Keesmaat, *Paul and His Story*, pp. 84–87; Pinnock, *Most Moved Mover*, pp. 135, 168; Hays, *Moral Vision*, p. 304.
29 Paul quotes a lament psalm (Ps. 44:22) in Rom. 8:36.
30 N. T. Wright, *Evil and the Justice of God*, p. 98.
31 J. H. Yoder, *The Politics of Jesus*, pp. 207–209; Hays, *Moral Vision*, p. 304.
32 Clark, 'Images and Concepts of Hope', p. 40.
33 Harrison, 'Paul, Eschatology and the Augustan Age of Grace', p. 87.
34 Pinnock, *Flame of Love*, p. 147.
35 Keesmaat, *Paul and His Story*, p. 132.
36 Welker, *God the Spirit*, pp. 245, 218.
37 e.g. Isa. 43:19, 65:17; Ezek. 37:11–14.
38 Hays, *Moral Vision*, pp. 338–339; Esler, *Conflict and Identity in Romans*, p. 337.
39 J. M. Washington, (ed.) *Testament of Hope*, pp. 135, 213, 297.
40 Wright, 'Paul's Gospel', p. 162; 'Coming home to St Paul?', p. 404.

6. The Kingdom of God and the Mission of the Church

1 I am borrowing this description of the church from Howard Snyder, *The Community of the King*.
2 Walter C. Kaiser Jr, *Toward an Old Testament Theology*, p. 143.
3 José Luis Sicre, *Profetismo en Israel*, p. 486.
4 Sigmund Mowinckel, *El que ha de venire*, p. 8.
5 Sicre, *Profetismo en Israel*, p. 186, seems to agree with Mowinckel. According to him, 'The word "messiah" is never used in the Old Testament books in the sense of the definitive saviour of the last days' (my translation).
6 Walter Brueggemann, *Theology of the Old Testament*, p. 616.
7 The NIV and other Bible versions do not translate 'the kingdom of God is *among* you' but 'the kingdom of God is *within* you.' In line with this reading, the footnote on Lk. 17:21 in the *NIV Study Bible* offers the following comment: '*the kingdom of God is within you*'. Probably indicating that the kingdom is spiritual and internal (Mt. 23:26) rather than physical and external (cf. Jn 18:36).' Although the rendering 'within' is grammatically possible, it should be discarded on two accounts: (a) It makes no sense when one takes into account that Jesus was addressing the Pharisees. How could he say that the kingdom of God was within them? (b) There is no evidence to support the view of the kingdom of God as 'spiritual and internal'. As Joachim Jeremias (*New Testament Theology*, p. 101) has observed, 'Neither in Judaism nor elsewhere in the New Testament do we find the reign of God as something indwelling in men, to be found, say, in the heart; such spiritualistic understanding is ruled out both for Jesus and for the early Christian tradition.' The NIV comment belongs to the category of what N. T. Wright (*Jesus and the Victory of God*, p. 290) in another context calls 'retrojections into the first century of a nineteenth-century Romantic ideal of religion in which outward things are bad and inward things good.'
8 Wright, *Jesus and the Victory of God*.
9 Brueggemann, *Theology of the Old Testament*, p. 208. Interestingly enough, Lk. 4:18–19 quotes Isa. 61:1–2 but with an addition and a subtraction, both of which are significant in light of Jesus' ministry. The addition is of a phrase taken from Isa. 58:6: 'to set the oppressed free.' The subtraction is of a phrase that in Isa. 61:2 follows the reference to the year of the Lord's favour: 'and the day of vengeance of our God.'

[10] I am borrowing this expression from Donald Kraybill, *The Upside-Down Kingdom*.
[11] Wright, *Jesus and the Victory of God*.

8. Poverty, Sin and Social Structures

[1] Adapted with permission from Ronald J. Sider, 'Justice, Human Rights and Government', pp. 171–174.
[2] For a longer discussion, see Ronald J. Sider, *Rich Christians in an Age of Hunger*, pp. 121–132.
[3] Adapted by permission from Sider, *Rich Christians In An Age of Hunger*, pp. 107–117. All rights reserved.
[4] *Sollicitudo Rei Socialis*, 30 December 1987, Sect. 36.
[5] Adapted by permission from Sider, *Rich Christians In An Age of Hunger*, pp. 133–182. All rights reserved.
[6] FAO, *The State of Food Insecurity in the World 2003*, p. 31.
[7] UNDP, *Human Development Report 2002*, p. 2.
[8] Michael P. Todaro and Stephen C. Smith, *Economic Development*, p. 544.
[9] World Bank, *World Development Indicators 2003*, p. 329.
[10] Ibid., p. 319.
[11] Todaro and Smith, *Economic Development*, p. 539.
[12] Ibid., p. 649.
[13] UNDP, *Human Development Report 2003*, p. 155.
[14] FAO, *The State of Food Insecurity in the World 2003*, p. 21.
[15] Quoted in Bread for the World Institute, *Hunger 1995*, p. 67.

9. Justice and Approaches to Social Change

[1] Walter Brueggemann, *The Land*, pp. 13-14.

10. The Tipping Point: Faith and Global Poverty

[1] This chapter has been adapted from Jim Wallis, *God's Politics*.
[2] Chancellor of the Exchequer Gordon Brown, speech at a conference on 'Making Globalization Work for All – The Challenge of Delivering the Monterrey Consensus,' 16 February 2004.
[3] Charlotte Denny and Larry Elliott, 'Bank Works for Change, Its Chief Insists,' *Guardian*, 27 September 2000.

[4] Romilly Greenhill and Elena Sisti, 'Real Progress Report on HIPC', Jubilee Research/New Economics Foundation, September 2003.
[5] Equal Exchange: www.equalexchange.com.
[6] Ten Thousand Villages: tenthousandvillages.com.
[7] International Fair Trade Association: www.ifat.org.
[8] Jim Wallis, interview with Clare Short, 'Lies Leaders Tell', *Sojourners* (January 2004), p. 21.
[9] World Vision on HIV/AIDS.
[10] Kofi Annan, interview with BBC, 28 November 2003, news.bbc.co.uk/2/hi/africa/3245014.stm.
[11] Adam Taylor, 'The Devil's in the Details', *Sojourners* (May–June 2003), p. 18.
[12] Ibid.

11. Poverty: What Does It Look Like and Can We Rise to the Challenge?

[1] This is a paraphrase of an analogy used by Jim Wallis.
[2] e.g. Minor Prophets, Beatitudes and Lk. 6:20.
[3] 1 Tim. 6:8–10.
[4] Lk. 16:13.
[5] Gen. 1:26ff.
[6] Jas. 2.
[7] Mk. 14:7.
[8] Stewardship as set out in Corinthians and the Covenants of the Old Testament, particularly Gen. 12. Consider this startling reminder:

> You eat to excess; Christ eats not even what he needs. You eat a variety of cakes; he eats not even a piece of dried bread. You drink fine Thracian wine, but on him you have not bestowed as much as a cup of cold water. You lie on a soft and embroidered bed; but he is perishing in the cold . . . You live in luxury on things that properly belong to him. Why, were you the guardian of a child and, having taken control of his estate, you neglected him in his extreme need, you would have ten thousand accusers and you would suffer the punishment set by law. At the moment, you have taken possession of the resources that belong to Christ and you consume them aimlessly. Don't you realize that you are going to be held accountable. (John Chrysostom, *On Matthew: Homily 48:8* cited by Walsh and Langan, 'Patristic Social Consciousness', p. 130.

9 Lk. 4:16.
10 Lk. 11.
11 Isa. 65; Rom. 8; Rev. 21, 22.
12 The idea of Material Poverty, Spiritual Poverty and Civic Poverty is taken from Jim Wallis, *Faithworks*, pp. 51–70.
13 See Jim Wallis, *The Call to Conversion*, p. 57.
14 As quoted by Fr Mathew Kariapuram SDB, research scholar in the Department of Christian Studies at Madras University (www.missionsocieties.org.uk).
15 Ibid.
16 See Mt. 19:24 for the original idea from Jesus himself.
17 For more information on poverty in the UK visit www.shelter.org.uk and www.poverty.org.uk from the New Policy Institute.
18 As quoted in Pope Paul VI lecture, 2005. For information see www.cafod.org.uk.
19 'The Salvation Army and the Poor: Voices of Our Global Family. Conclusions of the Task Force on the Internet/Lotus Notes Poverty Summit' available from www.salvationist.org.
20 Phillip Needham, in 'Towards a Reintegration of the Salvationist Mission'.
21 Oscar Romero, *Homily*, 18 February 1979.
22 See a helpful article 'What Evangelicals have done to Sin' by Jon Kuhrt. Available at www.fulcrum-anglican.org.uk.

12. 'This Stuff Works': Specific Action to Combat Poverty

1 A broader consideration of the impact that Christians and churches can have on the big issues confronting us today, including poverty and climate change, is contained in my *Louder Than Words*. By kind permission of the publishers this chapter draws upon sections of that book.
2 Ed Newell and Sabina Alkire, *What Can One Person Do?* This book is the perfect antidote to any feelings of impotence induced by the question it seeks to address!
3 Speech at the Christian Socialist Movement 'Faith in Politics' event, London, 2001.
4 See for example Wallis, *God's Politics*, pp. 3–40.
5 Paul Vallely, 'Not just one brief, shining moment', *The Tablet*, 1 July 2006, p. 6.

[6] *The Guardian 'G2'*, 28 December 2005, p. 5.

[7] While we may prefer working with agencies with a faith basis wherever possible, the issues we confront are too important for us to adopt a 'purist' or 'isolationist' mentality.

[8] See, for example, Clare Short, speech to the Assembly of the United Reformed Church, Portsmouth, July 2003. Available at hotline2003.urc.org.uk/content/clare-short-full.htm.

[9] Geraldine Bedell, *Make Poverty History*, p. 30.

[10] Tearfund, *Feeling the Heat*, 2006; Christian Aid, *The Climate of Poverty: facts, fears and hope*, 2006.

13. The Practice of Compassion

[1] David Benner, *Surrender to Love*, p. 40.

[2] 1 Jn. 4:18.

[3] Benner, *Surrender to Love*, pp. 84–85.

[4] Wayne Muller, *Legacy Of The Heart*, p. 27.

[5] Jn. 20:19–20.

[6] Phil. 2:6–8.

[7] Robert Putnam, *Bowling Alone*, p. 205.

[8] Ibid., pp. 212–213.

[9] Ibid., pp. 222, 237, 242, 228. There is still a great deal of debate about the value of choosing to live our lives in cyberspace. The best-case scenario is that the net will turn out to be like the telephone, which reinforces the community networks that we are developing. The worst-case scenario is that the net will turn out to be like television, which adversely affects the development of community networks. Even if the net turns out to be like the telephone rather than the television, the latest evidence would seem to suggest that at best the net will complement, but not replace, communities in real time and place.

[10] Ibid., pp. 23, 136.

[11] Ibid., pp. 92–94.

14. How Can We Bring This Book to Life?

[1] Ragged School Union meeting, April 1867. Quoted from an unpublished paper 'Shaftesbury and the Ragged School Union' by Richard Turnbull (April 1995).

[2] Jesus speaks of the greatness of service in Mt. 20:26 and 23:11 and in Mk. 9:35 and 10:43.

[3] Isa. 1:13–17; Jer. 7:2–8; Mic. 3:1–2; Amos 5:11–15, 21–25.

[4] You can read more about Paul's work in the booklet *Mystery in the Ordinary: the story of the Shaftesbury Centre in Eastbourne.* It is available from Grooms-Shaftesbury's Community Mission team (www.grooms-shaftesbury.org.uk).

[5] Kirsty Reilly attended the *Just People*? course at St Mary's, Bryanston Square, London. For information on the *Just People* course, see www.micahchallenge.org.uk.

Bibliography

Aasgaard, R., '"Role Ethics" in Paul: The Significance of the Sibling Role for Paul's Ethical Thinking', *New Testament Studies* 48 (2002), 513–530.

Allen, L. C., *The Books of Joel, Obadiah, Jonah and Micah*, New International Commentary, OT (Grand Rapids: Eerdmans, 1976).

Andrews, D., *Compassionate Community Work* (Carlisle, Micah Network and Piquant Editions, 2006).

Barna, G., *Growing True Disciples: New Strategies for Producing Genuine Followers of Christ* (Colorado Springs: WaterBrook Press, 2001).

Bedell, G., *Make Poverty History: How You Can Help Defeat World Poverty in Seven Easy Steps* (London: Penguin, 2005).

Benner, D., *Surrender to Love* (Downers Grove: IVP, 2002).

Black, D. A., *Paul, Apostle of Weakness. Astheneia and its Cognates in Pauline Literature* (New York: Peter Lang, 1984).

Bradstock, A., *Louder Than Words: Action for the 21st-century Church* (London: Darton, Longman & Todd, 2007).

Bread for the World Institute, *Hunger 1995: Causes of Hunger* (Washington DC: Bread for the World Institute, 1995).

Brueggemann, W., *The Land* (Philadelphia, Fortress Press, 1997).

—, *The Prophetic Imagination* (Minneapolis: Fortress, 2001).

—, *Theology of the Old Testament: Testimony, Dispute, Advocacy* (Minneapolis: Fortress Press, 1997).

Brunner, E., *The Mediator* (Cambridge: Lutterworth, 1934).

Byrne, B., 'Interpreting Romans Theologically in a Post-"New Perspective" Perspective', *Harvard Theological Review* 94.3 (2001), 227–242.

Chalke, S. and Mann, A., *The Lost Message of Jesus* (Grand Rapids: Zondervan, 2003).

Chester, T., *Good News to the Poor* (Nottingham: IVP, 2004).

— and Timmis, S., *Total Church* (Nottingham: IVP, 2007).

Clark, M. E., 'Images and Concepts of Hope in the Imperial Cult', in K. H. Richards (ed.), *Society of Biblical Literature Seminar Papers* (Chico, CA: Scholars Press, 1982), pp. 39–43.

Colwell, John (ed.), *Called to One Hope: Perspectives on Life to Come* (Carlisle: Paternoster, 2000).

Donnelly, E., *Heaven and Hell* (Glasgow: Banner of Truth Trust, 2001).

Elliott, N., 'The Anti-Imperial Message of the Cross', in R. A. Horsley (ed.), *Paul and Empire. Religion and Power in Roman Imperial Society* (Harrisburg: Trinity Press International, 1997), pp. 167–183.

Esler, P. F., *Conflict and Identity in Romans. The Social Setting of Paul's Letter* (Minneapolis: Fortress, 2003).

Food and Agriculture Organization (FAO), *The State of Food Insecurity in the World 2003* (Rome: FAO, 2003).

Forrester, D. B., *On Human Worth: A Christian Vindication of Equality* (London: SCM Press, 2001).

Georgi, D., 'God Turned Upside Down', in R. A. Horsley (ed.), *Paul and Empire. Religion and Power in Roman Imperial Society* (Harrisburg: Trinity Press International, 1997), pp. 148–157.

Harrison, J. R., 'Paul, Eschatology and the Augustan Age of Grace', *Tyndale Bulletin* 50.1 (1999), 79–91.

Hays, R. B., *The Moral Vision of the New Testament. A Contemporary Introduction to New Testament Ethics* (Edinburgh: T&T Clark, 1996).

Henry, M., *An Exposition of the Old and New Testament* (London: John Nisbet, 1903).

Jeremias, J., *New Testament Theology: The Proclamation of Jesus* (London: SCM Press, 1971).

Kaiser Jr, W. C., *Toward an Old Testament Theology* (Grand Rapids: Zondervan, 1978).

Keesmaat, S. C., 'Exodus and the Intertextual Transformation of Tradition in Romans 8:14–30', *Journal for the Study of the NT* 54 (1994), 29–56.

—, *Paul and his Story. (Re)Interpreting the Exodus Tradition*, JSNT Supplement 181 (Sheffield: Sheffield Academic Press, 1999).
Konig, A., *The Eclipse of Christ in Eschatology* (Grand Rapids: Eerdmans, 1989).
Kraybill, D., *The Upside-Down Kingdom* (Scottdale, PA: Herald Press, 1978).
Lewis, C. S., *The Screwtape Letters* (London: Geoffrey Bles, 1942).
Mahaney, C. J., *Humility: True Greatness* (Portland: Multnomah, 2005).
Moltmann, J., *The Church in the Power of the Spirit. A Contribution to Messianic Ecclesiology* (London: SCM Press, 1977).
Mowinckel, S., *El que ha de venire: Mesianismo y Mesías* (Madrid: Ediciones Fax, [1951] 1975).
Muller, W., *Legacy Of The Heart* (New York: Simon & Schuster, 1992).
Needham, P., 'Towards a Reintegration of the Salvationist Mission' in J. D. Waldron (ed.), *Creed and Deed: Toward a Christian theology of social services in The Salvation Army* (Oakville, Ontario: The Salvation Army, 1986).
Newell, E. and Alkire S., *What Can One Person Do?* (London: Darton Longman & Todd, 2005).
Oakes, P., *Philippians. From People to Letter*, SNT SMS 110 (Cambridge: Cambridge University Press, 2001).
Owen, J., *Overcoming Sin and Temptation*, eds Kelly M. Kapic and Justin Taylor (Wheaton, IL: Crossway, 2006).
Pinnock, C. H., *Flame of Love: A Theology of the Holy Spirit* (Downers Grove: Intervarsity, 1996).
—, *Most Moved Mover. A Theology of God's Openness* (Carlisle: Paternoster, 2001).
Price, S. R. F., *Rituals and Power. The Roman Imperial Cult in Asia Minor* (Cambridge: Cambridge University Press, 1984).
Putnam, R., *Bowling Alone* (New York, Simon & Schuster, 2001).
Sicre, J. L., *Profetismo en Israel: El profeta, los profetas, el mensaje* (Estella (Navarra): Editorial Verbo Divino, 1992).
Sider, R. J., 'Justice, Human Rights and Government', in Ronald J. Sider and Diane Knippers, *Toward an Evangelical Public Policy* (Grand Rapids: Baker Books, 2005), pp. 163–193.

—, *Rich Christians in an Age of Hunger*, 5th edition (Nashville: Word Publishing, 2005).
Snyder, H. A., *The Community of the King*. 2nd edition (Downers Grove, IL: InterVarsity Press, 2004).
Stott, J., *The Message of Galatians* (London: IVP, 1968).
Thacker, J., *Postmodernism and the Ethics of Theological Knowledge* (Aldershot: Ashgate, 2007).
Todaro, M. P. and Smith, S. C., *Economic Development*, 8th edition (Boston: Addison Wesley, 2003).
Uehlinger, C., 'The Cry of the Earth? Biblical perspectives on ecology and violence', *Concilium* 1995/5, 41–58.
United Nations Development Programme (UNDP), *The Human Development Report 2002* (New York: UNDP, 2002).
Wallis, J., *The Call to Conversion* (Abingdon: Marston Books, 2006).
—, *Faithworks: Lessons on Spirituality and Social Action* (London: SPCK, 2002).
—, *God's Politics* (San Francisco: HarperSanFrancisco, 2005).
Walsh, W. J. and Langan, J. P., 'Patristic Social Consciousness – The Church and the Poor', in John G. Haughey (ed.), *The Faith that does Justice: Examining the Christian Sources for Social Change* (New York: Paulist Press, 1977), pp. 113–151.
Washington, J. M. (ed.), *Testament of Hope. The essential writings and speeches of Martin Luther King, Jr.* (San Francisco: Harper Collins, 1986).
Watson, T., *A Body of Practical Divinity* (Edinburgh: Archibald Fullarton, 1832).
Welker, M., *God the Spirit* (Minneapolis: Fortress, 1994).
Winter, B., 'Roman Law and Society in Romans 12–15', in P. Oakes (ed.), *Rome in the Bible and the Early Church* (Carlisle: Paternoster, 2002), pp. 67–102.
Wolterstorff, N., *Lament for a Son* (Grand Rapids: Eerdmans, 1987).
World Bank, *World Development Indicators 2003* (Washington DC: World Bank, 2003).
Wright, N. T., *The Challenge of Jesus* (London: SPCK, 2000).
—, 'Coming home to St Paul? Reading Romans a hundred years after Charles Gore', *Scottish Journal of Theology* 55.4 (2002), 392–407.

—, *Evil and the Justice of God* (Downers Grove: IVP, 2006).
—, *Jesus and the Victory of God* (Minneapolis: Fortress Press, 1996).
—, 'Paul's Gospel and Caesar's Empire', in R. A. Horsley (ed.), *Paul and Politics. Ekklesia, Israel, Imperium, Interpretation. Essays in Honor of Krister Stendahl* (Harrisburg: Trinity Press International, 2000), pp. 160-183.
Yoder, J. H., *The Politics of Jesus* (Carlisle: Paternoster, 1994).

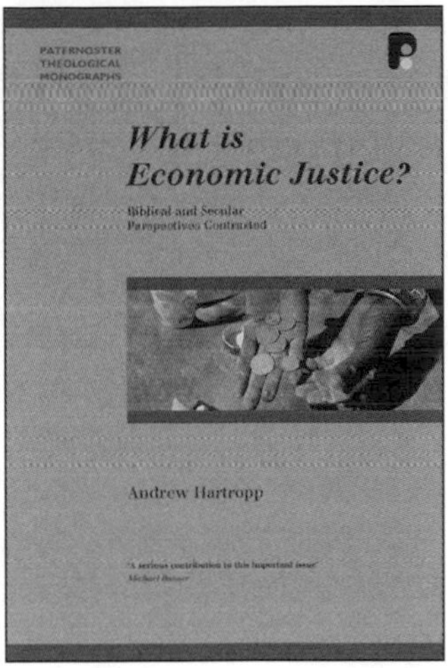

What is Economic Justice?

Biblical and Secular Perspectives Contrasted

Andrew Hartropp

Although the language of 'economic justice' is used right across the political spectrum today, there is no consensus about what it means. Secular perspectives are in deep and confusing disarray. This is of little help to the poor or the rich. Can the Bible do better? Most certainly, according to this book. It argues that a biblically-rooted account of justice in economic life has three great strengths.

First, it is harmonious: although there are a number of strands to a scriptural perspective on economic justice, they are clearly woven together, and they find their unity in the person of the God. Secondly, it is substantial: a biblically-rooted understanding of economic justice is able to engage thoroughly and critically with leading secular perspectives. Thirdly, it is contemporary: a biblical perspective applies in powerful and relevant ways to current economic issues in our globalized world. Whereas secular approaches tend to focus either on justice in production and exchange ('free trade' versus 'fair trade') or justice in distribution (equality versus freedom), a biblically-rooted account shows that both of these aspects are central to economic justice.

Andrew Hartropp is a church minister and an economist. He lectured in economics for five years at Brunel University, West London, and has doctorates in both Economics and Christian Ethics.

978-1-84227-434-7

Grace and Global Justice

The Socio-Political Mission of the Church in an Age of Globalization

Richard Gibb

What does it mean for the twenty-first-century church to conceive of itself as a community defined by the covenant of grace? *Grace and Global Justice* explores the ramifications of this central Christian doctrine for the holistic mission of the church in the context of a globalized world. Gibb shows how the church can be a voice for justice on behalf of the global poor by affirming its mission as a community of grace.

'Extremely insightful.' – **Richard Mouw**, President and Professor of Theology, Fuller Theological Seminary

'This study is warmly recommended for its theological insights and its careful integration of international political theory and biblical faith. – **Mark Amstutz**, Professor of Political Science, Wheaton College

'An insightful and pertinent analysis.' – **Alan Torrance**, Professor of Systematic Theology, University of St Andrews

'In much evangelical theology the terms "grace" and "global justice" are rarely teamed together, but it is the basis of Gibb's forceful and richly-resourced argument that they must. This is vigorous theology . . . It provides a model for others to follow.' – **David F. Wright**, Emerutus Professor of Patristic and Reformed Christianity, University of Edinburgh

Richard Gibb is Assistant Minister of Charlotte Chapel, Edinburgh.

978-1-84227-465-1